MYSTERIOUS
NORTHAMPTONSHIRE

MYSTERIOUS
NORTHAMPTONSHIRE

DANIEL CODD

First published in Great Britain in 2009 by
The Breedon Books Publishing Company Limited
Breedon House, 3 The Parker Centre,
Derby, DE21 4SZ.

This paperback edition published in Great Britain in 2013 by DB Publishing,
an imprint of JMD Media Ltd

ISBN 978-1-78091-305-6

Printed and bound in the UK by Copytech (UK) Ltd Peterborough

CONTENTS

Dedication

For Charlie: wherever you grow up, so you know what is back home.

Acknowledgements

Janet Codd, Neville Codd (for their support, suggestions and proofreading!), Jade Oliver, H. Carey (for pointing me towards the Dutch Doll legend), A. Howe (for his mention of the 'phantom monk' of Lamport), R. Bray, J. Copping, *et al* (for their contributions to Northamptonshire folklore), Northampton Archives, N.S. (for her suggestions for images, and for relating to me some memories of the stories of Raunds and of the surrounding area that she grew up with), *Northamptonshire Chronicle & Echo*, Northampton Central Library (including Jon-Paul Carr), the staff at Rothwell Church (for providing the history of the Bone Crypt), Geoff Stone, and the many people to whom I am indebted to for passing on anecdotes or providing further information concerning well-known legends. Wardens and staff of Lyveden New Bield, Rushton Triangular Lodge and Wellingborough Museum for their kind assistance. Also thanks to the Friends of Delapre Abbey Society and the wardens of St Guthlac's Church at Passenham; St Mary's at Woodford; Holy Trinity at Rothwell and St Peter's at Stanion for allowing me to see the Dun Cow rib. All illustrations are copyrighted D. Codd, except: page 128 (Friends of Delapre Abbey Society) and page 135 (Wellingborough Museum).

FOREWORD

Although Northamptonshire will forever be known by such monikers as the 'rose of the shires' or 'the shire of squires, spires and springs', for the purposes of this book an article in *The Gentleman's Magazine* of 1861 seems to best sum the county up. It is described as 'a county that can offer the oldest church, the oldest font, the oldest Christian monument, the oldest council chamber…a county wherein were fought such decisive battles as Northampton and Naseby, one linked with the fortunes of so many queens, with so noble a cathedral (at Peterborough), so plentifully stored with nobility and gentry, the language of whose common people is the purist of any shire in England. The worst foot of soil is equal with the best of any other county; it touches nine counties, yet derives all its rivers from itself – a county with so many gifts of nature and enrichments of art.'

Northamptonshire is a beautiful and mysterious county, a perception made possible by its picture postcard countryside and swathes of ancient woodland. Villages such as Rockingham appear too perfect to be true, almost as if they were 'made' to a specification of an English idyll that everyone wishes existed, and this goes for many places here. Many of its treasures are nestled away and can often take some finding, such as Lyveden New Bield, and there must be some monuments – such as the late 13th-century Eleanor Cross in Geddington – that people simply pass by every day without concerning themselves with the history of this remarkable, almost-unique antiquity. Even the Naseby battlefield takes some finding, and there is a curious sensation that one (if they so desired) could drive

through the entire county without actually realising anyone lived here; it can seem that the major M and A-roads are almost trying to hustle travellers through the county so that it can be left to its peaceful self. In places it seems that the only inhabitants are the sheep, which seem to populate the fields in their thousands. It is certainly difficult to associate the county with the massacres, battles, disastrous fires and ferocious rioting that history tells us has occurred here. For example, during the chaotic reign of King John we are told that a surge of beggars at the gate of the Hospital of St John claimed several lives, and more were murdered by the vergers who descended on the crowd with knives and clubs. Not the Northampton we recognise today.

The Eleanor Cross, Geddington: an ancient treasure of Northamptonshire.

The spectacular natural surroundings of Northamptonshire have been the basis for many of its stories, particularly those that relate to so-called 'healing springs', and in preparing this compilation I have made some observations about the supernatural and folklore across the county in general.

Firstly, it is clear that, while we were out-and-about researching this book, many people found its broad-ranging subject matter fascinating, and there are few people who after a moment's hesitation will not cautiously admit to knowing that somewhere 'is haunted', or that 'so-and-so reckons they saw a UFO', or that 'actually, I remember being told such-and-such as a child.' Pub-goers and dogwalkers always seem extremely forthcoming.

Secondly, it can often be frustratingly difficult to get to the bottom of certain stories. For example, it seemed to be common knowledge that Charles Dickens saw the ghost of a woman in white at Rockingham Castle in the mid-19th century, but I cannot seem to pin this story down to anything concrete in his writings or journals. There *is* a more substantive ghostly legend at Rockingham Castle of which I was made aware: during (and following) the governorship of Alain le Zouche, Baron le Zouche of Ashby and steward of Rockingham Forest (d.1314), the castle was supposed to be haunted by the ghost of a murdered ancestor. Every Holy Rood Day (14 September) the ghost of the baron's grandfather, another Alain who himself had no actual connection with the castle, strode about the place, his noisy footsteps echoing. He had been assassinated at Westminster Hall – now better known as the Houses of Parliament – by the Earl of Warren and Surrey in a row over land in 1268. However, the anecdote about Dickens appears to have little foundation other than that he stayed at Rockingham at the invitation of friends and that Chesney Wold in *Bleak House* is to some extent based on Rockingham. Possibly someone can prove me wrong – it would be wonderful if there were more truth to the anecdote than this – but this illustrates the problems of getting to the bottom of

The Welland railway viaduct, Harringworth: a Victorian treasure of the county.

Northamptonshire's folklore. Separating fact from fiction is often difficult with many Northamptonshire legends, so the reader is warned to be careful in accepting the 'fact' of some of these stories. I have tried as best I can to try and track down some legends to their source, but often when the only source is a vocal one this sometimes becomes nigh on impossible.

It is also apparent that Northamptonshire's spooky and paranormal themes follow those of the surrounding counties, and I have found many instances where a particular legend has a variation in another part of the Midlands. Many beliefs from times gone by (such as the goblin-like Shag Foal, or phantom coaches of the type held to haunt Boughton House) were common fare in days past, just as the flying black triangles and huge predatory 'panthers' of today are themselves mirrored in other parts of the East Midlands.

This can sometimes prove a little disappointing to the researcher, especially when an old (but good) story is found to be a carbon copy of one from somewhere else. However, Northamptonshire also provides superb examples of strange, supernatural and paranormal events that I have not heard repeated anywhere else: from the well-known legend of the Dutch Doll of Finedon to the weird time-loss incidences at Little Houghton. One or two of the legends of saints and their miracles appear to be unique to this county as well, as does the legend of the Wansford floating man.

That said, the curious and mysterious history of this county, on the whole, is bettered nowhere else. Come, then, and take a tour round mysterious Northamptonshire – a land of legend and folklore, of urban myths, of the supernatural and paranormal, and of the unsolved and bizarre. It is worth pointing out that in many instances the sincerity of the reports indicates that the phenomena described within these pages does exist – or else that we are continually seeing things 'we are not really seeing.' For the purposes of modern accuracy, Peterborough is classed as Cambridgeshire and is not included in any great depth. This book is not a history book and I apologise in advance for any unwitting historical inaccuracies the sharp-eyed may pick out, and I can only assure the reader that all sources drawn upon were considered reliable ones.

Many of the sites noted herein are privately owned, so please be careful. In truth it is up to the reader to form their own opinions on the phenomena herein and delve further if they are intrigued.

CHAPTER I

ENIGMATIC EVENTS FROM NORTHAMPTONSHIRE'S HISTORY

As with elsewhere there is much lore surrounding times of violent conflict in the region. In some instances it is the mere lack of historical certainty about people and events that fascinates; for example, the *exact* site of the final battle that crushed Boudica's anti-Roman rebellion in the year AD 60 is unknown, although it is long held to have been somewhere along Watling Street (the A5), the ancient trackway that stretched from Dover through the English midlands and into Wales. It has been claimed that the clash, in which 80,000 Britons and several hundred Romans died, occurred at a site known locally as Cuttle Mill Lane between Paulerspury and Pury End, two miles south east of Towcester (itself the site of the Roman town called *Lactodorvm*). The Roman historian Tacitus wrote that Boudica poisoned herself, and although she was afforded a lavish burial it is unclear where she was interred. These events have given rise to much speculation in Northamptonshire. Coinciding with a resurgence of the warrior queen's legend, during the late-19th century the site was frequently raided at night by men armed with spades and lanterns who expected to find a queen's ransom in buried treasure linked to the legendary events said to have occurred there nearly two millennia earlier.

Just to the south of Paulerspury is Whittlebury, and in October 2004 *The Northampton Chronicle & Echo* covered the claims that Boudica herself might actually lie buried in a field known locally as Dead Queen Moor, having dramatically killed herself in Whittlewood Forest. Similarly frustrating for scholars have been attempts to place the locations of the 12 battle sites ascribed to the semi-mythical King Arthur by the Welsh scribe Nennius in his *Historia Britonum* (*c*.AD 835). There is the barest of possibilities that the decisive clash between Arthur's forces and the Anglo-Saxons at somewhere called Mount Badon actually occurred at *Bannaventa* – a small Roman settlement on agricultural land at Whilton Lodge, north east of Norton. It has also been speculated that the fabled king led his men into battle on the other side of Daventry, at Badby.

Quite often it is something tangible that is discovered which surprises. The antiquarian John Cole noted that a lock of hair, about a yard in length, was dug up in the churchyard of All Hallows, Wellingborough. Writing in 1837, he observed that it had been found a 'great number of years ago' and had been preserved in clay. It was certainly ancient, and local supposition was that it had once adorned the head of 'some ancient British Queen'. In Cole's time it was kept in the vestry of the church. Another discovery in Wellingborough – that of an ancient British bead coloured green and opaque – indicated to Cole evidence of trade between the county and the ancient Greeks and Phoenicians, via a trading route with Spain. Such trade is reckoned to have been ongoing in the sixth century BC when Britain was referred to as Albion. At this time, to the civilized Greeks, Britain and Ireland were still lands of myth whose actual existence was not recorded until *c*.530 BC by a Greek sailor. Even then many back home in Greece thought that the whole rumour of two large chilly, rainy islands to the north west of Spain was an invention.

Hidden among the shadows of history is the story of Aelfgifu of Northampton, a mistress of King Cnut of England, whose ruthlessness would appear to have put Lady Macbeth to shame. Northamptonshire's association with royalty and conflict has further led to a persistent supposition that Duke Arthur of Brittany, the 16-year-old nephew and rival of King John of England, was assassinated in Northampton as a result of the power struggle. Perhaps it is not surprising that legends are linked to periods of violent upheaval in the county, as this chapter illustrates. This is particularly true of the events surrounding the execution of Mary, Queen of Scots, at Fotheringhay Castle on 8 February 1587 and the decisive battle at Naseby on 14 June 1645.

Apart from the historical conundrums, there are other legends that speak of buried treasures in the county. During the imprisonment of Mary, Queen of Scots, at Wingfield Manor, Derbyshire, from 1569 onwards, two thieves robbed her of money, horses and jewellery and then fled south into Rockingham Forest. The two were apprehended and carted to London where they confessed to hiding the stolen property on Geddington Chase. Edmund Brudenell of Deene Hall attempted to find it but was unsuccessful, and so it is said that Mary's priceless relics are still hidden there, and have been since 1576. Occasionally there have been rumours of conspiracy in the county: a disastrous fire which struck Kettering in 1679 and burnt out half the town was blamed on militant Catholic agitators, since it began in a sturdy-framed house where no candles had been lit and had spread so rapidly. 'Firing' of towns was a charge often levelled at mysterious terrorists in 17th-century England.

Other stories concern that strange world where history, rumour and wishful thinking converge (such as is often the case with folklore) and are 'mysterious' by virtue of the fact that the tale cannot be *absolutely* proved or disproved one way or the other. One example of this is the song entitled *The Mistletoe Bough* by T.H. Bayly (d.1839) which tells the story of a lovelorn young woman, 'Lord Lovell's bride', who dances before her proud father and erstwhile husband at a Christmas wedding ceremony before taking herself off to play hide-and-seek. She subsequently vanishes off the face of the earth, to the dismay of her mystified family and friends – until years later: '…an old chest that had once laid hid; Was found in the castle – they raised the lid; A skeleton form lay mouldering there; In the bridal wreath of that lady fair.' This is supposed to have been based on an actual event (or rumours of an actual event) and taken place at Titchmarsh Castle, of which nowadays only earth mounds remain. Titchmarsh Castle was built at the behest of Sir John Lovel *c.*1304 and survived not even a

The earthwork remains of Titchmarsh Castle.

century. It took the secret truth of the legend of the 'Mistletoe Bride' with it as it slipped into disrepair, and it now finds itself one of the numerous locations up and down Britain where this famous story is supposed to have occurred.

On the other hand, some incidents are real, but simply bizarre. The area south of Towcester is famous for an incident involving a gun-toting vicar, who in 1776 happened to encounter an army captain who was out searching the countryside with a post-boy for a highwayman who had earlier robbed him. The clergyman, the Revd John Risley of Tingewick, Buckinghamshire, joined the group, and they finally ran the highwayman to ground near Stony Stratford. A brief shootout followed during which the armed vicar aimed and shot the bandit off his horse. The corpse was carted off to Towcester but could not be identified, adding another strange element to an already curious case. Revd Risley suffered the indignity of being tried for murder before being acquitted and judged entirely blameless for the fatal shooting. The killing of an adulterous parish priest by an enraged butcher wielding a meat cleaver sounds like almost by-the-book folklore, except that according to Daniel George's *A Book Of Characters* (1959) this actually happened in Wappenham. On 23 January 1685 a clergyman of doubtful authenticity called Theophilus Hart was caught in bed with the wife of the village butcher, George Tarry, who promptly hit Hart on the head with a meat axe and killed him.

Thankfully, these days things are a little calmer but there are instances of the darker side of human nature that sometimes goes unsolved. *History Of The British Turf* (1879) tells us that the 1884 Derby winner, Running Rein, vanished forever after being brought first to Northampton and then Sywell. This was in the middle of a protracted legal case attesting that the horse had been too old to compete, and therefore should not have been entered; huge amounts of money were at stake and it appears that the poor animal became Northamptonshire's answer to Shergar – killed so that the case would collapse because it could not be proved either way.

One of the most famous crimes of the 20th century concerned the human remains found inside a burning Morris Minor in Hardingstone Lane, Hardingstone, on Bonfire Night 1930. It later transpired that a salesman named Rouse had battered a vagrant to death, forced the corpse into the car and then set it alight in an attempt to fabricate his own suicide in a car fireball. However, two boys had encountered a breathless Alfred Arthur Rouse as he scrambled through a hedge and walked past them in the moonlight. Police put the pieces together and Rouse was eventually hanged, but the identity of his victim has never been conclusively proven, even the murderer never knew. Today there are occasional reports of dead drug 'mules' and other murder victims whose identities are never discovered, or of murder victims never found despite convictions. In other instances some people who simply vanish without trace are assumed to be the victims of foul play. Such incidents are thankfully rare – although it is a reminder that even with such a sophisticated police force now in place, sometimes this is not enough when there is no real place to start an investigation. However, it does illustrate that some of Northamptonshire's historical enigmas not linked to the supernatural are mooted in the real world: shadowy characters, bizarre burials, weird crimes and the whereabouts of Oliver Cromwell's remains are all mysteries that have intrigued county folk throughout the centuries.

SKELETAL REMAINS

In the mid-1700s the making of turnpike roads in Northamptonshire turned up a great many curiosities. The remains of Roman-era funeral pyres found at Titchmarsh, near the banks of the River Nene, around 1756 had revealed that the corpses of the wealthy had at one time been incinerated along with carcasses of slaughtered boars, stags and oxen. The ground had actually changed colour because of the intensity of the repeated fires, and when another such place was found north of Higham Ferrers there was excited speculation that such sites were 'evidence' that Great Britain had Trojan ancestry. Briefly, British mythology tells us that in biblical times refugees from the Trojan Wars arrived in the British Isles, defeated a race of giants who inhabited the land and set up a capital at New Troy (modern-day London). There is no actual evidence of this other than established legend, but the manner of the incinerations – with the ashes being placed in urns in cone-shaped holes at the site of burning – reminded antiquarians that this was how Virgil spoke of the Trojan army dealing with their fallen comrades. Quite often coins were found among the ashes, as well as animal bones and pottery: payment placed with the remains for Charon, the ferryman of Hades, whose job it was to carry men's souls over the Stygian Lake after their decease.

Unexpected deposits of skeletal remains, often dating back centuries, still occasionally surface to provide mysteries for archaeologists, historians and scientists to ponder over. In the 19th century, for example, when the Wellingborough-to-Kettering road (A509) was being dug through the hills, there was a surprising find within the hill itself: an immense stone 'of nearly five hundred weight' blocked a natural dry well – in which was entombed an entire human skeleton. Quite what the circumstances were behind this odd, lonely interment is unclear.

In the spring of 1847 a startling discovery was made by men digging for gravel in the sandy ground at Shooter's Hill, south of Great Addington. A cluster of skeletons was unearthed, along with beads, urns and spearheads, and archaeologists speculated that Shooter's Hill might have been the site of an ancient Druid sacrificial altar. There were many finds that linked the discovery to the Druids, and a number of the skeletons appeared to have had their heads lopped off before the bodies were placed face down with a pile of stones representing the head. Strangest of all was the suggestion that 'no earth had ever been raised over them', indicating that they were not physically buried, just that in time they had sunk into the earth, laying undisturbed for millennia. How they escaped the ravages of animals and the weather was unclear, but perhaps the ritualistic overtones of the scene indicated that the Druids kept watch over the corpses until they were mere skeletons. Whatever had happened there, it was well known locally that Shooter's Hill was so-called because of a terrible warlike clash that had occurred there centuries before. Could the name of the place have been a folk-memory of events of the year c.AD 60 when the Roman army set about wiping out the warlike priestly caste known as the Druids?

On 12 November 2004 local media reported the unearthing of the skeletons of five members of a farming family: a woman, two men, an adolescent and an infant. The discovery was made in fields at Whitehall Farm, Nether Heyford, between Daventry and Northampton, just east of Weedon Bec, and the remains were dated to the sixth or seventh century. This detail alone is intriguing; it places these people as possibly being alive in the era when several mysteries noted in this book may (or may not) have occurred in the locale, such as the admittedly unlikely guess that one of King Arthur's battles was fought at nearby *Bannaventa*, or the numerous tales of Anglo-Saxon miracles.

An example of a bizarre death was uncovered during excavations that started in 1994 in King's Meadow Lane, Higham Ferrers. The female skeleton, unearthed in 2003, was dated to around AD 800, and, although missing the head, neck and arms, it displayed evidence of having been executed – possibly while her legs were tightly bound to her torso, her knees at her chin. It then appeared that she had been hanged after death, by the neck, the arms and – bizarrely – the feet. It was speculated that the brutal execution appeared to coincide with the death of King Offa of Mercia on 29 July AD 796. Since Higham Ferrers was at that time a royal estate, and since the dead woman appeared to have been of some social standing, it was possible that she had been an unlucky victim of the power struggle that engulfed the region following Offa's demise. Once again, the true story of this death, the motive and the identity of the murderers has been lost to the ages.

AELFGIFU OF NORTHAMPTON

There are many folk from Northamptonshire's past of whom we know all too little. For example, around 1200 the county was terrorised by a bandit-queen called Emma Brunfustian who directed a band of highway robbers and burglars. Assize rolls from 1203 tell us that she was a familiar figure at Stamford, Daventry and Northampton markets, where she attempted to sell wares stolen from her victims. She was an associate of Adam Falc and Hudde the Forger, and with others they pillaged parts of the county; it is written that 'she killed men and led robbers to rob houses' until they were arrested. However, the details of her crimes – and her ultimate fate – are lacking. But one of Northamptonshire's most enigmatic characters flourished some 160 years before this...

Of particular fascination to historians is a shadowy member of the Anglo-Saxon nobility named Aelfgifu of Northampton, the details of whose intrigues have now also been very much lost to the ages.

Aelfgifu was the 'handfast wife', or concubine, of King Cnut and she bore him two sons, thus ensuring a legacy of dynastic warfare for the kingdom of England. In 1030 Cnut presented her with the regency of Norway, but her rule, alongside the couple's eldest son Svein, was so unpopular that revolution in 1035 forced her back to England. Upon Cnut's death in December 1035, Aelfgifu set her sights on the throne of England for her second son Harald 'Harefoot', Svein having died violently in Denmark around this time. What followed was an ugly period of outrageous slander and inter-factional warfare, with parties, kingdoms, brothers and half-brothers taking sides, all of which culminated in the murder of Alfred Aetheling, the stepson of Cnut and his *court* queen Emma of Normandy. Aelfgifu apparently connived with Earl Godwin of Wessex to have Alfred, the most immediate threat to her son's position as future king, captured when he returned to England in early 1036. Alfred and his retinue were ambushed west of Guildford and the event turned into a massacre of horrifying proportions: hundreds of Alfred's supporters were butchered, and the young prince himself was grabbed and blinded as he boarded a ship. He was then transferred to the monastery at Ely where he died on 5 February. With all her rivals for the throne of England either dead or abroad, the utterly ruthless Aelfgifu saw her son Harald 'Harefoot' crowned in December 1037; her work done, she then slipped into obscurity and died, possibly of a stroke, in 1040 aged about 45 – with much blood on her hands.

Aelfgifu had been born around AD 995, the daughter of Ealdorman Aelfhelm of Northumbria and Wulfrun, and brought up on one of their Northamptonshire estates. Cnut took her as a lover when she was around 20 years old, but it is also said that he shared her with Olaf II Haraldsson of Norway until his death in 1030, which led to her disastrous stint on the throne of Norway and her eventual return to England. To further confuse things, *The Anglo-Saxon Chronicle* (a contemporary, although sketchy record of events) disputes that Harald was ever even Aelfgifu of Northampton's son. What a fascinating tale the life of this Northamptonshire *femme fatale* would make – unfortunately most of the detail of the story has been lost in the shadows of history. Noted scholar and historian Frank M. Stenton went so far as to write in his *Anglo-Saxon England* (1943) that, '...it is probable that for part, if not the whole, of his [Harald's] reign, his mother Aelfgifu of Northampton was the real ruler of England.'

ROYAL RUMOURS

Northamptonshire's association with royalty and conflict has led to a persistent legend that Duke Arthur of Brittany, the 16-year-old nephew (and rival) of King John of England, was killed in Northampton as a result of the power struggle for the throne.

In fact the young duke had vanished without trace in early 1203 after being captured in battle the previous year at Mirebeau, France, and was later transferred as a captive to Falaise. He was a hero to the local Breton people and his arrest caused widespread unrest, which caused King John to consider having Arthur blinded and castrated in retaliation. This plan would almost certainly have been self-defeating to the king's interests, so the diplomatic Hubert de Burgh – charged by John with Arthur's captivity in France – announced to the world that Arthur had died of a broken heart. This failed to stem the popular uprising, so Hubert backtracked and said the duke was still alive. By now it was being rumoured that John had had his young hostage murdered and one contemporary account alleges that Duke Arthur was transferred to the castle at Rouen under William de Braose, where King John himself murdered his nephew during a drunken rage. The corpse, it was said, was tied to a heavy stone and cast out of a boat into the River Seine with de Braose's complicity: here a humble fisherman later dragged the body up in his nets where it was identified and taken for a secret burial for fear of King John's wrath.

There is at least some circumstantial supporting evidence for these historical accounts, although much of it still appears to be hearsay. Perhaps due to a veil of secrecy surrounding his disappearance, it has often been said that the young duke met an entirely different end: William Shakespeare took the bare foundation of these events and set the grim finale in Northampton. In the play *The Life & Death Of King John* the captive Arthur leaps to his death from the walls of Northampton castle, crying 'O me, my uncle's spirit is in these stones; Heaven take my soul and England keep my bones!'

King John is known to have stayed in Northampton some 30 times. A contributor to *Notes And Queries* in 1863 asked on what authority Shakespeare had set the death at the castle; in truth, the very vagueness of the circumstances of the duke's disappearance is probably the answer.

CRIME ENIGMAS

I have heard it said that if one wishes to understand what it was like to live in another era then one should study the murder cases of the period to gain an insight into the social conditions, judicial procedure and political and religious circumstances that brought the crime about. Records for Northamptonshire naturally become sketchier the further back one looks, but nonetheless even in the chaos of the English Civil War there are written pointers. Cotterstock parish registers briefly recorded '1641. Edward Spratton was buried the second day of June, who was suddenly slain at Mr Norton's gates the same day.' Perhaps this unfortunate man was murdered by soldiers of the undisciplined, marauding armies that frequently passed this way. Within the church of St Mary and St Peter at Weedon Lois there is a Victorian brass plaque commemorating the bravery of the Revd William Losse, who was shot and stabbed by Parliamentary soldiers who invaded the church on 2 July 1643. The spectacle was played out before the congregation, and Revd Losse was murdered for standing up to the troops. Lost parish registers make it impossible to ascertain whether he died instantly: he had sought shelter in an attic and the soldiers had randomly fired at it. Enough blood, however, seeped through the wooden trapdoor for them to assume they had killed him. Even so, scant as it is there is at least some evidence of events. Sometimes, however, the proof is lacking and it can even be unclear whether certain alleged crimes *actually ever happened*.

Much like the legend of *The Mistletoe Bride* is the legend of Mr Fox, better known as the story of *The Oxford Student*. Briefly, the legend concerns a student called Fox who gets a serving girl pregnant. She agrees to meet him in an apple orchard and there finds a hidden, ready-dug grave. So the girl climbs an apple tree, and there sees her lover arrive, armed with a spade and an accomplice. All becomes clear: Fox had intended to murder her at the site of this tryst and bury her with his companion's help. Eventually they leave and she reports him to the authorities. He is subsequently hanged. The tale appears in J.O. Halliwell-Phillips's *Popular Rhymes & Nursery Tales* (1849) and he placed it in Oxfordshire; however, the story had been around for decades, if not centuries, and many counties lay claim to being the location of the actual event: Buckinghamshire, Lincolnshire and Bedfordshire among them. In Northamptonshire it is reckoned that this event happened at Yardley Hastings, south east of Northampton, or else Brackley near the Oxfordshire border, but whether it was a real historical event is open to question. 'Fox' was often a byword for a kind of folkloric bogeyman, and this tale may be nothing more than a nursery rhyme. However, it is intriguing to speculate on its basis in fact, and this is so with numerous other whispers of brutal, dark deeds in the county.

Lost in the mists of time are the details – indeed any real proof – of a brutal and bizarre crime noted by mid-16th-century antiquary John Leland while travelling through Northamptonshire compiling his *Itinerary* (1535–1543). In St Peter's Church, Brackley, there was to be found an image of a former parish vicar who had apparently fallen foul of 'a Lord of the Towne' in times past. The quarrel had arisen when the vicar had taken a horse he believed was his right following 'a mortuarie' (which one assumes means a burial he performed). The Lord, one Neville, had the priest thrown into a grave, still wearing his clerical robes, and buried alive for this, although in turn Neville suffered punishment of a sort for the killing. He went to Rome where he repented for absolution.

There is little more to this, and Leland seems to have *heard* about the tale from the Tudor inhabitants of '*Barkeley*' rather than studied it, which presumably accounts for the lack of detail or coherence in the story. St Peter's as it now stands has its origins in the Norman era, and so the crime could have happened anytime from the late Norman to the early Tudor era.

This curious tomb was pointed out as belonging to the slain priest.

The gatehouse to Rockingham Castle.

Upon visiting the ancient church in 2008 I managed to locate what is alleged locally to be the grave of the murdered priest in the 'old' corner of the churchyard. There I was told that the priest's faithful dog had thrown itself into the grave after the body and had also been buried alive. It is at this point that the story begins to sound suspiciously like a myth, and with nothing to evidence it conclusively, bar the strange grave, the historical truth of this crime has to be classed 'unproven'.

This lost piece of town history is just one of many enigmatic crimes in the county throughout the centuries. There are similar, unverifiable legends linking Robin Hood to Northamptonshire which the Edwardian poet C.H.M.D. Scott even put into rhyme. The origins of the outlaw have proved famously impossible to pin down, although perhaps the first allusion to him appears in William Langland's poetic masterpiece *Piers Plowman* (*c.*1377), which refers to '…rymes of Robyn Hode.' Scottish poet Andrew of Wyntoun's *Orygynale Cronikil Of Scotland* (*c.*1420) is the first to make reference to 'Lytil John and Robyne Hode', who had been active in 'Yngil-wode and Barnysdale' about 150 years earlier. Around 1492 the ballad *A Lyttel Geste Of Robyn Hode* put the story into the context with which today's generation is familiar.

Court records from the Law Society show that in 1354 a Robyn Hode was thrown into prison in Rockingham Castle for trespassing in the royal forest of Rockingham. The castle has indeed stood since the era of William the Conqueror, and although the peasantry were allowed to collect fallen and dead wood, that was about all they were allowed to do within the forest. Could a minor act of rebellion by a Northamptonshire poacher *really* have captured the public imagination at the time so thoroughly that a mere two decades later '…rymes of Robyn Hode' were already well known?

Alas, the name was a common one at the time, and there are other contenders for the 'historical' Robin Hood in the Midlands and north of England. There is even a suggestion that 'Rabun-hod' had been a cover-all terminology for any bandit or outlaw for decades before the first allusions in print

The Bocase Stone, said to mark the site of a tree where Robin Hood hid his weapons.

to one 'Robyn Hode'. Nevertheless, there are ancient stories of Robin's activities in Northamptonshire, and he is said to have had headquarters at Corby at one time. It was here that the king, lost while out hunting, encountered Robin and his band of outlaws. They led him to Corby and fed him before letting him go on his way. At nearby Brigstock, Robin and his men are held to have been ambushed on Lady Day (25 March) as they left St Andrew's Church in the village. In the pitched battle that followed, Robin's would-be captor – Sir Hugh de Hanville – was killed and Robin is said to have run from the scene into the woodland of Rockingham Forest. He threw his bow and arrows into the hollow of a tree and, disguised as a peasant, evaded his pursuers and managed to make it back to his men. Alice Dryden's *Memorials Of Old Northamptonshire* (1903) notes that the tree where Robin stored his bow and arrows was known locally as the Bocase Tree, and it had stood about half-a-mile from Fermyn Woods outside of Brigstock. The tree itself had been chopped down centuries ago, but in the 17th century it was decided to mark the site with the Bocase Stone. Dryden wrote that it was, '...almost certainly one of the forest boundaries, close on 4ft high, with two inscriptions cut: *In This Plaes Grew Bocase Tree* and *Here Stood Bocase Tree.*' The stone — most likely a gathering point for discussions about forestry rights and archery practice — can still be found, albeit with some difficulty.

Within the walls of St Mary's Church, Woodford, village legend says that a foul deed occurred. Jane Blois was the wife of Sir St Andrew St John, and she died around 23 January 1710. It is said that she was laid out in the church prior to her funeral at Ketton, and the unscrupulous sexton began to remove her rings. He was unable to do so and began to cut off her fingers in order to get them — then Jane woke up and began screaming, for she had not been dead at all. A good tale but highly unlikely to have actually happened, conforming as it does to the universal myth about supposedly dead people waking up in church to terrify criminal vicars.

In Rothwell the mysterious discovery of thousands of skeletons in a 'bone cavern' beneath the Norman-era Holy Trinity Church has prompted much excited speculation. The story goes that around 1700 a luckless gravedigger accidentally discovered the mysterious cavern when he fell 12ft down through the floor and into the crypt. When his eyes became accustomed to the gloom he shrieked in terror — for he was surrounded by a mass of bones and thousands of skulls that leered at him. He never recovered from the shock and is said to have died a wreck, forever traumatised by the event.

Quite where these grim remains under Rothwell Holy Trinity Church came from is not known.

The crypt probably dates from the 13th century, and the suggestion that the skulls displayed signs of extreme violence prompted several theories. The mid-18th-century publication *History Of The Hundred Of Rowell* calculated there to be some 30,000 skeletons, the bones of which were 'carefully packed in alternate strata of skulls, arms, legs and so forth.' Apart from displaying fatal injuries, most of the bones were rumoured to be of men in the prime of life, and this prompted speculation that all were the immured victims of a battle between Anglo-Saxons and ancient Britons. If that were so then the bones must have been transferred there from somewhere else *after* the crypt was built in the 1200s. Others thought that the skeletons belonged to those slain at the Battle of Naseby, although this is unlikely – that conflict appeared to be too recent. The author of *History Of The Hundred Of Rowell* was a medical gentleman who inspected the bones. In his opinion they were not likely to have been the victims of ancient conflict, but did display signs of having previously been buried in the earth, implying they were dug up and transported to the crypt from somewhere else. As to the 'battle injuries', he pondered that most were '...rather to the spade and foot of the sexton' than to violence.

These days Rothwell's 'Bone Crypt' contains about 1,500 skeletons, rather less than the fanciful 30,000 allegedly observed in the 18th century. They can still be seen as the crypt is open to the public, allowing them to ponder over the ghoulish mystery. In this instance there is almost too much evidence. How the crypt actually came to be is plagued by uncertainty, as is the enigma of who the hundreds of skulls belonged to...

ARCHITECTURAL CURIOSITIES

Some of the curiosities in Northamptonshire take the form of buildings. Maybe the best known example of this is Lyveden New Bield, a half-finished Elizabethan manor house, work on which began in 1595 at the behest of the Catholic peer Sir Thomas Tresham. This was during the Protestant reign of Elizabeth I, and New Bield's isolated, deliberately hidden location in the parish of Aldwinkle-St-Peter is an uncompleted testament to Sir Thomas's faith. It is rich in Catholic symbolism, being designed in multiples of the numbers three, five, seven and nine (three and nine signifying the Trinity, five the wounds of Christ and seven the instruments of the Passion). Also, it is clear it was meant to be inhabited (as opposed to it being a 'folly'). It was probably meant to serve as a 'secret house' for use when the principal house, nearby Lyveden Old Bield, was being cleaned or was being threatened. But it was never finished: Sir Thomas died on 11 September 1605 and his son and heir Francis died within three months, after becoming implicated in the Gunpowder Plot.

The Victorian historian Alice Dryden noted of Lyveden, 'The secluded New Bield, the work of the builder, must have always been roofless, since it was left unfinished at the death of Sir Thomas. Its desolate rooms are now filled with wild plants and low elder bushes.' It is bordered by a wide, deep moat, and nowadays the grounds, earthworks, the nearby orchard and, of course, the building itself are preserved by the National Trust. If anywhere should be haunted it is Lyveden New Bield, and it does not take much to imagine the ghost of Sir Thomas staring sadly from one of the upper windows. However, I have been told that there are no ghosts here, which is strangely logical, since Lyveden was *never inhabited*. What *is* fascinating is that the building stands *exactly* as it did over four centuries ago after the workers left halfway through their grand project – leaving what can only be described as a 'snapshot', a photograph in time of a bygone era, showing itself as it did all that time ago, having somehow escaped the ravages of war, disaster, looters and the elements. (There is, according to tradition, a ghost that haunts nearby Lady Wood. It was in the woodland hereabouts that a band of soldiers from the Black Watch regiment retreated after staging a mutiny in 1743. A company of dragoons was sent to flush them out, and a bloody battle was only narrowly averted, although three of the rebellious Highlanders were later shot for their actions. It was written in 1912 by military historians that 'at least one of them died during their sojourn in Lady Wood, and that a corner of land near it was lately known as the "soldier's grave".' It is said that a ghostly lone figure in the dress of an 18th-century Highland soldier has been glimpsed near the two spiralled 'snail mounts' which lie between the ruin and the woodland. He apparently plays a sad lament for his comrades, whose uprising was so short-lived.)

Equally curious are the rumours of underground tunnels. There is a certain romance about hidden subterranean passages that hints at secret trysts, plots and hazardous escapes, but for the most part the legends are unlikely and familiar. Sir Thomas Tresham's other legacy to Northamptonshire's architecture is Rushton Triangular Lodge. The familiar legend says that a fiddler was dared by his friends to investigate a mysterious underground tunnel that led away from the building. As he went the fiddler played his instrument so that those above ground could follow his progress – until suddenly the subterranean music ceased. The fellow's comrades raced back to the lodge and attempted to enter the tunnel themselves to find out what had happened – only to discover that the tunnel had totally collapsed and they could not get in. Variations on this story are almost universal across Britain, although I was also informed that the fiddler later re-emerged and claimed to have walked all the way to Australia!

Of course, Rushton Triangular Lodge is the type of building to inspire such romance. There is also believed to be an underground tunnel leading from Haunt Hill House on Kettering Road, Weldon, to St Mary's Church in the village; here, one local tradition avers that someone went into the tunnel and never reappeared, and this has supposedly resulted in 'phantom knocking' from beneath the floorboards of this strange-looking Jacobean building. However, under Northampton itself there *is* better evidence of a labyrinthine tunnel network which radiated out from the site of All Hallows Church. The church stood until a great and devastating fire tore through the town on 20 September 1675, destroying hundreds of homes and shops and leaving 11 people dead. However, the central tower and crypt survived, and All Hallows was subsequently rebuilt as All Saints five years later. The *actual* passages are thought to have been built for the hasty escape of the clergy if violence or fire threatened, and they are supposed to radiate in eight directions towards where, at one time, would have stood other religious properties. Local lore speculates that one tunnel linked All Hallows Church to Northampton Castle and that Thomas Becket, Archbishop of Canterbury, may have used it to flee the castle as a confrontation with the king in 1164 turned violent. This array of tunnels, although having a basis in fact, has now grown in stature thanks to urban myth. The vaulted passages have become a veritable underground ant's nest-like labyrinth that incorporates ancient pub cellars, crypts, and religious houses: almost a 'town beneath the town'. Apparently if you know the right people you can navigate the entire town of Northampton underground, even avoiding collapsed sections of the subterranean passages. The *Northampton Chronicle & Echo* commented of these romantic theories in February 2008: 'Is there really a whole other mysterious world beneath our feet?' Apparently, some readers recalled exploring the maze-like tunnel networks decades ago in their childhood.

'WANSFORD IN ENGLAND'

A plausibly comical tale from the extreme north east of Northamptonshire, where the county border follows the route of the River Nene via the border with Peterborough, has all the elements of a folk tale, yet may just be one of those bizarre stories that is actually based on a *real* event.

John Morton noted in his *Natural History Of Northamptonshire* (1712) the legend of a man who had fallen asleep on a haycock (rolled bale of hay) in a field along the banks of the 'River Nyne' somewhere near Wansford (now just on the Peterborough side of the border) when a flash flood deluged the previously dry meadow and took the haycock (and its sleepy occupant) with it. When

Lyveden New Bield — a snapshot of history.

the fellow awoke and looked about him, he panicked, for it appeared that he was now floating, '...for ought he knew in the wide ocean', such was the devastating extent of the flooding in the region. A local shouted at the bewildered new arrival and asked him where he was from. The man, believing he had floated to a domain of fairies or a foreign country, replied 'Wansford in England!'

This anecdote had first appeared 74 years earlier in *Drunken Barnaby's Four Journeys To The North Of England* by poet Richard Brathwaite (d.1673). 'Barnaby Harrington' was a pseudonym for Brathwaite himself, and the prose was probably based on his own escapades while travelling. 'Barnaby' arrives at Wansford but immediately flees after seeing the place daubed with signs declaring it a plague village. He finds himself in a meadow, resting on a haycock: '...Though from death none may be spared, I to die was scarce prepared. On a haycock, sleeping soundly, the river rose and took me roundly!' He finds himself afloat seemingly in the middle of nowhere. A group of people gathered and asked if he had drifted from Greenland – 'Barnaby' replies, 'No; from Wansforth-Brigs in England.'

Quite whether this actually happened to Brathwaite himself, or whether he incorporated it into his prose after visiting Wansford and hearing the story is unknown. Forty years after his death, however, it was a well-known story in that part of the Northamptonshire–Peterborough border, as John Morton later noted in 1712. In 1857 the story was still around; a contributor to *Notes And Queries* upon visiting 'Wandsford, in Northamptonshire' (as it was then) heard it differently though. The haymaker had drifted a great distance following the flooding of the Nene and ended up in Wansford, rather than drifting away from Wansford. Either way, he noted, the sign on the village coaching inn commemorated the event as a historical 'fact'. That inn is now the Haycock Hotel; it dates back to *c*.1620 and so it may have been there when 'Drunken Barnaby' visited during his brief excursion to Wansford. The pub sign can still be seen.

As history, the tale might raise some eyebrows, although there is credulity to the prose of Drunken Barnaby's exploits and much of it is thought to have been based on fact. There is a sense that, over time, the unfortunate fellow who found himself drifting over the vast sea of the flooded Nene

Wansford is proud of its legend.

landscape has covered an ever more epic distance; either to Wansford or away from it. The Nene valley has a history of extensive flooding, so the story is at least credulous. But who that unfortunate fellow actually was, how far he drifted, and whether the tale is *real* is now a happily unanswerable question, which leaves Wansford with its own unique legend that cannot be proved either way. The village is actually now known as Wansford-*In-England* on account of the story.

THE MYSTERY OF CROMWELL'S BURIAL

When Oliver Cromwell passed away on 3 September 1658, so great was England's dependency on him that even to the very last many refused to believe that God would allow him to die – even up to the point when he took what was clearly a fatal decline after six months of ill health. In his last hours he was heard to cry out 'Truly God is great' from his deathbed, leading some to expect his salvation at the last moment. England's display of nervous uncertainty over the future of the nation illustrates the immense respect the Lord Protector had earned in his lifetime; all a far cry from the barbaric treatment meted out to his corpse following the restoration of the monarchy on 29 May 1660.

The death of such a national figurehead was always going to be the subject of debate. When he died at Whitehall aged 59 the decline in his health was seen as symptomatic of his contracting malaria (possibly in Ireland) and urinary infections, aggravated by a broken heart: he had been forced to sit by the bedside of his beloved daughter Bettie as she died from a painful illness the very month before. There were contemporary suggestions that Cromwell's physicians were mismanaging his health, and there were even rumours that one of them, Dr Bates, was part of a Royalist plot to engineer his demise.

Cromwell's son and heir Richard was not suited to public office and was deposed, and 20 months after Cromwell had died Charles II arrived at Dover and re-took the throne of England. The shift in government saw an immediate reaction against the old regime, and it is at this point that the story of Cromwell enters into the realms of mystery. On 20 October, 10 of those involved in the trial and execution of King Charles I were themselves brutally executed at Tyburn, London – judicially murdered as revenge for Charles's 'martyrdom'. In January 1661 Cromwell's corpse was exhumed from its resting place in Westminster Abbey and subjected to the grim ritual of a posthumous execution: the body was hanged 'in a green seare cloth' (it had been excellently preserved through embalming) for a full day before being taken down and cruelly decapitated. The head was stuck on a pike outside the abbey for a quarter of a century. The remains of two others who had been prominent in signing the king's death warrant, Henry Ireton and John Bradshaw, were also exhumed and suffered similar treatment. At some point around 1684 Cromwell's skull was either taken from its pole or blown off during a gale, and it was passed around for almost three centuries before finally being buried at Sidney Sussex College, Cambridgeshire, in 1960. What happened to the rest of the corpse has forever been speculation.

It is likely that following the ritualistic execution the disinterred body was thrown into the burial pit at Tyburn (at the junction of Edgware Road and Oxford Street), where 'Tiburn House' formerly stood and now stands Marble Arch. Possibly, the skeleton of the Lord Protector lies there, but no one knows for sure. It may have been thrown into the Thames. However, there is a persistent rumour that his remains were spirited away either by his daughter Mary (who took them to Newburgh Priory, Yorkshire) or his supporters, who took them to the site of his most famous victory – the battlefield at Naseby in Northamptonshire.

This is a very romantic notion, and it gained great currency in the Victorian era. In 1852 a certain AB contributed to *Notes And Queries* the supposition that Cromwell's burial at Westminster had been a mock one to thwart the very event that subsequently happened – exhumation and posthumous execution.

Apparently the Lieutenant of the Tower, Mr Barkstead, being a confidante of the dying Cromwell, had enquired of his master where he wanted to be buried, and Cromwell had confirmed that he wished to be interred at Naseby. At midnight, soon after the Lord Protector's death, the body (having been embalmed and enclosed in a lead coffin) was secretly conveyed to Naseby Field where a group of fellows, Barkstead and his 15-year-old son among them, '...found about the midst of it a grave dug about nine feet deep, with the green-sod carefully laid on one side, and the mould on the other'. They lowered the coffin into the hole by moonlight and carefully filled it in, taking care to disguise the earth as though it had never been disturbed. Similar care was taken to plough the field and sow it with corn to further disguise it.

AB cited as his source for this *The Compleat History Of England* and the notion so fascinated him that around 1854 he took himself to Naseby. Here he talked to an aged clergyman who claimed to have compiled authentic documents which proved that Cromwell's remains had arrived 'at Huntingdon, *on their road elsewhere.*'

However, there are problems with this story. Apart from the romance of the notion, and the folkloric aspect of the ready-dug grave, if Cromwell's *intact* corpse was transported to Naseby just after his death, then whose body was exhumed in January 1661 for post-mortem execution? A corpse whose well-embalmed features were apparently still half-recognisable? Presumably the head impaled outside Westminster belonged to some unknown vagrant then, except that the skull was the subject of a scientific study in 1935 — which declared that it was indeed Cromwell's head. *Harleian Miscellany*, a contemporary discussion of the events following Cromwell's death, even related the talk among 'fugitives after the Restoration' that a corpse substituted for Cromwell's in Westminster Abbey was none other than that of the executed King Charles I!

Nonetheless, the supposition prompted excited speculation in *Notes And Queries*. One correspondent, Mr Markland, commented that 'There was something mysterious in the disposal of his [Cromwell's] body; and various authors, those of opposite opinions [we are told] positively assert that it was never carried to Westminster Abbey' in the first place. There were, apparently, rumours of a plot to cause an explosion within the abbey on the day of Cromwell's funeral, and it is possible that some might have discussed substituting Cromwell's corpse for another one. If his body *was* secreted away in the dead of night for burial elsewhere, then it presumably happened *after* his post-mortem execution in 1661 and was minus its head, given the conclusive findings of the study of the skull in 1935.

At any rate Mr Markland explained that he had been told that the Lord Protector's remains had ended up in an unmarked grave in the family plot in Northborough, Peterborough. This was apparently common knowledge locally. Another correspondent to *Notes And Queries* asked, 'Has this subject been properly investigated?' Perhaps now too much time has passed, although Naseby is the favoured site in the popular imagination.

It is a fascinating idea that the skeleton of the great man still lies there, nine-feet-down, and not surprisingly the ghost of the Lord Protector himself is sometimes said to be glimpsed standing alone in Naseby Field, as if surveying the scene of his great victory.

BIZARRE BURIALS

In 1979 a curious party took place, hosted by a 64-year-old Northamptonshire grandmother. Mrs Christine Farnham decided to hold her own funeral party while she was still alive, so she could enjoy it. In July of that year the village hall was rented out, and invitations were sent out to family and friends, including some as far away as Canada. A great time was had by all at this wake, including the 'deceased' Mrs Farnham, who told reporters, 'Now I'll die happy.'

This odd behaviour calls to mind some of the more bizarre circumstances under which people were interred in days gone by, either through choice or circumstance. In a piece submitted to *Notes And Queries* in 1873 there is the odd tale of one David Dix Dunham, who had previously been a soldier but who then made a living as a small farmer at Hargrave. He lived at Three Shire House – so-called 'in consequence of the three counties of Huntingdon, Bedford and Northampton meeting there.' In the 1830s Dunham's wife died, and since he had quarrelled with the parish priest he was unwilling to allow the body to be buried in All Saints' Church. So Dunham simply placed his wife in her coffin and walled it up in an outhouse. Seven years later his daughter died aged 27, and she too was interred beside her mother in a similar fashion. Dunham died in 1861 at the age of 85, and his surviving son – equally eccentric and difficult – had to be persuaded not to let his father also rest in the bricked-up outhouse but to instead bury all three in the neighbouring parish of Covington, Cambridgeshire, in one grave. The publication noted that since then the son himself and his wife had been interred in the family plot, where a single recumbent stone 'records their names and years with this inscription – *Shall Not The God Of All Do Right?*'

An even more ghoulish interment was noted the previous century. *The Book Of Days* by Robert Chambers (1864) records the truly macabre burial of the Revd Langton Freeman, who was born in 1710. Freeman had been the rector of Bilton in Warwickshire and was a lifelong bachelor. During his lifetime he became known in the vicinity for his unbelievable meanness, which led to him scrounging food from the larders of wealthier neighbours and even Sunday dinners from labouring men, despite being reasonably well off himself.

Freeman died on 9 October 1784 and at that time he had retired to the village of Whilton in Northamptonshire, where he dwelt in an old manor house. In his will, written the previous year, he made amends with those he had taken advantage of by compensating them. His will also made some utterly bizarre provisions which he wished to be strictly adhered to after he had passed on. The will was dated 16 September 1783 and stated that he, Revd Freeman, was a God-fearing man and in very sound mental health. But he wished to '...commend my soul to God through the merits of my Redeemer.' He instructed that his body was to be left on the bed that he passed away on for four-or-five days, until his body became 'offensive.' Then his corpse was to be carried on that same bed to the summer house of his manor at Whilton, where he would be laid out and wrapped in a strong double winding sheet. The entire contents of the summer house were to be left as they were when his body was carried inside, and all the doors and windows were to be locked and bolted. The summer house was then to be surrounded with newly planted evergreens and finally enclosed with a fence of 'iron or oak pales' painted in a dark blue hue. His nephew, Thomas Freeman, was granted the old manor house – provided that this bizarre ritual was adhered to.

By the time Robert Chambers wrote of this story it was well-known near-history and the conditions of Freeman's will had entered local lore. Chambers wrote that the terms and conditions *appeared* to have been complied with by the nephew in his lifetime, but with the passing of the decades the summer house fell into ruin. By the time he wrote down the tale the fences had gone and the evergreens had been torn up – although the summer house that had become a mausoleum still stood. Time and the elements had left it looking like a ruined hovel, and there was a hole in the roof through which (so it was said) two years previously some inquisitive chaps had gained entry into the summer house.

What they saw was deeply disturbing. Within the gloomy confines of the dilapidated summer house, by the light of their candles, their eyes fell upon '...a dried up, skinny figure, having apparently the consistence of leather, with one arm laid across the chest, and the other hanging down the body, which, though never embalmed, seems to have remained perfectly incorrupted.'

Robert Chambers noted that Freeman's will was real, and it appeared to be a matter of fact that there was no record in the parish register of the reverend being buried. However, despite the recentness of the alleged encounter with the mummified corpse (two years previously), there seems to be something unrealistic about the supposition that the conditions of the will were actually adhered to in 1784 – and Chambers may in fact have been recording contemporary urban legend rather than real events. Would a body really be left out in a winding sheet for 80 years, in those God-fearing times? Surely a corpse would decay over such a length of time in a summer house? What this leaves is the supposition that Revd Langton Freeman's body was buried in unconsecrated ground – but whether immediately after his death, or after generations laid out in his summer house, is now impossible to tell.

It would certainly not be surprising if locally they claimed that he still lies somewhere in Whilton, stretched out and mummified on his deathbed in the bracken-covered remains of his ruined summer house.

THE DISAPPEARANCE OF LYDIA ATLEY

There is little doubt that in 1850 Lydia Atley was murdered, and yet there is still a tantalising mystery surrounding her disappearance.

Lydia's vanishing caused quite a stir in early-Victorian Ringstead. She had been seduced by the local butcher, one Weekly Ball, who quickly tired of her and moved on to other conquests. Lydia, whose age was estimated to be around 30, was not the type of woman to take rejection lightly, however. Heavily pregnant, impoverished and suffering from scurvy, she seems to have told anyone in the village who would listen that the unborn child was Weekly Ball's and that she would make sure she got all monies due her. Ball was threatened with exposure (he was married) unless he paid up, and after a while it seemed that an end to the matter, if not exactly a reconciliation, was imminent. Lydia told a friend that Ball had asked her to come to his orchard one night and settle things.

The meeting duly took place, and a passing labourer later declared that he had heard the two former lovers arguing heatedly from the orchard. Lydia was heard to remark, 'I believe you mean killing me tonight, Weekly Ball!' The following day she had vanished and was never seen again.

The investigation, if it could be called that, was a hasty exercise, despite it being clear that no one profited from Lydia leaving Ringstead other then Ball. However, the entire affair resurfaced in February 1864 when a labourer named Warren, working on a ditch near to the site of Ball's orchard, unearthed a skeleton. Subsequent investigations showed that it was around the same age and height as Lydia and appeared to have been buried no more than two decades earlier. It was also missing two teeth, as Lydia had done. The skeleton was unclothed.

Weekly Ball was arrested and tried for Lydia's murder, although at the end of it he was acquitted. It had simply not been possible to prove that the skeleton had been that of the missing woman, and Ball's defence had argued that the location where the skeleton had been unearthed was a gypsy burial site. Might not the skeleton have been that of a gypsy woman?

After Ball was cleared of Lydia's murder the villagers in Ringstead shunned him, and he was ultimately forced to leave. Even so, poor Lydia Atley suffered no justice, either in life or death. It is in keeping with much of the subject matter of this book that, as well as the very tangible disappearance of Lydia, there was shortly thereafter an even more inexplicable event being reported by the folk of the village. Christina Hole's *Ghost Lore Of England* (1941) explains that the ghostly figure of a woman was observed appearing from the orchard and drifting to the place where, in later years, the skeleton would be unearthed. Sometimes the wraith would make its way to St Mary's Church. However, it could not bring itself to enter the churchyard and always turned away from the church to drift sadly back towards the orchard before being lost to view. After the mysterious skeleton was unearthed in 1864 it was decided that it was Lydia's ghost that had been seen, but the discovery did not stop the ghostly woman from appearing. She '…continued to appear for some years afterwards and then gradually ceased to haunt the place.'

CHAPTER 2

SIGNS AND WONDERS

INTRODUCTION

Northamptonshire boasts numerous splendid examples of Anglo-Saxon churches, and the proliferation of myths concerning saints from this era stands as testimony to this. In the town of Northampton itself, where it might be expected there would be more recent tales of signs and wonders, the lack thereof can perhaps be attributed to the Dissolution of the Monasteries, the Great Fire of 1675 and maybe the fact that all the town's religious properties were overshadowed by Peterborough Cathedral; the Soke of Peterborough being at one time part of Northamptonshire. Northampton Cathedral (The Cathedral of Our Lady Immaculate and Saint Thomas of Canterbury) only dates back to 1840. This is not to suggest, however, that Northampton does not boast some truly impressive houses of historical and religious significance. The Church of the Holy Sepulchre dates to the early 12th century and remains one of a tiny handful of round churches built in England to resemble its namesake in Jerusalem. The Abbey of St Mary de Pratis (better known as Delapre Abbey) also dates to the 12th century, and remains one of only two examples of a Cluniac nunnery built anywhere in England. The Northampton diocese itself has its roots dating back to the early part of the seventh century, and where the current Norman-era St Peter's Church stands in Marefair there is evidence that at one time there was a more primitive Anglo-Saxon church. During the reign of Edward the Confessor (1042–66), according to a single source, the *Nova Legenda Angliae*, a devout manservant was repeatedly told in dreams that a great servant of God lay buried beneath the flagstones at the church. So he appealed to the priest, one Bruning, that they might search and dig, and shortly after they unearthed a grave. A crippled woman called Alfgaeyva of Abingdon then found that she could walk after a miraculous light had appeared before her at this grave site. Not long after, Bruning opened the tomb within the grave and found tattered and delicate scrolls which identified the bones as being those of the martyr Raegener, or Raegenerius. Raegener was the nephew of the Christian martyr-king Edmund, who, like his uncle (according to tradition) had been brutally murdered for his faith *c.*AD 870. Many more miracles of healing are said to have subsequently occurred at a shrine made for the saint within the church.

There are also numerous stories of sainthood and martyrdom associated with the county at large. Perhaps Patricius (Patrick), patron saint of Ireland, was a native of Northamptonshire. Indeed, there is a period of some six centuries where the vagueness (or total lack) of historical data concerning such characters in Northamptonshire meant that for hagiographers there was fertile ground for allegations of divine intervention and supernatural occurrences.

It is also an unfortunate symptom of human nature that religion sometimes becomes the mask for other, less spiritual, events. During vicious rioting at Stamford, Lincolnshire, in 1190 one John of Stamford fled the town to Northampton with treasures plundered during the devastation. He sought lodgings in the town under the roof of an undesirable character and one morning John was found slain and dumped outside the town's walls and his avaricious host had fled, taking with him the treasure. Historian A.P. White wrote in his *History Of Northampton* (1914) of how baseless rumours swept the town: 'John of Stamford had been murdered by the Jews; John of Stamford had died a martyr for the Christian Church; miracles had been performed at John of Stamford's tomb; John of Stamford was the greatest saint of the age. Before long, visitors were flocking in from all the neighbouring villages and towns to worship at the shrine of that blessed martyr, St John of Stamford, and the dead thief's burial place in All Saints' Church was thickly covered with votive offerings.' Things were getting out of control, and so Bishop Hugh d'Avalon of Lincoln was summoned. At that time the diocese of Lincoln covered Northampton and the bishop is recorded as tearing down the votive offerings at John's tomb. He then bravely faced the swelling crowd of burgesses and threatened them with excommunication if they should continue to worship at the tomb of a common thief.

The bishop's brave actions failed to eliminate the anti-Jewish rot that was emerging in England during this time. Variations on the theme of persecution persisted across Britain for centuries. In September 1557 a shoemaker from Syresham called John Kurde was dragged to the 'stonepittes' outside the north gate of Northampton and burnt to death. He had been tried in All Hallows Church the previous month on a charge of denying the doctrine of transubstantiation. John Foxe wrote in his *Book Of Martyrs* how John Rote, the vicar of St Giles in Northampton, had attempted to get Kurde to recant, promising him his freedom. Kurde's answer was that he had his pardon by Jesus Christ, and at this the wood blocks at the foot of the stake to which he was tied were lit. Foxe's *Book Of Martyrs* dealt with unjust Protestant deaths, and Northamptonshire's most famous martyr is of course Mary, Queen of Scots – a Catholic.

Such a depth of faith as John Kurde's in the 21st century would seem to some to be fatally unnecessary, but in centuries past God's hand was seen in virtually every aspect of life. Folk were, quite literally, God-fearing and His wrath was often observed by the clergy to be manifested physically as punishment for some sin or other within the community. Oliver Cromwell himself had always believed in submitting to providence, or God's will. A month after the decisive battle at Naseby on 14 June 1645 he wrote of the encounter, 'And to see this, is it not to see the face of God! You have heard of Naseby: it was a happy victory...of which I had great assurance; and God did it.' On 26 December 1648 he addressed Parliament with these words: 'Since the providence of God hath cast this upon us, I cannot but submit to providence.' He was, of course, referring to moves to try King Charles I for treason. Even by the 19th century the folk of the county based their community life around religious superstitions.

It is remarkable to note that the great fire that destroyed much of Wellingborough in July 1738 left All Hallows Church largely unscathed as the terrified townsfolk sought shelter there. One can guess that God's hand was seen in this 'miracle'. The seriousness with which such beliefs were taken during this time is indicated in a pamphlet of 1783 entitled *The Northamptonshire Female Dreamer, Or Wonderful Revelations Of East-Hadon, and Ravingthorp: By An Angel*, which indicates that even dreams could be interpreted as the manifest word of the divine. Much later, it was said that a large grassy mound within the grounds of the old vicarage at Great Oakley was made by a former vicar, the Revd Sutton, in the 1840s so that he and his successors could alight it and feel closer to Heaven while contemplating. However, it may reassure some to know that such evidence of faith is far from gone in these cynical days. In a small spinney on the edge of the village of Little Houghton, so they say, can be found an ancient tree – with the face of Jesus Christ visible in the bark.

The curiosity was first seen by 64-year-old chapel organist Rita Clayson, whose story appeared in the *Northampton Chronicle & Echo*. She first spotted the simulacrum on the bark of the tree as she followed the footpath during a walk from Brafield-on-the-Green, the day before Good Friday 2005. She later returned with a camera and took photographs of the 'face', which were subsequently distributed among the parishioners.

I have heard numerous stories of county folk who have experienced very good luck after the unaccountable discovery of a pure-white feather in their living room, or after having found one on their desk at work, or at their feet while walking. This they commonly take as evidence that they have a 'guardian angel' watching over them. It is good to know that faith in Northamptonshire has, from whatever quarter, apparently not dimmed and this chapter is designed to illustrate the miraculous, the mysterious and the marvellous attached to such faith.

LOST IN TIME: LEGENDS OF SAINTS FROM THE DARK AGES

Patricius was born *c*.AD 415 in the years immediately following the Roman withdrawal from Britain. His father was a Romano-British civic official and a Christian deacon. The boy Patricius may have been born near Carlisle, but his deathbed *Confessio* (confession) has his origins worded thus: 'I had as my father the deacon Calpornius, son of the late Potitus, a priest, who belonged to the small town of *Bannavem Taberniae*; he had a small estate nearby.' Some have read this as meaning that the great man hailed from *Bannaventa*, the small Roman settlement now to be found on agricultural land at Whilton Lodge, north east of Norton (a possible, though unlikely, site of one of King Arthur's 12 battles a century later). When he was 16 years old Patricius was abducted by pirates who were coming ashore to raid the old Roman highways. Patricius was taken across the Irish Sea and sold into slavery in Ireland. After six years, however, he escaped and managed to sail to Gaul (France) before eventually returning to his family to follow in his father's footsteps and train as a deacon. His *Confessio* explains how at this point he experienced a vision in which he read a letter, *The Voice Of The Irish*, in which 'the voices of those who dwelt beside the forest of *Foclut* which is near the western sea' (i.e. Ireland) begged him to walk among them once more and save them. Thus, it is plausible, if not possible, that one of the most famous saints ever to have walked the earth – Saint Patrick – had his origins in Northamptonshire and, indeed, may have received his calling there.

If legend is to be trusted then *Bannaventa* was also the site of the martyrdom of Saint Cadoc, Abbot of Llancarfan in Glamorganshire. His early life was less than spiritual; although he was the son of King Gwynllyw, a regional South Wales king, he led a band of robbers that numbered in the hundreds – until his father ordered him to a monastery in Caerwent, Monmouthshire. Thus began his spiritual journey, and the *Life Of Cadoc* (*c*.1100) ascribes to him many pilgrimages and church-buildings before his violent death aged around 83 at somewhere called *Beneventum*. He had settled in this town and had taken the position of abbot, turning his attention to rebuilding the dilapidated church; however, his tenure did not last long. Around the year AD 580 he was brutally murdered by a band of Saxon mercenaries within the church itself as he celebrated the Holy Mysteries. One soldier ran Cadoc through with a spear. It has been speculated that his martyrdom at *Beneventum* occurred at the Roman town of *Bannaventa*. The region was at the time overrun with marauding Saxons, and there was a tradition that the Britons were not allowed to come into the town to recover the body of the dead holy man. Eventually the Saxons relented and the monks of Llancarfan were allowed to remove the murdered abbot's remains and take them back to Glamorganshire.

It is curious to note another martyrdom in this area, although the saint concerned is much less venerated. Goscelin's *Life Of Saint Warburg* (*c*.1095) notes the story of a pious cowherd called Alnoth who lived a life of simplicity on the grounds of the monastery at Weedon Bec. Werburgh, daughter of Wulfhere, King of Mercia, one day saw her steward assaulting the cowherd for some oversight. At this she positioned herself between the steward and the beaten cowherd and threw herself at the feet of her own steward, beseeching him to leave Alnoth alone as he was more worthy of entering Heaven than any other person present. The plea apparently had an effect on the brutal steward: Goscelin recounts that he suffered some sort of fit and collapsed, grovelling at the feet of Werburgh, begging forgiveness. Thus saved, Alnoth chose to live the life of a pious hermit in the dense woodland at Bugbrooke until he was killed by two brigands *c*.AD 700. He was buried at Stowe and for generations the local peasantry venerated his memory with pilgrimages there and held a festival in his honour.

THE STORY OF SAINT RUMBALD

According to the Norman-era work *Vita Sancti Rumwoldi* by Bishop Wulfstan of Worcester, a miracle occurred at Walton Grounds between King's Sutton and Aynho.

In the year AD 662 there was born of the royal line of Mercia a child named Rumbald (or Rumwold, Rumald or Grumbald etc). The infant boy was the grandson of King Penda, although by the time he was born the warrior-king was long dead, slaughtered along with hundreds of his men in a bitter clash along the banks of a swollen river called Winwed (somewhere near Leeds). Penda was a pagan king, responsible for the murders of several regional kings as he expanded his power-base. However, when his little grandson was born some seven years later there took place a miracle quite unlike any other recorded in the annals of Christianity.

It has been speculated that Rumbald's mother was Penda's daughter Cyneburh, an exceptionally pious Christian who had married a pagan Northumbrian ruler, Ealhfrith. She refused to grant him his conjugal rites unless he took the Christian faith. After Ealhfrith had done so, Cyneburh fell pregnant with Rumbald. The then-king of Mercia, Wulfhere, summoned Cyneburh (who was his sister) and her husband to the royal court. It was during the journey to the king that Rumbald's mother went into labour. The cortège was forced to stop at Walton Grounds, which at that time formed part of the Mercian royal estate.

Here something incredible took place. Immediately after he was born the tiny infant began to talk, saying repeatedly in Latin, 'I am a Christian, I am a Christian.' He continued to talk, requesting baptism and asking that his parents name him 'Rumbald'. He then proceeded to provide a full and learned confession of his faith before those assembled. The infant then appointed his own godfathers. Following this, the child's eyes fell upon a large hollow stone, and he stated that he desired it to be brought to him as his font. His father's servants struggled to shift the stone; however, the two priests that Rumbald had requested as his godfathers managed to pick the stone up as though it weighed nothing at all. Afterwards he was baptised by Bishop Widerino and assisted by a priest named Aedwold.

When the ceremony was over the infant Rumbald, still only hours old, walked in the direction of Brackley, and there he preached constantly for three days. At the cessation of this he predicted his own death and requested that he be buried at three spots: first King's Sutton, then Brackley the following year and ultimately Buckingham as the final resting place. Having given these orders, he instantly passed away – a mere three days old. The date was 3 November 662.

The infant's desire to be buried at three successive locations was granted following his death. Cults based on this legend subsequently grew up at these three locations. The story was firmly established in local lore by the time William Camden travelled the land compiling his historical *Britannia* (1586). Of Rumbald's association with Brackley he wrote, '…being canonized by the people among the Saints, [he] had his commemoration kept both heere and at Buckingham.' However, less than a century later the churchman and historian Thomas Fuller (d.1661) was entirely sceptical of the whole incident. Fuller was himself born in Aldwincle, Northamptonshire, yet despaired of such fanciful tales, declaring his view that '…thank God we live in times of better and brighter knowledge.'

Nevertheless, the legend of this curious story has persisted. A nearby natural well between King's Sutton and Upper Astrop became known as Saint Rumbald's Well. The well is in the grounds of Astrop House, and as with many of the natural springs in Northamptonshire it garnered a reputation for healing qualities in the years following the Civil War. A certain John Howe wrote in August 1680 that he had returned to London '…leaving his company deeply engaged in water-drinking at Astrop.' A decade later the famous traveller Celia Fiennes described the well as containing 'steele water', and in 1740 writer Thomas Short explained how St Rumbald's Well had become the focus of pilgrimage

Holy water stoup at the entrance to King's Sutton church. It was likely filled from nearby St Rumbald's Well in former centuries.

for travellers suffering from consumption, jaundice, dropsy, rheumatism, alcoholism, manic depression and 'female obstructions.' By this time the story of the miraculous infant who had given his name to the well would have been around for over a thousand years.

It is likely that the naming of the well was a 17th-century invention, designed to capitalise on the romantic popularity of a saint whose cult had only died out the previous century. It seems the well was not actually discovered until 1664, and so any associations with the infant saint would have been speculative at best.

The well is now in a very neglected condition. In King's Sutton itself, stonework in the font of St Peter and St Paul's Church is commonly thought to have been used to baptise Rumbald. Sadly, the headless effigy that adorns one of the entrances, so I was told, was supposed to have at one time been a likeness of the infant saint that was later defaced by rationalists attempting to rubbish the legend. However, the field at Walton Grounds – where he is believed to have been born and where a chapel is thought to have once stood until it was torn down in the 1500s – can still be pointed out.

WERBURGH & THE GEESE OF WEEDON BEC

Weedon Bec has an association with the aforementioned Saint Werburgh (or Werburg, Werburga, Warburg, etc), and the association is a curious one, a strange, almost comical story of a miracle that she performed.

Werburgh was born in Staffordshire of the Mercian royal line and took the life of a Benedictine nun at Ely, Cambridgeshire. She would have been a close blood relative of the infant Saint Rumbald.

Her greatest achievement was overseeing the reformation of convents in the English midlands, including the nunnery at Weedon Bec. She was ordained Abbess of Ely and eventually died *c.*3 February 699/700.

At that time Weedon was part of a royal estate, and Werburgh may have spent her time there overseeing the converting of the royal residency into a nunnery. During her time at Weedon, so it was said, there was a bizarre occurrence that began one day when Werburgh was told that flocks of wild geese were landing in the fields of the convent's farmstead and eating the corn. She ordered her

Weedon's church supports a weather vane in the image of a goose commemorating the story.

servant to round up the geese into pens. After looking at his lady with uncertainty, the servant did as he was bid – confused by her order to have the geese penned in when he knew they would simply fly out and continue to attack the corn.

However, once the geese were rounded up they defied conventional wisdom and docilely let themselves be penned in. Werburgh then approached the geese and began to scold them for their conduct, and it is at this point that the ancient tale enters the realms of fantasy.

The popular version of the story follows these lines. Werburgh forgave the troublesome geese and asked that they fly away. However, shortly afterwards the flock was back at the convent, the head gander waddling forward and croaking loudly as though angry. Werburgh was brought to the incensed goose and she apparently understood what it was 'saying'. As it circled round her feet it complained that the flock had discovered one of their number had gone missing, apparently during their brief incarceration. The servant was shuffling uncomfortably, and Werburgh charged him with having killed and eaten the missing goose. With the eyes of Werburgh, the assembled nuns and hundreds of geese upon him, the servant confessed to his act of gluttony.

Werburgh ordered the servant to gather up the carcass and bones of the dead goose and bring them from the kitchens. Then, with a sign from her hand, the bones of the goose fleshed out and gradually its carcass began to move as it was brought to life once more. Then its wings feathered and soon it was waddling about among its fellows. Werburgh rejoiced in the event, singing, 'Birds of the air, bless the Lord!' Eventually the flock took off, and forever after, it was said, no wild geese would ever trouble the fields of Weedon Bec.

The Elizabethan antiquarian John Leland noted during a visit to Northamptonshire that near the south side of the parish church of St Peter and St Paul there was still to be found a chapel dedicated to Werburgh, although she had actually been buried at Hanbury in Staffordshire. Although her connections with Weedon are valid, the story of the geese may in fact have *originated* in Chester before somehow transposing itself to Weedon. The body of Werburgh was later removed from Hanbury to be reburied at Chester, some three centuries after her death.

Around the time her corpse was moved to Chester, Werburgh's hagiographer, Goscelin of Saint Bertin, was writing her *Life* and this is the first work to note the legend, although it has been suggested he may have elaborated (or even 'borrowed') the story from his *Life Of St Amelburga* to promote the cult of Werburgh and pilgrimage to Chester. The story was further elaborated by the English Benedictine Henry Bradshaw in a second *Life* of the saint compiled during his time at Werburgh's monastery in Chester during the latter part of the 1400s. However, at some point the story had become inextricably linked with Weedon Bec. As late as 1791, John Bridges, the vicar of St Sepulchre, Northampton, wrote in his *History And Antiquities Of Northamptonshire* that vulgar superstition held to that very day that no wild geese had ever been known to feed in the fields of Weedon.

Although this is the most familiar miracle associated with Werburgh, Goscelin also credits her with providing frequent examples of clairvoyance, healing and other marvels.

The 'Sweet Melody of Birds' at Oundle

Bishop Wilfrid was one of the most influential and controversial figures of the Anglo-Saxon church. By the standards of the period, Wilfrid's life is relatively well chronicled, thanks mainly to the work of a Ripon monk called Eddius Stephanus. His *Vita Wilfridi* was written shortly after the bishop's death at Oundle on 12 October AD 709.

Wilfrid was born c.AD 634 in the kingdom of Northumbria, and much of his youth was spent drifting after a conflict of interests with his stepmother. His inclination for a life of religion led him, under the patronage of Eanfled, Queen of Bernicia, to Lindisfarne, Canterbury, Rome and Lyons. He returned to England following the murder of his new patron, the Bishop of Lyons; it is written that the bishop's executioners would not allow Wilfrid to divulge the circumstances of the killing. Wilfrid himself faced personal danger: on another return journey from France in 666 (following his consecration in Compiegne) he and his retinue were shipwrecked on the coast of Sussex during a thunderstorm. A mob of pagan ship-wreckers repeatedly attacked the boat until changing winds and tides took the stranded vessel back out to sea.

By this time Wilfrid was already a leading champion of the Roman Christian doctrine in England, and had been promoted to the position of bishop of the see of York in 664. He founded the great monasteries at Selsey, Ripon and Hexham but in 677 was driven into exile following a quarrel with King Egfrith of Northumbria. During this period he spent much of his time trying to reassert his position, but during the years of exile south of the River Humber he was responsible for setting up many more monasteries – including one at Oundle, Northamptonshire.

Wilfrid returned to Ripon upon the death of King Egfrith in 686 or 687, summoned by the new king of Northumbria, Aldfrith. However, Aldfrith was a supporter of the Celtic Church and Wilfrid was ultimately once again forced into exile. He did not return to his homeland of Northumbria until the year AD 704, having outlived Aldfrith. Wilfrid is justly remembered for bringing English Christianity into line with European Christianity, and there are many tales told of him. He earned the nickname 'rain-maker' during his time spent attempting to convert the heathens of Sussex. It was a period when 40 or 50 peasants would link hands and jump off cliffs to their deaths rather than face starvation; yet upon the very day he began to baptize converts in Sussex it started to rain, thus saving the harvest. He also brought the skill of fishing to the region – previously the locals had only been able to catch eels.

Wilfrid was already renowned in his lifetime as the people's saviour, and it was upon his visit to the monastery at Oundle that he fell ill and breathed his last, aged 75, on 12 October 709. He had been ill for sometime, and he clearly knew that his horseback ride to the monastery at Oundle would be his last trip: he appears to have recognised that he was going there to die.

His death and burial, according to Stephanus of Ripon, were surrounded by instances of supernatural occurrences: Wilfrid died on his bed, merely turning his head on the pillow and expiring. At the very hour of his death many witnesses within the monastic community at Oundle testified that as they sang psalms they were distracted by a 'sweet melody of birds and clapping of their wings, as if they were flying up to Heaven...' As the brethren reverently carried Wilfrid's body out of the house to a tent where it would be washed and prepared for burial, this curious noise was heard a second time. Throughout the incident no flocks of birds could be seen and many saw the phenomenon as an invisible appearance of angels sent to guard the bishop as his soul ascended to Heaven.

The bishop was to be laid out post-mortem on the muslin garment of Abbott Bacula, and a nun who performed the task of washing the fabric found that the act had healed her withered hand. The abbot's robe was afterwards treated as a holy relic and given to the abbess, who was entrusted with its preservation. The clergy solemnly sang psalms and washed the bishop's body, but whenever they stopped they could still hear the 'bird-like melody and wafture of unseen wings above them.' After Wilfrid's body had been removed for burial at Ripon, a small cell was erected where the tent had previously stood and a wooden cross was put up. In the years that followed many miracles of healing were purported to have occurred at the site among the peasantry of Northampton and Huntingdon.

Stephanus of Ripon's autobiography of Wilfrid was finished around the year AD 720, 11 years after the bishop's death. Within it he mentions a miracle that occurred when a band of exiled nobles attempted to burn the monastery at Oundle to the ground. They had been pillaging and murdering their way along the valley of the River Nene, and at Oundle they set the monastery aflame. As the site burnt, one part of it remained unscathed: the cell where Bishop Wilfrid had passed away. The marauders threw dry straw onto the conflagration, but to their amazement it actually began to put out the flames. One of the young noblemen, furious at the turn of events, entered the cell and threw straw all around the inside. However, before he was able to set it alight he was struck with terror at the appearance of an ethereal young man dressed in white who held a golden cross before him. At this the outlaw fled from the cell screaming that the spot was defended by the angel of the Lord. The great thorn hedge that surrounded the monastery grounds was alight also; however, as the flames approached the miraculous cell they mysteriously died away. Similarly, as the fire approached the wooden cross erected at the site of the washing of the body it too died away. Stephanus of Ripon noted that all of those who took part in this incident were eventually captured, blinded and slaughtered in an atrocity which he saw as the work of divine retribution. The stories of these miracles are interesting as Stephanus was not writing centuries after Wilfrid's death, but merely in the decade that followed. This is therefore evidence that the stories were *contemporary* with the time of the bishop's death, as opposed to myths which grew with future generations.

Bishop Wilfrid is thought to have established the monastery at Oundle sometime between the years 666 and 669, but quite where is unclear. Stephanus of Ripon chronicled that the bishop died in 'provincia quae uocatur In Undalem'. 'Undalem' *is* Oundle, but the text implies that it was a region or province, rather than a town. Francis Peck's *Annals Of Stamford* (1727) noted, 'As I rode through Oundle in April 1723, I saw there a very ancient chapel, now converted into a barn or workhouse, which I am persuaded by the great antiquity of its structure, belonged heretofore to that very monastery wherein Wilfrid, our founder, died.' However, the site is not specifically located. During renovations at St Peter's Church in Oundle, thought to date from the 13th century, the pillars were found to stand on the footings of a building from a much earlier period. Could this, then, be the site of the primitive Anglo-Saxon monastery where angels made a visitation to earth in honour of the great Bishop Wilfrid?

Wilfrid was subsequently canonized, and Stephanus of Ripon's story of his life is remarkable in itself, being the earliest surviving historical work by an Anglo-Saxon scholar.

BECKET'S WELL

The association of King Henry II of England and Thomas Becket with Northampton is well documented. The pair would often hunt in the woodland of the deer park that enclosed the castle and sizeable surrounding town. In January 1155 the king appointed Becket, then Archdeacon of Canterbury, as his chancellor. On 23 June 1162 Becket was consecrated as Archbishop of Canterbury upon the death of his mentor Theobald. This was eight and a half years before the developing power struggle between the two men escalated into a bloody tragedy of Shakespearian proportions.

Cracks and rivalries had already started to appear in Becket's friendship with the young king. In September 1158 Becket, in his position as the king's chief ecclesiastical representative, had travelled to France to iron out the betrothal of Henry's three-year-old son to King Louis VII of France's infant daughter. The wealth displayed on Becket's baggage train absolutely stunned Parisians: 200 of his staff, each with their own servants, were followed by packhorses laden with treasures and portable altars, hawks, hounds and horses – each of which was led by a groom and had a monkey sitting on its back. This extravagant, almost vulgar, display of wealth unfortunately put to shame the king's own cortège in the memories of the French. Henry had himself visited France a month earlier, but Becket's cavalcade outshone his easily.

The simmering rivalry between the king and his archbishop came to a head in 1164. Upon his consecration Becket almost immediately entered into arguments with Henry over lands and properties which he felt had been taken illegally by the king. Henry, equally arrogant and stubborn, resisted this, feeling that his weaker predecessor, King Stephen, had granted the church the lands (and too much power) too readily in the first place. Quarrels over other ecclesiastical matters grew. Henry wanted royal courts to punish members of the clergy with the death sentence if they were convicted of murder, as had happened in his grandfather's time. In Stephen's reign, however, the clergy were allowed to be tried by their brethren, which often resulted in abbots and priors merely being defrocked if convicted of a serious crime. The king had the 'Constitution of Clarendon' drafted, which demanded total and absolute ecclesiastical obedience to the crown.

Henry further began to demand that monies he had provided Becket with to further royal interests be accounted for and that he hand back what he insisted was crown land. By this point the king was flying into violent rages, and discussions on the issues were being abruptly ended by him without conclusion. Subsequent items on the agenda were similarly left unresolved.

Thomas and his retinue were at this time being accommodated at the priory of St Andrew's, an 11th-century Cluniac monastery that stood (before it was razed c.1538) in the 'north parte of the toune, hard by the north gate' of Northampton. As the acrimonious negotiations – in effect a trial – hit a brick wall and descended into veiled threats of violence, Becket began to sense that Henry intended to demand his resignation. The archbishop was, at this point, in weak bodily health due to kidney stones, and to make matters worse he found little support from the clergy of St Andrew's, who were fearful of the king's wrath. So were many others, and the whole affair can now be seen to have been marred by labyrinthine political agendas, often involving personal grudges between the clergy and the barons; between the weak and the strong; and between those who feared the idea of the king's rule in England being absolute and those who hated Becket and resented his power.

On 13 October 1164 Becket took a final mass at St Andrew's in which he invoked the first martyr, St Stephen: an act indicating that he felt his course of action may cost him his life. Outside the priory, in his episcopal robes and bearing a great cross before him, he climbed his horse and set off, accompanied by a mere handful of attendants, the only ones who – in the face of Henry's rage – remained absolutely loyal. Notwithstanding this, the common townsfolk of Northampton crowded the muddy streets and withstood the pouring rain to applaud the archbishop as he made his way to Northampton Castle for what turned out to be his last meeting with the king.

Archbishop Becket entered the castle, convinced a martyr's death awaited him. Inside he was left alone with hostile courtiers, jealous barons and cowardly clergy, some of whom attempted to get him to lay down his cross; the archbishop refused, expecting violence and claiming it would protect him greater than any sword.

In a chamber upstairs the weak and worldly bishops of St Andrew's were reporting to Henry how they feared Becket was going to defy the king and take the issue to Rome. For the entire episode Henry had refused to stand face to face with Becket, sending messengers to and fro, all the while berating the trembling bishops for their cowardice – Becket had commanded them to take no further part in the proceedings, and they were now caught between a rock and hard place. As messages passed and Becket remained stubbornly immovable to the will of the king, Henry's rage grew until it exploded into such a fury that it seemed the very walls of the castle shook. The justiciar Robert of Leicester was ordered downstairs to proclaim Becket a traitor and to cast sentence upon him as such. However, Becket, who had still not set eyes upon the king, interrupted Leicester and bellowed, 'Who are ye that ye should judge me? Ye are but princes of the palace, lay persons! I am your spiritual father, and by my authority I forbid you to pronounce the sentence!' He then turned to leave as those assembled threw objects at him, but he found the door locked; luckily an attendant managed to secure a key and the archbishop was hustled outside where a mob of overjoyed townsfolk gathered, preventing the king's supporters from rushing out to arrest Becket. Common folk, kneeling before Becket, lined the dirty streets all the way back to St Andrew's Priory.

In the very early hours of 14 October 1164 Becket took the decision to flee Northampton. When the king's men invaded the priory grounds looking for the archbishop, they found him gone.

Writing in 1914, A.P. White noted in *The Story Of Northampton* that '...a local tradition says that in his flight he drank from the well near Cheyne Walk that bears his name.' It is reliably recorded that throughout the entire confrontation Becket was in poor health. At the time of his flight he was disguised as a Gilbertine monk and accompanied by three faithful attendants. During a ferocious thunderstorm he is alleged to have alighted his horse at the well (at that time just outside the town walls) and drank its waters, with the result that it provided him with the rejuvenation required to keep going. White considered the story unlikely as Cheyne Walk lay in a contradictory direction to the route Becket would have taken when he fled via the Great North Gate of the town in the direction of Grantham, Lincolnshire. That is unless he deliberately sought out the well before proceeding. Perhaps not surprisingly, 'Becket's Well' gained a reputation locally as a healing spring where the sick and crippled could be taken, and in the early Victorian era, still outside of the town boundary, it was enclosed in stone. Here it continued to be a popular destination for tourists and the sick. In 1948 the well was closed off in the belief that it was now unsuitable for drinking, and as the town had grown around it by this point it gradually fell into a state of disrepair. Happily, however, months of hard work restored it to its former glory in November 2006.

Folklore has attributed a similar feat to Becket at nearby Deanshanger monastery. In his flight he hid at several Gilbertine monasteries and during one incognito residence he went unrecognised by all, with the exception of a common farm labourer. Perhaps mindful of the event at Cheyne Walk, the farm labourer asked the new arrival if he could sort out the village's undrinkable water supply. Becket complied by purifying the town's spring. Again, there is area for contention with this story:

The Holy Sepulchre, Northampton, built by crusading knights returning from Jerusalem.

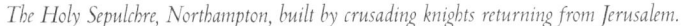

Deanshanger is a good deal south of Northampton and in the wrong direction to the route of his flight. It is possible that in both instances these 'miracles' are an intertwining of the association between Northamptonshire's numerous 'healing springs' and older legends about the archbishop thumping his crozier into the ground and producing a spring of pure water (such as at Otford, Kent).

Whether it is true or not, just over six years later the power struggle between King Henry II and Thomas Becket reached its conclusion upon the archbishop's return to England. A fragile peace made at the French town of Freteval on 22 July 1170 led Becket to return home where he was formally reinstated as Archbishop of Canterbury on 1 December. Parading as though the ruler of the kingdom wherever he went, Becket caused further trouble by punishing bishops who had officiated at the crowning of Henry's son as heir to the throne – that responsibility, he insisted, was Canterbury's. The simmering animosities were still there, and Becket made almost no attempt to keep a discreet profile; nothing had changed, his enemies were still everywhere and a contingent of three archbishops (whom Becket had excommunicated after learning of their part in the coronation) carried their grievances to King Henry in France. On Christmas day he notoriously thundered, 'What a pack of fools and cowards have I nourished in my household that not one of them will avenge me of this turbulent priest?'

As a Northampton historian, A.P. White wrote of Becket's end at Canterbury Cathedral on 29 December 1170: 'What need to tell again the story of Becket's return, of the hasty words of Henry, and of the cruel murder in the cathedral that made the archbishop known to future generations as St Thomas, the Martyr of Canterbury?'

THE PARSON AND THE BEAR

In the winter of 1642 there occurred in Wellingborough an incident which brings to mind the mystical affinity between man and beast that is sometimes recorded about notable holy men, such as St Francis of Assisi or Bishop Hugh of Lincoln. The extraordinary event is drawn upon in John Cole's *The History & Antiquities Of Wellingborough* (1837), which itself draws from *Mercurius Rusticus* – a Royalist newsletter, which, like its Parliamentary rivals, eagerly printed such partisan incidents. In the chaos of the Civil War a local notary, Mr Zouch Tate (who is presumed to be a supporter of parliament at a time when Wellingborough was for the king), sent a mob of 300 'watermen' to cause havoc in the town. This rampaging mob plundered their way through Wellingborough, at one point murdering a barber and taking his performing bear with them as a whimsical 'captive'. Among the human prisoners rounded up was Thomas Jones, who had been vicar at All Hallows Church for some 40 years. The aged Mr Jones was at the time in poor health; he was lame from an accident but was nonetheless forced to march with the other prisoners along the muddy road in the direction of Northampton.

The infirm vicar naturally began to fall behind, and at this point the mob accompanying the procession grew tired of merely jeering at him and decided to set the captive bear on him for sport. However, the great animal – a female – ran up to the vicar, put her head down and allowed him to sit on her back; she then quietly and calmly carried the old man. Everyone in the crowd was astonished at this, and so Mr Jones was dragged off the animal's back and placed atop a restless horse that had been bucking and trying to escape the grim convoy for most of the journey. This animal also settled down once the vicar sat on its back and quite calmly trotted along now as though nothing were amiss. Someone from among the crowd, who had been involved in the killing of the barber, straddled the bear himself, whereupon the animal turned on him and mauled him so violently that he died.

It is written in *Mercurius* that the Revd Jones was thrown into a straw-lined cell in Northampton gaol, where a wooden bed and single blanket had been left for him. Despite this treatment, in the middle of the winter, and being forced to subsist on meagre rations of bread and water, he managed to survive for three months until he was freed. It was already being said that a miracle had occurred and the popular vicar of 40 years had been saved by God's hand.

Sometime after this the brave reverend was arrested a second time for preaching against the rebellion in Wellingborough and carted off to Northampton once more. Here he was kept in even worse conditions in solitary confinement. Not surprisingly, he died during his incarceration – not of ill health or infirmity, it was whispered, but because his gaolers had deliberately starved him to death. The Revd Jones had been murdered, and by the time *Mercurius* was written it is apparent that local folk were already considering him a martyr. His condition post-mortem was observed to be painfully thin and it was clear he had been starved. To add insult to injury, John Gifford, mayor of Northampton and colonel of the town regiment, had the corpse thrown unceremoniously into a hole and covered as quickly as possible. His name was also removed from parish registers, according to Cole writing in 1837.

The story reported in *Mercurius* could still be cited as an actual event by those writing in the years following the war. There were witnesses, including members of the clergy who had personally known Jones, who would defend it as being a true anecdote, and there is some justification for the story being at least *based* on an actual event, which was perhaps elaborated on by the people of Wellingborough and Royalist journalists. A mighty stained-glass window in the north aisle of All Hallows Church, Wellingborough, commemorates this curious story.

PROVIDENCE AND DIVINE JUDGEMENT

One aspect of religion in times past was the sincere belief that all that happened, both good and bad, was due to God's will. Often something that manifested physically, such as thunderstorms, was interpreted as the divine displeasure of the Lord. To understand this mindset one has to remember that people were quite literally God-fearing. As noted earlier, Cromwell himself believed very strongly in submitting to providence and thought that all things were God's will. Thus, any misfortune – not just in war, but in everyday life – was in fact the wrath, or will, of the Lord personified. For example, Glass's *The Early History Of The Independent Church At Rothwell* (1871) noted how in 1658 the minister of Rothwell, one John Beverley, entered into the records of Holy Trinity Church the death of a parishioner's baby 'by God's stroke'. The minister had quarrelled with the parishioner about the child's level of education some time before its death. Beverley clearly thought that the infant's death was divine judgement for the unseemly slanging match, a strangely unsympathetic sentiment from a holy man.

In tune with this, the weather played an important part in the lives of county folk in more than one sense. It was often regarded as an omen of misfortune – if not the very word of the Lord himself. One very famous legend tells how William de Drayton, a wayward son of the de Vere line (of Drayton House, west of Lowick), was a notorious poacher of the king's game in the 13th century, in the days when the village, and the Drayton estate, was part of the thickly wooded Rockingham Forest. Ballads recalled how on one occasion William was trapped by the local sheriff and his soldiers during an immense thunderstorm. As the sheriff blew his bugle he was struck and instantly killed by a bolt of lightning, which local folklore has attributed to the hand of providence; William's mother, knowing of his criminal escapades, had prayed that God protect her son.

A violent thunder and lightning storm in 1601 left many people dead in Everdon, south of Daventry, and tracts were regularly published on such disasters with extravagant titles such as *A Brief & Seasonable Improvement Of The Late Earthquake In Northamptonshire, Jan 4th 1675-6*, or *The Great Flood, Or Sad & Lamentable News From Northampton & C[ounty] On Tuesday And Wednesday 5th & 6th Instant May, 1663*.

The flooding of 1663 left many people dead, although God's hand was seen in the miraculous escape of an infant who was washed a mile out of Weedon Bec when the swollen Nene broke its banks, only to be safely deposited in a mill.

Perhaps understandably, flooding, lightning, thunderclaps and other aerial phenomena such as comets were also regularly viewed as biblical portents of disaster – the physical manifestation of the wrath of God. Ministers would terrify their flock by announcing that such events heralded the end of the world and that time was up for the sinful folk of Northamptonshire. This would especially extend to rare natural phenomena, such as earthquakes. The year 1750 was a remarkable one for earthquakes: in London a soldier prophesied that tremors shaking the capital were the forerunner to a disastrous quake that would level the city and destroy the nation. This did not happen and the soldier was thrown into an asylum, but it is curious to note that earthquakes hit various parts of Britain later that year. The one that shook Northamptonshire on 30 September was doubtless seen by many as heralding the end of the world.

Plague, pestilence and warfare were also often seen as the manifestation of the Lord's anger. Thus, when plague broke out in the county in October 1605 it was seen as divine judgement and prompted the mayor of Northampton, George Caldwell, to crack down on drinking and gambling dens in the town. Remarkably (or so it appeared at the time) his crusade coincided with the outbreak of plague diminishing and thus proved that God had been appeased, albeit at the expense of some 500 lives within the town walls.

Conversely, upon the Great Fire of Northampton on 20 September 1675, in which 11 died and much of the town was razed, God's intervention was seen in ensuring that the disaster was not much worse. Many more could have died but for the fact that it had been a cold, late summer; coal had been stockpiled, which in many cases 'ate up' the fire and slowed down its spread, while the Lord had assured that it was a year of plentiful harvest – and so famine would not strike the region afterwards. However, following the Great Fire of Wellingborough on 28 July 1738, a local parson, Dr Doddridge, blamed God's wrath rather than his mercy. He thundered, 'It was the hand of the Lord that kindled your fire, and his breath that fanned it into such a terrible blaze!' Doddridge went on to describe how the speed, direction and difficulty in controlling the fire all evidenced divine judgement on a populace who had 'been addicted to riot and intemperance.' Clearly the aspects of divine 'involvement' in these two fires are at odds with one another.

Sabbath breaking was one of the sins particularly likely to bring down Heavenly wrath, and there were numerous verbal warnings against this in which the sinner is turned to stone, or else falls asleep, never to wake up. In Northamptonshire the folklorist Thomas Sternberg noted in 1851 a fairy tale told to children which contained this message – and which involved a unique punishment for the Sabbath-breaker. A villager had stolen a '*furze* faggot' on a Sunday and for this he was condemned to spend the rest of his days alone on the moon – a veiled warning to children in the form of an explanation for the 'man on the moon' that they were also told of. As Sternberg points out, 'It is the Sabbath-breaking that constitutes the principal offence, and not...the theft.'

These fairy-tale warnings did actually mirror factual events: The *Northampton Mercury* of 17 June 1786 reported on the death of young Lewis Gregory who had drowned while bathing in the River Ouse near Olney. There was great consternation among the mourners when the unfortunate lad was interred at Hanslope, Buckinghamshire, for he had been a fit and healthy 21-year-old and had unaccountably drowned on a calm, sunny day. The minister who conducted the service was in no doubt why this had happened: young Lewis, he cried, had incurred the wrath of the Almighty because he had fallen among those who, '...make a common practice of misspending the Lord's day' and who '...daringly and sacrilegiously profane the Sabbath by undue and illicit practices by walking and bathing in defiance either of respect to God or decency to man...'

JOHN WESLEY'S FOOTPRINTS

In 2008, in the process of researching this book, I was told a fascinating anecdote by a gentleman in Brackley. Apparently, the founder of Methodism, John Wesley, had found the people of Towcester so disagreeable to his philosophy that he had been unable to preach to them on any level. Despite much spirited effort he had despaired of the townsfolk and sadly given up all hope of converting them to Methodism. His repeated attempts at preaching there, however, 'left imprints of his feet *emblazoned in the stone*' – a phenomenon that had a gradual effect on the apathetic populace long after Wesley had departed in despair and exasperation. This site was subsequently where Towcester Methodist Church on Brackley Road was erected around 1893.

This story is an interesting one which I have heard of nowhere else. The person who told me this recalled being told it themselves during a childhood visit to Towcester's Methodist Church in the 1960s.

It is true that John Wesley (and other Methodists) made repeated visits to Towcester. They encountered little success during their open-air sermons; it was not that the populace were violently opposed to his preaching (as some places in England were), but merely that their apathy stunned and saddened Wesley. His own diary records that as late as December 1784 he preached to '…poor, dead Towcester. But is not God able to rise the dead? There was considerable shaking among the dry bones. And who knows but these dry bones may yet live?'

Twenty-five years of preaching in Towcester as part of a nationwide crusade revealed only occasional successes. In 1760 a sermon had produced 'One person whose soul God keeps alive, although he has little to converse with.' A Methodist emissary apparently reached one Sarah Spencer, who in 1774 had a premonition of her own death at a young age and spent much of her remaining days trying to convert the townsfolk. She died, with her weeping father by her side, on 7 June that year.

Wesley's life story is a fascinating one: his sermons were bedevilled by violent clashes, and claims of supernatural events also cling to him. His old home in Epworth, North Lincolnshire, was famously haunted. Even more telling is the legend that his footprints are supposed to have been emblazoned into the marble work of his father's tomb at St Andrew's Church in Epworth. *Notes & Queries* discussed this matter in depth, repeating the old story that John Wesley had been denied access to Epworth Church and so had preached from his father's tomb. The imprints of his feet could be observed there for generations afterwards, and I cannot help but think that this is where the story I was told about Towcester originates. An 1840 book, *The Works Of The Reverend John Wesley*, tells us that Methodism did not make much of a foothold in Towcester despite Wesley's years of crusading in the 1700s. Perhaps this is why to have a Methodist Church in Towcester at all is seen as so remarkable nowadays.

THE MYSTERY OF RUSHTON HALL'S HOLY RELIC

Somewhere within the grounds of Rushton Hall, at Rushton, north west of Kettering, legend states a holy relic lies hidden. Work commenced on the hall around 1438 at the behest of Sir John Tresham, and centuries of additions, improvements and enlargements using mainly local stone have provided the foundations for the hall as it stands today: an exceptionally impressive structure, both imposing and magnificently graceful, its great rooms adorned with sizeable stone and timber fireplaces. The first Sir Thomas Tresham, who died on 8 March 1559, was a leading Catholic politician who served as Sheriff of Northamptonshire and MP for the county. He was also held to be a member of the Knights Templar, and recently – in the wake of the success of *The Da Vinci Code* – it has been speculated

Rushton Hall.

that the holy relic rumoured to lie safely hidden away within the grounds of Rushton Hall is none other than the Holy Grail itself.

In Christian mythology the Holy Grail is alleged to have been a plate, dish or cup used by Jesus Christ at the Last Supper, and there is a wealth of lore linking the relic to Britain. Robert de Boron's *Joseph d'Arimathie* (1202) is among the earliest references which links the various elements of the myth as a whole, and he drew upon earlier accounts of Joseph travelling to England as a tin merchant (such as William of Malmesbury's early 12th-century *Gesta Regum Anglorum*). The legend says that Joseph had come to Britain via an ancient Phoenician trade route – and had been accompanied by the boy Jesus. The story follows that, after the crucifixion of Jesus Christ, Joseph had the Grail taken to Great Britain, and there a line of guardians was established to keep it safe. The remains of Saint Joseph of Arimathea and his followers are *alleged* to have been uncovered at Glastonbury in Somerset sometime in the mid-14th century. The aforementioned Welsh saint, Cadoc, is widely held to have been one of the guardians of the Holy Grail. Maybe he brought it with him to *Beneventum*, which has been tentatively identified as *Bannaventa* near Norton in Northamptonshire. Here Cadoc met his violent end at the hands of a marauding Anglo-Saxon soldier.

The tale was a popular one in the Middle Ages and is still so today. Belief in the Holy Grail and speculation as to its whereabouts have never ceased. Although the legend of it being brought to England might be more romance than fact (forming the basis for one of the most famous myths concerning King Arthur), speculation on the topic has continued right up to the current era and has now become inextricably linked with the Knights Templar. The Knights Templar – or, to go by their full title, The Poor Fellow Soldiers of Christ and of the Temple of Solomon – began life as a charitable organisation which protected pilgrims to the Holy Land in the aftermath of the First Crusade. As their power grew, speculation clung to the Templar order that during their residence near the Temple of Solomon, Jerusalem, in the early 12th century they had begun excavations in a search for relics and had made finds of huge religious significance.

The Knights Templar had chapters in Britain, and the Church of the Holy Sepulchre in Northampton was built *c*.AD 1100 at the behest of Earl Simon de Senlis and the Templars themselves, its curious circular design reflecting the Church of the Holy Sepulchre in Jerusalem. So then it might be idly speculated that the Holy Grail was either brought to Northamptonshire by Saint Cadoc in Anglo-Saxon times, or else brought from the Holy Land by the Templars during the Crusades. The Templar order was purged in 1312, the knights in England arrested and their property seized by King Edward II. However, the aura of mystery and secrecy that clung to the order has led to fanciful suggestions that they engineered their own demise to 'drop off the radar', and that the order persisted in some form following the purge, but under a cloud of even further secrecy.

In the wake of the movie *The Da Vinci Code* the ancient legend that Sir Thomas Tresham had been a member of a Knights Templar order that had survived beyond the purge was resurrected. On 18 May 2006 Keith White, who had been employed to maintain Rushton Hall for the past quarter of a century, told the *Northampton Chronicle & Echo*, 'The knights supposedly returned to this country with a holy relic and there are some who believe that it is buried at Rushton Hall.' Legend says that the mysterious artefact is wrapped in leather and encased in lead.

The Tresham family created an oratory at Rushton Hall, and this room still houses an invaluable representation of the Passion – Christ on the cross – that was removed from St Peter's Church (which once stood on the grounds of the hall). It dates back to 1577, and so would have been positioned in the oratory long after Sir Thomas Tresham's death in 1559; nonetheless, on the plaster panel are depictions of several people pointing to different letters in the inscription on the crucifix. Mr White told the newspaper, 'The letters they are pointing to are supposed to be part of a code or anagram which is meant to reveal where the relic can be found.' Within the grounds of Rushton Hall can be

The entrance to All Saints' Church in Northampton town centre. In the 1730s a preacher named Doddridge was amazed by the young religious mystic Mary Wills of Pitsford, who prophesised he would come here and who claimed many 'miraculous experiences'. These included surviving a poisoning and raindrops not touching her.

found the late-Elizabethan era curio called Rushton Triangular Lodge, itself rich in symbolism. Mysterious numbers are carved into the gables – 3509 and 3898 – and it has been speculated that the spacious area between the lodge and the oratory itself is the location where the holy relic lies buried.

These days Rushton Hall functions as the most elegant of countryside hotels. Quite what is hidden here is unclear. The Holy Grail is the first and most obvious suggestion, but the newspaper article hints that there is a belief locally that it might even be a relic from biblical times linked to Moses' parting of the Red Sea when the Hebrews fled Egypt. There may be a mystery of immense religious significance waiting to be unravelled here; conversely, it may be that the romantic aspects of such a speculative story are just so compelling that the legend will never completely die out.

After all, there is a suggestion that at one time mediaeval Holy Trinity Church in Rothwell may have harboured a sliver of the true cross. In addition it must be pointed out that (although not on the Hollywood-epic scale of the rumoured Rushton relic) a true holy relic *has* turned up in the county. In November 1809 a small cylindrical wooden box was found in 'the mortuary chapel' in the southeastern portion of the church of All Saints, Brixworth. The box was dated to the 14th century but the contents appeared much older: a tiny bone, and a piece of parchment that fell to dust upon being exposed to the air. The fact that there was a mediaeval fair and guild in the parish to honour Saint Boniface caused the relic to be credibly considered part of his larynx. Boniface was an eighth-century saint born in Devonshire who was ultimately martyred in Frisia and is today the patron saint of Germany. Although the tiny bone was kept safe in a container dated to the 1300s, the church in Brixworth probably dates to around the seventh century and would have existed in some form when Saint Boniface was actually alive.

CHAPTER 3

SUPERNATURAL EVIL

INTRODUCTION

There can be few people these days who live in Northamptonshire who are not at least aware that the county has an impressive history of documented witchcraft cases, and I have heard it said by many that England's last witch to be executed died in Northamptonshire: Northampton, Mears Ashby or Oundle being the locations most frequently specified. While this might not be quite true, the region does indeed boast fascinating and unsettling instances of witchcraft. The pattern of witchcraft is strange in Northamptonshire; there is as much historical written evidence of actual trials involving 'real' witches as there are folklore stories, and this is unusual. Many of the accounts paint a picture of a truly disturbing period in the county's history, particularly those that relate to the purge of 1612.

The region itself was the setting for one of the earliest recorded incidences of witchcraft. An anonymous Anglo-Saxon charter dated 1044 notes that around a century earlier one Wulstan Uccea was a *thegn* in the East Midlands who held estates at Kettering and Ailsworth (now part of Cambridgeshire). The latter had come into his possession because a neighbouring widow had had a grudge against his father, Alfsige. When the widow's house was searched an effigy was found of Alfsige with an iron pin stabbed into its heart, and following her conviction on a charge of witchcraft the widow was carted off to London Bridge where she was drowned in the Thames. Her Ailsworth estate thus passed to her victim's family, with King Edgar's blessing, while her own son was forced to flee after being branded an outlaw.

In 1316 Philip de Gayton died without an heir, and his lands at Milton Malsor and Collingtree, and Shrewley in Warwickshire, passed to his brother Theobald, who promptly died a few days later. Part of the lands then passed to his sisters Scholastica, widow of Geoffrey de Meaux, and Juliana. A third of the manor passed to his widow Margery. In 1321 Juliana was burnt to death, accused of witchcraft and of murdering her husband Thomas Murdac with poison. Her lands at Shrewley were declared the property of the king, and thereafter the lands at Malsor and Collingtree in Northamptonshire became the subject of bitter legal contesting. It seems that the remaining sister, Scholastica, had Margery de Gayton manoeuvred out the following year, and hence ruled Malsor and Collingtree herself until her death around 1353. In St Mary's Church, Gayton, can be found an effigy of Scholastica herself; for years the number of deaths surrounding her which aided her political advancement led to rumours that Scholastica de Meaux had used witchcraft to engineer the whole scenario with the intention of providing for her son, Sir John de Meaux.

During the mediaeval period even a queen mother was not safe from such accusations. In late 1469 the then Queen Mother, Jacquet de Luxemburg, was accused of using witchcraft to engineer her daughter Elizabeth Woodville's enrapture of the young King Edward IV. Edward and Elizabeth's first meeting five years earlier is supposed to have taken place underneath an enormous hollow oak tree subsequently called the Queen's Oak, between Wakefield Lawn and Yardley Gobion. When their secret marriage at Grafton Regis was made public it outraged many, who saw their opportunity to manoeuvre the king into a political marriage benefitting themselves disappear. Among these was Richard Neville, the Earl of Warwick, known as 'the kingmaker', whose anger at being thwarted in his desire to negotiate Edward's marriage began to simmer. A conspiracy was entered into to defame Jacquet and therefore illegitimise her daughter's marriage to the king: such accusations were in fact a form of political weaponry during a period bedevilled by bloody civil war. *The Rolls Of Parliament, 9 Edward IV* of 1470 later recorded how one Squire Thomas Wake (no doubt acting in complicity with the Earl of Warwick's supporters) caused a riotous furore in the town of Warwick by claiming that an effigy made of lead had been discovered which had been linked to Jacquet. Wake presented it to the lords during a visit of the king: it was about the length of 'a mannes fynger' and held fast with wire where it had been broken in the middle. Furthermore, Wake claimed, Jacquet had entrusted two more effigies to a certain 'John Daunger, parishe clerk of Stoke *Brewerne*, in the *counte* of Northampton.' These two effigies were claimed by Wake to have been of the monarch and Elizabeth Woodville, and to have been used with sorcery to bring them together under the Queen's Oak. As the wider power struggle swung violently to and fro, King Edward had the accusations thrown out. The story is a confusing one, and the political landscape shifted so frequently that it is quite likely Jacquet was an innocent victim caught in a conspiracy and subsequent propaganda war. Unfortunately the accusations still hounded her memory even after her death, during the rule of Edward's successor, the infamous Richard III.

Jacquet de Luxemburg died on 30 May 1472. Notwithstanding the damage to her character, perhaps Jacquet was lucky to escape the accusations physically unscathed; most of those involved in the politics of the age had much blood on their hands. However, all this was nothing compared to the nightmare of Puritan tyranny frequently visited upon Northamptonshire during the 17th century. These events left a brutal legacy in the 18th century and a lingering atmosphere of suspicion and accusations that persisted through Victorian times. Demonic bogeymen were also taking on different forms by this time. In 1843 rumours swept the county that the infamous bounding predator Spring Heeled Jack, with his icy claws, eyes of fire and a mouth that spat flames, was in the area. He was said to leap out of the darkness to attack mail coaches in the region, and a report of the time described him as '…the very image of the Devil himself, with horns and eyes of flame.' By the 1850s he was reckoned to be prowling the streets of the towns and villages in the midlands 'rattling his chain'. There were other demons to beware: folklorist Thomas Sternberg wrote that in Victorian times it was well known that a demon knight haunted the mediaeval woodland which encroached on the village of Whittlebury. The entity took the form of a hunter who led a ghastly retinue through the glades of Whittlewood Forest – although it was not pheasant or deer that the knight hunted…

Way back in history a local knight was said to have fallen in love with the daughter of one of the forest rangers. She was a young lady famed for her beauty and coquetry, and in the beginning she encouraged the knight's affections. Before long, however, she rejected him and her attitude towards him became contemptuous; finally, the distraught knight lost his mind, he stabbed himself with his own sword and died cursing his unrequited lover's name.

The young woman also died soon afterwards, and their spectres did not come back as mere ghosts: the knight took the form of a dark, demonic huntsman, leading a ferocious pack of hell-hounds as they charged and crashed though the woodland, him laughing maniacally and the dogs barking uncontrollably. Their quarry had taken the form of the ranger's daughter, now doomed in the afterlife to be forever fleeing from her murderous former sweetheart. This entity haunted many wooded parts of Northamptonshire: 'On a calm summer's night, when the pale glimmer of the young moon scarcely penetrates the dark foliage of the trees, he may be seen mounted on his silent-hoofed steed, slowly riding along the green-sward border of some old green lane or lonely road.' To see him was, and is still, an omen of death.

These days the local media occasionally reports on supposed 'satanists' desecrating churches. In 2005 it was reported that Holy Cross Church in Church Walk, Daventry, had been daubed with satanic symbols and other anti-Christian abuse. Sadly, that attack (linked to devil-worshippers) proved the forerunner to a rash of vandalism and robberies at county churches – including a ghoulish break-in at an 18th-century tomb in the churchyard of St Peter's, Raunds, in September 2006. That attack left parts of a skeleton exposed.

However, this chapter is largely concerned with the legacy of witchcraft in Northamptonshire: a county where unbelievable accusations of demonically supernatural incidents were written as fact, and a land where the 'Witchfinder General' Matthew Hopkins (a man undoubtedly more evil than those he sought out) presided over tyrannical trials and barbaric executions. Such is the county's association with these practices that in Charles Dickens's *Master Humphries Clock* it is briefly noted how one character reads, 'a dismal account of a gentleman down in Northamptonshire under the influence of witchcraft and taken forcible possession of by the Devil, who was playing his very self with him…'

WHEN THE DEVIL VISITED NORTHAMPTONSHIRE

For generations the folk of the region grew up with the story of Werbode and his diabolical end. Werbode was a knight at King Wulfhere of Mercia's court in the seventh century. He was a pagan, and the king's two sons refused to allow Werbode to marry their sister Werburgh since she was raised a Christian. Werbode's solution was to kill the two princes as they prayed. However, he instantly repented and took himself before Bishop Chad to confirm himself converted to Christianity. Because of this, a short time later Werbode was openly strangled before the king's palace in *Medeshamstede* (Peterborough) by the Devil himself – who took his soul to Hell.

It is more likely that Werbode hanged himself, but this story must have terrified folk in this part of the Midlands. There are many other legends of Satan's diabolical interest in the county. In Church Stowe a story circulated that when the ancient St Michael's Church was being erected on a hill there were persistent supernatural attempts to thwart this. In the night, tools, building blocks, even the trenches were mysteriously moved to the location where the church now stands. Nine times this happened, until the lord of the manor ordered a workman to see who was causing the chaos. The culprit was 'summut bigger nor a hog', which presumably means the Devil in one of his forms. In despair the lord ordered the workmen to erect the church on the site where the demon kept moving the materials. The nine attempts are supposed to be the reason why the civil parish is called Stowe Nine Churches.

North west of Towcester can be found Cold Higham, and in the south chapel of St Luke's Church, off Church Lane, can be found the oak effigy of what is thought to be Sir John de Pateshull (who died in 1349 aged about 58), although St Luke's has been dated to earlier than this so it could belong to someone else. His image is laid out on a stone tomb and shown helmeted and cross-legged, although the antiquarian Alice Dryden noted that this did not mean anything symbolically and was a 'mere English convention.' His right hand rests upon a sword and his left bears a shield. For some reason Sir John's wooden feet rest at the effigy of an ugly little creature which might be a lion, and this curiosity has given rise to the legend (as told to me by a churchgoer in August 2008) that Sir John led a very immoral life, during which he sold his soul to Satan. On his deathbed, knowing that Satan was coming to take his soul, Sir John insisted that he be buried *within* the church so that he might consider himself safe, but nevertheless Satan was too quick and managed to get inside and dart underneath his feet during the funeral service. The lady who told me this mentioned that the effigy represented the local supposition that Satan had indeed managed to take Sir John's soul, despite his precautions. It is a good story, but presumably the creature is meant to represent something else.

St Michael's Church at Church Stowe, apparently sited here by some kind of demon.

On 20 March 1593 a ferocious gale that assaulted Northampton was thought to be the huffing and puffing of the Devil. Roofs were ripped off houses and townsfolk feared to step outside; at All Hallows Church the roof was badly damaged and collapsed inwards, leading to the assumption that Satan's wrath had been aimed at the church. In days gone by, much in the same way that providence was seen in all walks of life and oddities were regarded as portents, negative events that affected day-to-day life were often seen as the work of the Devil. The St John family archives in Bedfordshire show that one Mr Gage of Northamptonshire wrote to Sir Roland St John on 20 February 1641 explaining that 'Satan, by his wretched ministers who are executors of his most damnable will, did never more reign than in these our latter days.' Mr Gage's son had recently died fighting in the English Civil War, and it is interesting to note how the prolonged conflict was decided in some quarters to have been engineered by Satan. Cromwell famously saw the subsequent Battle of Naseby as 'the face of God' and a turning point in the war, indicating a belief that events in Britain were following a divine path in an altogether greater battle between good and evil. In 1642 diabolical intervention was laid at the door of three simultaneous deaths in Towcester. The churchwarden's wife died, and he instantly went insane and died shortly afterwards. Following this, his sister-in-law also died, leading to much speculation that they had all been killed and taken by Satan for dark and unknown reasons.

This absolute belief in the Devil, and alongside it a curious attempt at scientific rationality, is evidenced by a pamphlet published in 1616 by a Stuart-era Northampton physician named Cotta who wrote in sincerity of how the unwary *could* be mistaken if they thought the Devil was at work. He wrote that people should 'be wary and cautiously wise, how [do] we make a true difference between a true work of the Devil and the strange likeness which phantasms.' What this indicates is that even the rational, in advising caution before leaping to conclusions, nonetheless acknowledged that the Devil was a *real* threat.

Fear of the Devil and his tricks persisted well into the Victorian era. Folklorist Thomas Sternberg writing in 1851 noted that in Northamptonshire '…we can only account for the vast number of Faust-like legends to this day current among the peasantry by supposing that, like the Puritans of old, they interpret literally the words of the apostle' which spoke of Satan roaming the countryside seeking those he wished to devour. The popular belief was that he possessed the traditional appearance of the Devil: horned, breathing fire, a tail, eyes like a *bason*, fangs like a dog, claws like a bear, and a voice that roared like a lion's. He was also referred to as 'Nick' or the 'Old Un'. Sometimes, in order to gain the trust of the peasantry, he would appear as 'a little old man, the form usually assumed by Lucifer on these excursions' and try and trick lazy or greedy farmhands into promising him their souls.

Perhaps the most impressive anecdote appears in *Notes And Queries* (26 June 1852), which involved a story then doing the rounds in western Northamptonshire. It was even being recounted by a Warwickshire preacher who would use the 'true' story as a furious warning to the sinners in his congregation to choose the path of righteousness. The story concerned the experience of one Providence B_____ (apparently a real person, '…a well-known man throughout the whole country-side' in that part of Northamptonshire) who was a member of the clergy. Providence had been employed in performing an exorcism on a yeoman's daughter who was possessed by an evil spirit, and making his way home late that night he found that he and his horse had become hopelessly lost in the gloomy countryside. Spotting an isolated inn through the woodland, Providence knocked on the door and asked to stay the night, and the ugly old crone who answered grudgingly obliged.

It was a couple of hours before a furious knocking on the door of Providence's room all but ordered him to come to supper. The cleric was engaged in prayer and refused, but the voice out in the corridor said he had no choice and had to join the other guests for supper. Once downstairs Providence found that the kitchen table was populated by 'little shrivelled up old men' who glared at him with undisguised hatred; it was then he spotted that all present, except himself, had tails and that he had been lured into a demonic trap. In panic, Providence shouted aloud a prayer: 'Jesus the name, high over all; In Hell, or earth, or sky; Angels and men before him fall; And devils fear and fly!' The wizened features of the assembled old men began to change colour, and, wailing, they morphed into blue smoke before disappearing up the chimney, leaving behind a foul smell of sulphur. At this Providence passed out. Local youths said that the tale was an invention and that Providence had been found drunk in a ditch following the evening in question; however, the cleric was well known for staying clear of alcohol.

These days it would appear that Old Nick has turned his attention elsewhere, but to the people of the village of Broughton this type of folk belief still manifests itself in the annual Tin Can Band, where scores of people gather at St Andrew's Church on the first Sunday after 12 December. Just as the clock chimes midnight they proceed to march around the village making as much noise as possible, blowing whistles, banging tin trays, buckets, dustbin lids, tin cans, kitchenware, and generally making an unholy din loud enough to keep villagers not interested in the spectacle from their slumber. The event seems to have been going on for more than two centuries, although its origins are hazy. It is generally thought that the noise is aimed at warding off evil spirits from Broughton, and may have had added merit in allowing fathers to show their sons where the village boundaries fell. The event has been known to become quite riotous (there was trouble in 2006 when the police were called out to investigate instances of vandalism) and an attempt to ban it in 1929 led to a level of defiance that almost resembled a mini-revolution. Local lore has it that should the custom not take place on the date then it must cease forever after, and thus the evil spirits would be allowed to drift their way back into the village. I understand that one year during World War Two a single lone canner trudged through a blizzard banging a saucepan in an heroic attempt to defend the village from demonic agents. Upon attending the Tin Can Band event a few years ago a friend of mine asked one participant what it was all about and received the reply 'It's to keep the Devil away.'

I wonder what the glaring, horn-headed Faustian figure of Old Nick, perhaps listening to the racket from the safety of the earthworks of Cransley Motte outside the village, makes of it all.

1612: 'A Brief Abstract of the Arraignment of Nine Witches at Northampton'

In 1603 King James VI of Scotland was crowned James I of England. In July 1597 the king had published his *Demonologie*, condemning all magic workers as guilty of sins against God – and although witchcraft allegations were hardly unknown in England, King James's accession to both thrones brought a new perceived urgency to the threat. His ferocious desire to crush the scourge of witchcraft spread south of the border with a ruthlessness that lasted for decades and left a legacy that lasted for centuries. Northamptonshire was frequently touched by this terror during those years of hysteria.

Two pamphlets document a disturbing sequence of events in the county which in many ways conform to the archetypal Stuart-era witch story: a contemporary pamphlet entitled *The Witches Of Northamptonshire...*, and a slightly later handwritten manuscript entitled *A Brief Abstract Of The Arraignment Of Nine Witches At Northampton, July 21, 1612*. The events depicted were disturbing to the populace of Northamptonshire at the time because of the unholy accusations; they are disturbing to the reader of today because of the level of hysteria that is portrayed at every level, even the judiciary.

The whole affair started off with a petty feud between neighbours in the village of Guilsborough. Nowadays the idea of this kind of animosity leading towards groundless accusations of witchcraft is almost a laughable cliché, but the Guilsborough incident shows that this was often the case, and also demonstrates just how frighteningly quick everything could get out of control. A certain Mistress Elizabeth Belcher, 'a virtuous and Godly gentlewoman of the same town of *Gilsborough*', entered into an argument with a woman called Joan Vaughan (or Varnham), during which Mistress Belcher physically attacked the other woman for some perceived slight. It is clear from the start the pamphleteer has no sympathy for Ms Vaughan: she is a 'maide, or at least unmarried' and, together with her mother, Agnes Browne, was 'as farre from Grace as Heaven from Hell.' The mother, old Agnes Browne, is described as being 'of poor parentage, and poor education.' Nevertheless, Joan walked away from the confrontation apparently vowing revenge, while Mistress Belcher shouted that she feared neither Joan nor her mother.

Soon after this Mistress Belcher fell sick, suffering from violent fits, during which she yelled out in delusion, 'Here comes Joan Vaughan, away with Joan Vaughan!' Rumours in the village soon spread that she had been bewitched, and things became worse when her brother, William Avery, arrived to visit his ill sister. Avery was shocked to see his sister's condition and had little difficulty placing the blame. He stormed in a fury to Agnes Browne's house with the intention of bringing the woman and her daughter before his sister – where he intended to draw their blood with a pin and thus thwart their power over Mistress Belcher. However, Avery found that he could not cross Agnes Browne's threshold. He later stated that he would become immobile at a certain spot, which he blamed on the power of 'the Devil, who was standing sentinel' before the witches' house. Soon after, Avery himself started suffering from convulsions and fits of insanity as his sister had before him.

These fits provided disturbing 'proof' that there was a plague of witchcraft on Guilsborough. Avery claimed that during a dream he had 'seen' a hideous wart on the body of Agnes Brown. Upon later inspection this 'black wart' was actually said to have been discovered under her left arm. Avery also claimed that he had been confronted by the bloodied spectre of a man, and the ghostly apparition beseeched Avery to leave his mistress, old Agnes Browne, alone. By 6 April the whole village knew that something was very wrong. Avery was claiming ever more weirder phenomena, and pointing the finger at old Agnes Browne: she was ordering moles to suckle his toes, and she even appeared naked above the waist before him during one of his delusions and offered him two knives to stab his sister to death and then kill himself with. In terrified hysteria he denied the apparition. One evening in the gloomy confines of his back yard he saw a dark, ugly, leering figure who dared him to come outside to confront him. In his madness, Avery claimed, he had screamed at the creature, 'Thou Devil! Thou filthy rogue! Thou damned whore! Thou hast done thy worst to my sister, and brought knives to me to kill my sister and my child that I might be damned as thou art, but I defy thee…thou hast committed 14 murders, sparing young nor old, women nor children…' Avery claimed that this monstrosity had, on occasion, managed to invade his house, but could not harm him: he had the Saviour on his side.

The accusations were flying thick and fast, and Agnes Browne and Joan Vaughan were arrested on the orders of Sir John Saunders of Cottesbrooke and carted off to Northampton gaol. Here it was decided by the magistrate to allow the injured party – Avery and his sister – into Agnes Browne's cell to draw her blood with a pin. This they did and were almost instantly cured of the sickness and fits that plagued them. Avery was certainly not too weak to knock Agnes Browne to the floor, causing an injury that made blood spray from her eye.

However, it appeared that the witches could still cause trouble from within the prison. As Avery and Mistress Belcher rode home in a stagecoach away from Northampton town they saw coming towards them a man and a woman both riding the same black horse. Sensing that they were cronies of the witch, Avery cried out that he and his sister were doomed: as the strange couple on the black horse passed them, the two horses leading Avery's own stagecoach both dropped down dead. Apparitions of witches were hounding him, Avery claimed, wailing and bemoaning the name of one Joane Lucas, who they blamed for their coven's downfall.

Quite what that was meant to achieve is unclear since Joane Lucas was under arrest herself, suspected of being involved in events. In fact a 12-year-old boy called Hugh Lucas (a relation?) later testified that Joane had looked at him in church and he had collapsed and gone into convulsions upon arriving home. Clearly in the accusations there was something catching. William Avery himself claimed that during his fits he suffered delusions which came true, including the death of a fellow villager's horse in the lane before his very eyes; the wife of this villager, seeing Avery in his madness, began to convulse and suffer from fits herself. By the time she was taken home she was screaming that she had been bewitched just as Avery and his sister had been, and that chairs were dancing in the house before her eyes.

In fact, the madness in the air spread like a plague in May of 1612. As well as old Agnes Browne and her daughter, and Joane Lucas, there were arrests in Raunds, Thrapston and Stanwick as well as elsewhere. Those accused were dragged before magistrates to answer the charges: one Alice Wilson was threatened with execution by the justice if she would not say, 'I forsake the Devil'. Alice is held to have averred that this was impossible for her to say.

There is a perception that many of those arrested, some 14 in all, never stood a chance. Avery's performance in court was spellbinding. Upon entering the room he immediately went into a very convincing fit, although when the seizure had passed he was able to talk quite lucidly to the jury. Supernatural phenomena had plagued him endlessly: the accused witches came to him in visions, and his horse mysteriously threw him. He foretold that if one were to go down the stone steps of Northampton gaol at two in the morning the witches could be heard talking in an unknown tongue. At this, a Master of Arts at Trinity College, Oxford, stealthily took himself into the prison where he allegedly heard the accused women muttering and chattering to each other in words that could not be deciphered. This is a telling point: either those held were *real* witches – or the public at large were so fearful of them that they had already made their minds up and were 'inventing' evidence to help secure their conviction. Avery's sister, Elizabeth Belcher herself, put on a similar display of hysterics and martyrdom before the court.

Following their trial at the assizes of Northampton Castle, Agnes Browne and Joan Vaughan were sentenced to death and hanged on 22 July, convicted of witchcraft and an additional charge of using a spell to cause the death of a young child. It was written that they were 'never heard to pray, or call upon God, never asking pardon for their offences'. It later emerged that Agnes, Joane and one Katherine Gardiner – 'all birds of a winge' – had allegedly ridden on the back of a great black sow in the direction of Ravensthorpe two weeks before their arrests. Here lived another notorious witch, old Mother Rhoades, but before Agnes and the others got there Mother Rhoades had died. In the wake of the trial it was whispered that Mother Rhoades had said with her dying breath that three old friends were coming to see her; they would be too late, but no matter because they would all meet again 'in another place within a month after.' Clearly this was meant to be viewed as a prophecy that all would meet in Hell very soon.

The arrest of the witches in Guilsborough was the spark that lit the flame. Simultaneously, Arthur Bill of Raunds (of whom the authorities had long been suspicious) was arrested and accused of using witchcraft to cause the death of Martha Aspine and of bewitching his neighbour's livestock. As it was believed he came from a line of witches, his parents were also arrested and all three were subjected to trial by water. They were tied up and thrown into the water where they were observed to float. At this Arthur's cowardly father turned prosecution witness. There was a slight delay while a small ball that now suddenly obstructed his throat had to be physically removed; the pamphlet makes it clear that Arthur had used sorcery to block his father's throat and stop him giving evidence. It did no good: there was no hope for Arthur Bill. A comment that he made was interpreted as an accidental confession that he had 'certaine spirits' at his command. His mother died in gaol after managing to cut her own throat, and Arthur went to the scaffold crying that the law was corrupt as it had condemned an innocent man. He refused to confess to the murder of Martha Aspine and was hanged at the same time as Agnes Browne and her daughter. *The Witches Of Northampton* reckoned that Arthur was supposed to have three familiars called Grissill, Ball and Jack, but we are not informed what role they played in the affair or what form they took.

In Thrapston another drama was being played out. Ellen Jenkinson is written of as being a woman of notorious character, and once again the scenario seems to have stemmed from pure animosity between neighbours. One Mistress Moulsho claimed that if Ellen were searched then 'witch marks' would be found upon her body: she was and they were. It was next alleged that as Mistress Moulsho's maid had put out some washing, the girl had noticed that a smock bore disgusting stains that resembled 'toades, snakes, and other *ougly* creatures.' The maid told Mistress Moulsho, who smiled and replied, 'Here are fine hobgoblins indeed.' Knowing who to blame, the gentlewoman stormed round to Ellen Jenkinson's house and threatened that if her linen were not clean by the time she got back then she would return and rip out Ellen's eyes with her own hands. By the time Mistress Moulsho arrived home the linen was absolutely spotless. Ellen Jenkinson was later arraigned on a charge of using witchcraft to cause the death of a child, but it seems to have been the gentlewoman's testimony that swayed the jury most. Upon being sentenced to death Ellen screamed, 'Woe is me, I now cast away!' She was hanged with the others.

A fifth victim, Mary Barber of Stanwick, also met her fate due to the 'bloody assizes' at Northampton. She appears to have been little more than a crude backward woman caught up in the violence of the moment, and whom the pamphleteer reserves nothing but the worst insults: '...she gave way to all the passionate and unearthly faculties of the flesh'. Mary was thrown into Northampton gaol alongside thieves and murderers on a charge of bewitching a man to death because of her foul desires until on 22 July 1612 (with the other four so condemned) 'like birds of a feather they all held and hanged together for company at Abington gallowes hard by Northampton.'

The fate of the other eight or so suspected witches who were initially arrested is unclear. Arthur Bill's treacherous father may have been given his freedom for betraying his son and wife. Although Alice Harrys, Katherine Gardiner, Joane Lucas and Alice Abbott were also arraigned alongside the women who were hanged, by the end of it all it seems Joane Lucas was the only other one convicted, although it would appear that she was not executed, and the others may not even have been punished. Alice Wilson, her mother Agnes and her sister-in-law Jane were the final three who made up the nine arraigned on 21 July 1612, and although they faced some very serious charges they do not appear to have been severely punished. However, one can imagine the humiliation of these unfortunate women as they were paraded before the court, bloodied and dirty, and ordered to 'touch' their accusers to see if it stopped the endless fits that the likes of Avery were performing before the magistrate. Surely if they escaped harsh punishment, the stigma of the whole episode stayed with them long afterwards.

The image of the three witches riding atop a giant black sow to Ravensthorpe illustrated the contemporary pamphlet *The Witches Of Northampton*, and has in many minds become the archetypal image of the traditional witch. Three stern-faced, bonneted old hags sit behind each other atop a monstrous hog, old Agnes Browne at the front with a lantern and stick. In the town hall hangs a tapestry created by the Women's Institute based on this ideal. It is often said, incorrectly, that this is how the witches were arrested. It is also said that a young Oliver Cromwell was brought to the gallows to see the mass execution. He would have been 13 at the time if this is true; however, it may simply

The witches of Guilsborough ride atop a hog in this village sign.

be a myth that has become intertwined with the story due to Cromwell's later associations with the county in adulthood.

This story is a very famous one, analysed fully in folklorist C. L'Estrange Ewan's *Witchcraft And Demonism* (1933) and a host of other books on the topic for 80 years prior. What is unclear about all this is whether *any* of those so charged actually practised witchcraft. None seem to have confessed and it is hard to get past the thought that in those days no one would have *openly* admitted they performed such activities unless they were braggarts or half-witted. Therefore, were they actually practising witches? Or were they groundlessly accused during those fear-driven times? The accuser in each case is of a higher social standing than the supposed witch and it is clear that those accused stood no chance right from the very first. In each case the additional charge of causing death by witchcraft seems to have been dragged up from somewhere, probably to legitimise the time and expense spent on the proceedings. These days a 'witch-hunt' is the phrase used to describe the relentless, often unjustified, victimisation of a particular group. It is evident then that today we can see in the era of *actual* 'witch-hunts' something similar was clearly going on, something made all the more bizarre because the accusers (who could themselves be viewed as fanatically brainwashed, mentally unbalanced or just murderous troublemakers) were ultimately the ones with blood on their hands. As author Wallace Notestein commented on this case in *History Of English Witchcraft* (1911): 'It is quite impossible to grasp the social conditions, it is impossible to understand the opinions, fears and hopes of the men and women who lived in Elizabethan and Stuart England, without some knowledge of the part played in that age by witchcraft.'

THE 'WITCH FINDER GENERALL'

In the 1640s chaos reigned in England. The nation had been reduced to anarchy in the face of civil war, and many villages found themselves lacking protection from taxation, outbreaks of sickness, hunger and the abuses of undisciplined armies who marched through the parishes. As mentioned earlier, many saw the hardship their communities suffered as symptomatic of a larger war than that between Royalty and Parliament; it was the very struggle between good and evil itself. Into this mix was thrown Matthew Hopkins, the 'Witch Finder Generall', a figure demonised for over three and a half centuries now…a man who rode from parish to remote parish, village to isolated village, accompanied by a male assistant and a female searcher, who offered to alleviate the villager's sufferings by identifying the evil that plagued them.

Many such places had lost much of their male population to the war. By the time the long-haired, bearded Hopkins, in his familiar cloak and black steeple hat, rode into Northamptonshire with his assistants in 1646 he had travelled East Anglia and the English Midlands 'curing' the curse of witchcraft for two years. There was never a shortage of those who wished to have their neighbours prosecuted for harming livestock or relatives. Although the true number of luckless 'witches' identified by this time is unclear, hundreds had been accused and Hopkins had presided over scores of executions – all the while dubiously claiming to have been given the task by Parliament and charging fees wherever he uncovered a suspect.

In Northamptonshire Hopkins and his assistant, John Stearne, obtained confessions from numerous witches (outlined fully in *Witchcraft & Demonism* (1933), among others). At Woodford they heard accusations that one Anne Goodfellow had been accosted by the Devil, who had taken the form of a talking white cat. The creature tricked Anne into compliance by pretending to be a benevolent spirit – the ghost of a deceased aunt in fact. Speaking in a low voice the cat asked Anne to denounce God, Christ and her baptism in order to receive everything that she desired. She agreed to these terms, whereupon the cat bit her second finger and drew blood to seal the covenant. It was all a sham: Anne had sold her soul but received nothing for it and ended up standing trial before Matthew Hopkins.

In Thrapston an old man referred to as Cherrie fell into disagreements with his neighbours to such an extent that he also sold his soul to the Devil. He expressed the desire that his neighbour's tongue might rot out of his head, and following this curse the man was indeed taken sick with some kind of mouth ailment that got worse and worse until he died. Again Satan had deceived his subject: old Cherrie was tormented by imps who would prick him to draw blood. In an effort to keep them away from him he had them cause an outbreak of livestock disease among the cattle herd of Sir John Washington, who had formerly been a good friend. Cherrie was apparently arrested at a bridge (probably the bridge over the River Nene) on his way into Thrapston – his coat was ripped and he had a rope around his neck, and it appeared that he had been on his way to hang himself. Furthermore, his throat was blocked with something that had to be forced out of his windpipe. Perhaps the wretched man had tried to choke himself to death. Either way he was discovered dead in Northampton gaol on the very day he would have been arraigned – confirming everyone's suspicions that he was guilty.

At Denford an unnamed young man got into an argument about cattle rights with his neighbour, a man called Cocke. The young man sent an imp to attack Cocke's cattle, causing the beasts to foam at the mouth and run wild. It took great effort to rein them in, and for this crime the young man was executed by hanging.

It seems in the two latter instances at least that those accused were the victims of superstitious neighbours who were suffering misfortune among their cattle herds. In 1648 Stearne published an account of his and Hopkins's conduct entitled *A Confirmation & Discovery Of Witchcraft* in which he absolved himself of any wrongdoing. He also commented that Hopkins died peacefully after a long consumptive illness the previous year. This, it seems, left many feeling cheated, and there is a persistent legend that Hopkins was given a dose of his own medicine. He was, according to the wishful thinking of folk-justice, subjected to one of his own trials, during which he was tied hand and foot and 'swum' to see if he would float. He did, and thus proved that all along he had himself been an agent of Satan. This is said to have happened in Manningtree, Essex, and Hopkins either drowned or was strung up and hanged by a lynch mob. However, this ending to the brutal saga of the 'Witchfinder Generall' appears to be as much fiction as his demise in the movie of the same name, in which Hopkins is corned and slain by a Cromwellian soldier whose sweetheart he had mistreated.

The 17th Century

The persecution of witches in Northamptonshire did not end with the activities of Hopkins and Stearne. Researcher Margaret Alice Murray outlines the full horrific tale of one Anne Desborough in her *Witch Cult In Western Europe* (1921). Around the same time as Hopkins was 'finding' witches in Northamptonshire, Anne Desborough found herself standing before Joseph Coysh, Master of the Word, and justicar Thomas Becke in Bythorn, Cambridgeshire, both of whom heard her confession of witchcraft.

About 30 years earlier (*c.*1616) Anne had been asleep at her home in Titchmarsh, Northamptonshire, when there appeared in the room 'a thing like a mouse, but somewhat bigger.' It bit her, whereupon she woke up to find the little brown creature demanding that she give it her soul. Terrified, Anne had prayed to God and when she opened her eyes the thing had vanished. That had been in 'the first weeke of Clean Lent.'

However, it returned five days later and brought with it a similar, though smaller, creature which was also brown but had a patch of white about its belly. The bigger one said, 'We must suck of your body' and the trial heard that marks on the woman's body had indeed been found where the creatures had suckled at her. Anne agreed to forsake God, and named the bigger creature Tib and the smaller one Jone. She took them as her Gods and agreed they could take her soul when she passed on; in return Tib would injure men at her behest, while Jone would undertake to destroy her neighbour's cattle if Anne so desired. They appeared before her every 24 hours.

There were occasionally voices which dissented against this madness, especially in the cases of bewitched children, notably the clergy, some of whom rationalised that they were being put up to it by the parents. These opinions seem to have been in the minority, however, for in such an age any sympathy towards 'witches' might lead toward accusations against one's own person. In April 1674 there was another sensational witchcraft trial in Northampton, reported in a pamphlet entitled *A Full & True Relation Of The Tryall, Condemnation & Execution Of Ann Foster*. These events are also outlined fully by writer Margaret Alice Murray, but in particular by Edwardian scholar Montague Scott who saw the case as being a typical example of the longevity of the phenomenon.

At Eastcote, north of Towcester, a rich grazier named Joseph Weedon had refused to sell an old woman some mutton, and she had departed muttering veiled threats. A few days later he found in his field a horrific spectacle. Thirty of his sheep had been killed, their 'bones all shattered in their skins.' Suspecting witchcraft, Weedon threw one of the carcasses onto the fire, an act commonly believed to bring the witch into the open. It worked, and one Ann Foster suddenly rushed up and enquired as to why he was burning the sheep. At her appearance Weedon stabbed her in the hand with a knife to draw blood – a trick thought to deprive witches of their power. However, he badly injured the old woman, and, fearing her threats of getting the law involved, he gave her 20 shillings to treat the wound. Ann walked away telling Weedon that the 20 shillings was the Devil's money and that he had once again given her the power to bewitch him. On 22 May his house and barn caught fire, and the old woman appeared at the scene, mockingly telling those present that they would never be able to quench the fire. At this she was arrested, and seems to have confessed to her crimes quite freely, even threatening to kill the entire village if given half a chance.

Ann Foster was thrown into Northampton gaol, where her gaoler reported that other prisoners were in nightly terror because the Devil himself was appearing in the prison to suckle at the teat of the accused witch. It took the form of a thing like a rat and appeared at the dead of night. It would seem the wretched woman was chained up and immobile while rodents were free to crawl over her body. At length the gaoler was forced to unchain Ann because almost all her body was beginning to swell and balloon – probably because the rat bites were becoming infected as she ended her days in the filthy dungeon. Eventually she was dragged before the Northampton Summer Sessions on 22 August 1674, where she was convicted. She expressed a wish to be burned to death, but even this she was denied: she was hanged on the gallows.

Francis Hutchinson's *An Historical Essay Concerning Witchcraft* (1718) notes that numerous witches were tried by swimming in 1692 in Northamptonshire and the surrounding counties: 'Some drownd in the tryal.' This was the year of the famous witch trials in Salem, Massachusetts – clearly back home the scourge of witchcraft was still being taken just as seriously.

WITCHCRAFT IN THE AGE OF REASON

In 1705 there appeared a pamphlet entitled *An Account Of The Tryals, Examination And Condemnation Of Elinor Shaw And Mary Phillips...At Northampton On Wednesday The 7th Day Of March, 1705*.

Mary Phillips came from Oundle, and Eleanor Shaw from Cotterstock, a village just to the north. Both apparently had a reputation for immorality, and while sharing a dwelling they agreed to give their souls to Satan in return for working mischief. It was said at their trial that on the very night of their pledge the Devil appeared before them in a flash in the shape of a tall black figure. He 'had carnal knowledge of them, but was cold and unpleasant' before leaving them three little imps apiece – who, if the women allowed themselves to be suckled by the imps, would kill men and beasts on their behalf. Soon afterwards the horses, cows and pigs of neighbours began to die off at an alarming rate; it was repeated later that unless the two women kept the imps gainfully employed in this mischief, the imps would become bored and begin to hound the two women themselves. The imps in a 'hollow whispering low voice' reassured Eleanor and Mary that they would never feel the fires of Hell.

Unfortunately, the magistrate heard of what was going on, and the two women were arrested. A never-ending stream of neighbours were brought before the court to attest to the supernatural evil that the two witches had wrought upon the area, but the main charge was causing the death of the wife of Robert Wise of Benefield on or round about 31 December 1704. One witness claimed that she overheard Eleanor Shaw (via an open window) say, 'I have done her [Mrs Wise] business now, I am sure; this night I'll send the Old Devil a New Year's gift.' Eleanor's co-accused later claimed that Mrs Wise had been killed when Eleanor had made a wax effigy of her victim, stuck it full of pins and then melted it. One witness stated that two little black creatures 'almost like moles' had been sent to the unfortunate victim, and that they had sucked her 'lower parts'. This so petrified Mistress Wise that before her death she had sent for a local minister named Danks and asked him to pray for her. The pair were also accused of bewitching to death Elizabeth, the four-year-old daughter of Matthew Goreham of Glapthorn, and a 12-year-old boy from Southwick named Charles Ireland. Several

Children are told that this little fellow in Rothwell church is a genuine petrified imp, miraculously turned to stone.

testified that the boy had been suffering from fits and barking like a dog, and his mother suspected witchcraft. She obtained some of his water and corked it with some needles and pins in a stone bottle and buried it under the fire hearth. This established trick drew Eleanor and Mary to the house where they confessed to causing the young lad's fits. They promised to trouble him no more, but Charles never recovered and died shortly afterwards. Another pamphlet (which drew as its source a letter dated 18 March 1705, penned by a Northampton gentleman named Ralph Davis) linked the two women to some 29 deaths in the locality over a nine-month period – all of which had been considered natural until the trial.

After the arrest of Eleanor and Mary, the imps continued to visit them in gaol. A group of women testified that they had seen a 'little white thing about the bigness of a cat' that invaded the cell and sat upon Mary Phillips's lap. Eleanor was heard to mutter incomprehensibly, as though making an incantation, and the woman who heard her do this stated that her clothes had suddenly been thrown up about her head. The prison keeper, after threatening the two prisoners, was discovered dancing naked in the yard and no one could stop him for an hour. (One wonders why, if Eleanor and Mary were truly capable of such tricks, they did not simply free themselves and flee.) At length the two goalers threatened their captives with death if they stayed silent and freedom if they confessed, and to this end obtained a full confession. Mr Danks, the minister, was brought before the two women where he learned that the Devil had visited them several times, presenting them with a new, different coloured imp on each occasion who had sucked 'a large teat or piece of red flesh in their privy parts'. Such marks had been discovered on the two women upon their being searched.

Eleanor Shaw and Mary Phillips were carted to the gallows on the north side of Northampton on 17 March 1705, where before the stool was kicked away they admitted their guilt. Half-choked, they were then cut down from the gallows and burned alive at the stake. Both died cursing and ranting.

It is difficult to know what to make of this tale: it is very well known, but nonetheless the manner of execution seems highly unlikely. Perhaps they were hanged and then cremated *after death* rather than as part of the execution. The case caused much controversy among Victorian and Edwardian scholars. Many thought the pamphlets that chronicled the events were an outright fabrication, drawing upon inconsistencies in the narrative, the lack of independent confirmation of the story and its similarity to other contemporary works of a dubious source. Folklorist Wallace Notestein drew a line under the affair after much discussion in his *History Of Witchcraft In England From 1558 To 1718* (1911) with the comment, 'It seems probable, then, that the pamphlet…is a purely fictitious narrative.' However, C. L'Estrange Ewan, in his *Witchcraft And Demonism* (1933), thought that although it was an unreliable story, 'I consider that it bears the stamp of truth.' What it does indicate is that, even if the pamphlets recorded a fictional instance, it was still an era when such sensational accounts could be marketed as 'real'.

Whatever the truth it is clear that there were still genuine remnants of the belief in witchcraft in remoter parts of the county. In 1785 the *Northampton Mercury* noted how 'a poor woman, named Sarah Bradshaw' volunteered to be subjected to the 'ducking test' in Mears Ashby after being accused of witchcraft by her neighbours. She appears to have done this deliberately in order to clear her name, and it is recorded that she sank straight to the bottom of the pond, at which – her innocence proved – she was dragged out. The newspaper account appears to be quite sympathetic to the woman's ordeal, a sign of progress, certainly, but what it evidenced was the fear that still lingered in remoter parts of the community – a fear that persisted well into the following century and the Victorian era.

The generally enlightened attitude did not, however, mean that prejudice went un-manifested: it was just that the 'witchcraft' element was diminishing. *The Newgate Calendar* tells us that when a surgeon from London named Gordon moved to Northamptonshire he was subjected to a campaign of harassment by a local populace jealous of his success and suspicious of him as an 'outsider'. He was involved in frequent quarrels with locals, until one (falsely) complained that Mr Gordon had attacked him. A parish constable went to arrest Mr Gordon and was told to go away. However, he returned with a crowd of neighbours who rioted and began to stone Gordon's house. Mr Gordon's wife, terrified, told the couple's 18-year-old son Thomas to fire at the crowd; Thomas did so and killed the constable. The lad was executed at Northampton gaol on 17 August 1789. Many of the elements of earlier witchcraft accusations are still present here, but despite the bloody violence the superstitious aspect of the case appears noticeably absent.

WITCHES IN FOLKLORE

E. Lynn Linton in his *Witch Stories* (1861) summed up the generally enlightened attitude to the accusations of witchcraft that had gone before. He wrote of the barbaric murders of an elderly couple in Tring, Hertfordshire, a century earlier (in which a helpful Northamptonshire 'white witch' had been employed to point the finger of guilt squarely at the two victims): '…again in 1751 was witch blood actually poured out on English soil, and the cry of the *innocent* murdered sent up to Heaven in vain for mercy.' This reflects the Victorian acknowledgement that shameful, ignorant and hysterical events had occurred in England's — and indeed Northamptonshire's — near past. However, such traumatic and brutal events were bound to leave a stamp on the land and Thomas Sternberg, writing in 1851, concluded that the county's association with 'witchcraft' appeared to have been imprinted in the collective consciousness of Northamptonshire folk.

Sternberg noted the stereotypical suppositions of what witches looked like: to the popular mind they displayed wizened features, hairy lips, a fondness for black cats and a generally sinister aura. It was reckoned that to become a witch all one had to do was sit on the 'hob of the hearth' and say, 'I wish that I was as far from God as my nails are from dirt.' After this incantation the witch was immediately possessed with powers to do harm. Any person subsequently bitten or scratched by the witch then became one themselves. These aspects bear little in relation to the claims made about witches in the pamphlets of *actual* witchcraft trials and appear to be folklore aspects brought (or invented) into the witch mythology as memories and details of such trials dimmed. As elsewhere in the Midlands, witches were reckoned to be able to transform themselves into animals — notably black cats, and the Northamptonshire story of a tormented woodman cutting off a black cat's paw is almost universal, with one exception: he finds upon returning home that his wife has mysteriously had her hand chopped off, and realises that it was his *own wife* who was tormenting him in the form of a black cat. At Wilby it was long thought that the foxes or hares that led the huntsmen on such exhausting chases were witches; that was how the animals managed to escape. Witches were also thought to kidnap children by entering dwellings through keyholes.

Sternberg clearly found such beliefs absurd. However, the truly disturbing thing about all this is that almost certainly behind the fallacies, the beliefs and accusations still continued throughout the 19th century, perhaps under an unofficial vale of secrecy in various hamlets and villages away from the major population centres. There was substantial oral evidence, later collected by 20th-century folklorists, which indicated that this is what occurred in some neighbouring counties such as Lincolnshire. In the early 1800s it was still common practice in Northamptonshire to burn a live calf to halt a 'murrain' (disease outbreaks) sweeping through a 'bewitched herd'. Apparently a tourist in Northamptonshire watched this occur, and according to Theda Kenyon's *Witches Still Live* (1929) the shocked witness managed to coax from the surly farmers that this was a fairly common ritual. Sternberg himself acknowledged that aspects of this were also still going on in his time: 'Besides the somewhat doubtful power of the cunning man, certain charms were (and still are) resorted to in order to procure immunity from the arts of the witch.' These included a 'lucky bone' procured from the skull of a sheep and worn around one's neck, stones with holes bored through them to be worn as amulets and horseshoes nailed above thresholds. One 'credulous old dame' to whom Sternberg talked to preferred to rely on crossed cutlery; this lady suspected a neighbour of being a witch and so invited her round after hiding two crossed knives in the corner of her home. Upon arriving the 'witch' could not or would not sit down and eventually left in a baffled and agitated state. Of course, to Sternberg's informant this had proved the suspect's guilt. Across the county at large the linguist Anne Elizabeth Baker found that many folk in rural locations carried charms called *eldern*…something taken or made from the elder tree. She noted that the elder tree was supposed to possess protective powers 'from witches and wizards' for those who carried bits of it about their person. She also noted that this was the probable reason for there being so many elder trees planted beside cottages or in their grounds.

Around the turn of the 19th and 20th centuries children were being warned that certain locations were haunted by the ghosts of witches. Although these were perhaps imaginary tales created to frighten children it indicates that the 'witch' was still very much a piece of the collective psyche. In the early 1900s children were warned to stay away from a deep pool that was at the time found by Cold Ashby Road, Guilsborough. The village's link to the famous witchcraft trial of 1612 was probably the basis for the story that if children went too close to the edge of the water in the evening a filthy, scrawny, deathly white witch with matted hair and a drenched black shawl would crawl out of the water to eat them. It was even said in the mid-19th century an old witch at Syresham had been literally turned to stone by divine wrath – where she could still be spotted in her petrified state.

In August 1904 writer John Philipps Emslie saw a great many horseshoes over doors as he travelled Northamptonshire, including eight over the Sondes Arms in Rockingham. One suspects that, as in other counties in the Midlands, the lingering belief in witchcraft persisted well into the 20th century in Northamptonshire. Perhaps it still continues to do so in its darker, hidden corners.

'Something Diabolical'

Spiritualist Elliott O'Donnell (1872–1965) noted in his *Confessions Of A Ghost Hunter* (1928) the long-held rumours that some kind of nameless, formless – but evil – entity haunted the village of Guilsborough. It was whispered that this malicious creature haunted '…an old burial ground in the village' and that it also had a habit of appearing in a bedroom in a house on the other side of the village.

O'Donnell had relatives in Guilsborough, and he wrote how, sometime around the late-1800s to early-1900s, he found himself walking past this burial ground. It was very late at night and very dark, but he saw that something stood in the road before the old burial plot, and as he walked towards it O'Donnell found that he could not bring himself to look at it directly – for the dark shape exuded a sensation of extreme malice which irrationally frightened him.

Before he turned his head away from the creature to look at his own feet he formed a disturbing impression of the strange dark shape. It was exceptionally tall and dark, but '…the impression I got was that it was semi-human in appearance, the body to some degree resembling that of a human being, but the face being more like that of some very strange animal. It struck me as being wholly diabolical.'

This strange creature was silent as to O'Donnell's passing. He was later to learn that his father-in-law claimed to have been one of those to whom this phantasm had appeared at the house on the other side of Guilsborough. It is instantly notable that Guilsborough was the setting for the horrors of the witchcraft trials some three centuries before; the implication being that some menacing form of supernatural evil, perhaps linked to those terrifying times, still resided – or *resides* – in the haunted village.

Elliott O'Donnell also wrote that there was a certain field in Northamptonshire where something diabolical and murderous resided. Unfortunately, he does not give the location; his work *Haunted Highways And Byways* (1914) merely hints that the field was by '...a certain road in the midlands' where there could be found a big upright stone with the initials *M. T.* inscribed upon it. Here, O'Donnell said, in the recent past a Nonconformist minister named Deekon had attacked and murdered his mistress Mary Tebbutt before hacking her body so as to fit in a sack which was then thrown in the ditch that bordered the field. The killer's prison chaplain later told O'Donnell that all the while during his crime Deekon claimed he had been observed: he was being stared at by the misty form of a tall dark figure wrapped in a shroud, with a long head and a long, narrow, dark and bony face with parchment-like skin and no eyes, only cavernous sockets. It had whispered in Deekon's ear: 'Don't miss your opportunity! She'll ruin your career. Kill her.' It grinned at him maliciously, and Deekon feared that he was looking at some form of demon which had compelled the normally reserved man to turn on his mistress.

O'Donnell also recounted in *Byways Of Ghost Land* (1911) an experience a friend of his – Mr Pope – had undergone after journeying by train to Northampton and hence to a manor house alluded to as 'Killington Grange [which] lies at the extremity of the village.' This location is likely to have been renamed by O'Donnell (who hated the thought of the curious descending onto haunted properties), so it is not clear where 'Killington Grange' is. Nevertheless, Pope was attending a Christmas party and accepted a wager to stay in a grandiose bedroom in a certain wing of the property long said to be haunted. Pope recounted how, as he laid in a four-poster bed unable to sleep, his ears tuned into the fact that a high-backed ebony chair in the corner of the room was creaking as though someone were sat in it; worse still, he thought he could see '...two long, pale, and wholly evil eyes, that regarded me with a malevolency that held me spellbound.' A dark, shapeless form was sitting in the chair, barely visible in the gloom of the large room, glaring at him through lidless eyes, and he could hear a horrid sound like rasping breath.

At this drunken revellers crashed into his bedroom and the entity in the corner abruptly vanished. The following morning Pope was more fascinated than frightened and opted to spend a second night in the bedroom. The same pattern of events repeated themselves: the creaking chair, the glowing eyes, the sinister malevolence – all while Pope laid there in a state of speechless fascination that bordered more on fright the longer the experience went on. Again the spell was broken when newly arrived partygoers came to see if he was still awake. Both times Pope found that he fell into an untroubled sleep afterwards, and in the morning his fear of the night before had been replaced by the curiosity of a scientist.

On the third night, however, no partygoers interrupted the pattern of events, and the sinister entity that once more revealed itself in the chair gradually took on a terrifying form. As it noiselessly approached him through the gloom of the bedroom it displayed a 'dark and sexless face...surmounted with a straggling mass of black hair, the ends of which melted away into the mist.' Pope could see no body, but two long bony arms with 'crooked, spidery, misty fingers'. Petrified with fear, the thing glided towards the four-poster bed: 'I knew it was something repulsively, diabolically grotesque, but whether [it was] the phantasm of man, or woman, or hellish elemental, I couldn't for the life of me say.' The thing pressed its scrawny hands round Pope's neck and began to throttle him until, convinced he was dying, he passed out. However, he awoke later at daybreak.

Pope left Killington Grange later that day – Christmas Day.

CHAPTER 4

SUPERSTITIONS, PORTENTS AND CURSES

INTRODUCTION

Portents and omens of doom and disaster have taken many forms in Northamptonshire. Sometimes natural curiosities were regarded with awe and superstition. The antiquarian and archaeologist Revd John Morton, although generally not impressed by the lore of the peasantry, noted in *The Natural History Of Northamptonshire; With Some Accounts Of The Antiquities* (1712) that one of the many 'healing wells' in the county was also thought to act as an oracle in that its behaviour was somehow a clue to forthcoming events. He wrote that the well was referred to as 'Marvel-sike Spring, in Boughton Field, about two bows' shoot from Brampton Bridge, nigh Kingsthorp Road. It never runs but in mighty gluts of wet, and whenever it does is thought ominous by the country people, who, from the breaking out of that spring, are wont to prognosticate dearth, the death of some great personage, or very troublesome times. It did not run when I was there, on October 22nd, 1703, but the foregoing winter it did, and had not run before for two years. That winter it is well known was a very wet one.' (Morton was under-emphasising; in fact, thousands drowned in catastrophic flooding in November 1703.) The Marvel-Sike is supposed to have last overflowed sometime in 1916 when the final annual Boughton Green Fair was held, as if to bemoan a period of poverty in the village. However, it is unclear quite where the Marvel-Sike is nowadays. The more famous Drumming Well of Oundle was also reckoned to foresee major events in British history and drum a rumbling sound from its depths.

On 8 June 1607 a regional protest against enclosure led to a massacre in Newton, west of Geddington, when a force consisting largely of armed servants raised by the landowning Tresham family killed around 44 demonstrators in a bloody finale to what later become known as the Midlands Rising. The leader of the rebellion was said to be a tinker from Desborough called John Reynolds, who earned the pseudonym 'Captain Pouch' after he apparently told the swelling hordes of peasants that the mystical contents of his pouch would protect them all from physical danger. In the aftermath of the violent shambles 'Captain Pouch' was arrested and later executed; it is said that his protective pouch contained nothing but a piece of mouldy cheese. With hindsight the appearance in the sky of a fiery comet earlier that year (possibly Halley's Comet) was interpreted as an omen of the slaughter the little Northamptonshire parish was about to experience.

However, although times changed, the superstitious belief in natural and other phenomena did not. The beliefs gradually took different forms. In the Victorian era it was a widely held belief that a new moon on a Sunday foretold widespread flooding in the county. It has to be wondered what sequence of events generated this belief, but this sort of thing often went hand in hand with other superstitions such as the behaviour of wildlife. Thomas Sternberg recorded how Northamptonshire folk would attempt to see what the weather would do by hanging a dead cuckoo up by its feet and inspecting its tongue. They would use this as a kind of barometer, for apparently the dead bird's tongue would swell when rain was imminent, but become shrivelled up when the day was going to be fine. Even such a thing as the blooming of an apple tree after the fruit was ripe was considered unlucky, and this country rhyme was often repeated: 'A bloom upon the apple tree, when the apples are ripe, is a sure termination, of somebody's life.' Northamptonshire linguist Anne Elizabeth Baker noted in 1854 the 'popular and childish superstition' that white marks on fingernails were known as 'gifts', and to those with the know-how it was possible to predict future events much like reading tea leaves. The thumb touched the tip of each finger in succession and a bizarre rhyme was incanted – the outcome dependent on the number of 'gifts' or specks on the finger or thumb.

Sometimes the portents of doom took the form of something less-everyday, though. It is said that upon acquiring Rushton Hall in 1828 William Williams Hope had the notorious Hope Diamond stored within the premises. The diamond (supposedly originally stolen from a Hindu statue by a French thief in the early 1660s) attracted the legend that anyone who owned it suffered misfortune, and there is a long list of murder, suicide, disaster and bankruptcy attached to its owners. Hope was a diamond merchant and it is now said that he acquired the cursed stone from a relative. In 1836, eight years after the diamond's initial storage, Rushton Hall suffered a disastrous fire.

However, a significant number of portents of doom revolved around spiritual beliefs. Sometimes there was 'interaction' between the living and spectral entities. It was thought in Northamptonshire that when a sick person heard a sinister, ghostly knock three times on the wall of their room then they were about to die; this was followed by some invisible entity – presumably Death himself – saying the person's name audibly 'as it were, from the air'. There are also numerous ghost stories where the central theme is the apparition as an omen of coming misfortune (King Charles I himself is said to have been forewarned by an apparition that he should not fight at Naseby). Then again, to espy certain wraiths from a distance meant that one would surely die, and although there are numerous examples of this noted elsewhere, one will suffice for now. In the extreme south west of the county can be found the ancient Dower House at Fawsley, sometimes called the Old Lodge, an old manor

Beware the Old Lodge, hidden away deep in Badby Woods.

with beautiful twisted chimneys. Allegedly the oldest brick building in the county, today it is a picturesque ruin, hidden deep in Badby Wood and standing uninhabited since the death of Lady Anne Knightley in 1702. Here, it was once said, on New Year's Eve a ghostly huntsman dressed in green emerged from the ruins to ride around Fawsley Park, winding his horn. Anyone who espied this ghost was doomed to die, they whispered, as the huntsman was a harbinger of death itself. Quite who is supposed to have died and set this story in a motion can never be known, but as late as 1903 Alice Dryden noted in *Memorials Of Old Northamptonshire* that, 'Needless to say, the village people shun the place after dark.'

This story bears some similarity to the demonic huntsman of Whittlewood Forest noted elsewhere who was also regarded as a harbinger of death, and there are numerous others. Sternberg noted that such portents were universally diverse: the flowering of a tree twice in one year, the dropping of objects without any cause, the household clock striking 13. What all this indicates is that virtually anything out of the ordinary – or even the ordinary itself – was viewed with a depth of suspicious belief, even dread, that we can nowadays scarcely comprehend. Portents and curses took many forms, and it seems that in the past the folk of Northamptonshire saw the signs of impending disaster everywhere. As Sternberg put it, 'Almost every incident out of the common course of natural events, or which cannot be explained by the ordinary principles of rustic philosophy, is looked upon as ominous of approaching mortality.' We may scoff at this, but maybe – just maybe – the future can be read by the behaviour of animals, the weather and all manner of day-to-day occurrences. More worryingly, is the proof of forthcoming disaster all around us but we have forgotten how to see it?

THE BIRTH OF MONSTERS

In Elizabethan and Jacobean England – perhaps understandably – the birth of horrifically malformed infants was naturally viewed as either the work of a witch's spell or the result of a divine curse, 'punishment' for some unspoken sin committed by the parents or the community at large.

A pamphlet released in 1566 noted the birth of a horrendously deformed infant the previous year in Stony Stratford, on the Buckinghamshire–Northamptonshire border. It was entitled *The True Fourme & Shape Of A Monstrous Chyld, Which Was Born In Stony Stratforde, In North Hamptonshire.* Between six and seven o'clock in the morning of 26 January 1565 the child was born to an unnamed village woman and one Rychard Sotherne, who had fled. The child had two female bodies, with two sets of perfectly formed limbs, but from the navel upwards grew into one misshapen head that had a face comprising of two eyes, one nose, a mouth – but three ears, one of which was on the back of its head. It arrived screaming into this world and was christened by the attendant midwife, but lived for only two hours. After this, the bodie(s) of the unfortunate child were preserved and taken round the country as a sad and tragic curiosity, before finally ending up in London where it proved a popular attraction. It was pointed out that the child was born out of wedlock, and there is a clear Elizabethan warning that this is the punishment one would risk if they engaged in adultery or relations before marriage.

A printed tract (scribed by a curate named John Locke) that was published in August 1642 is one of the better-documented instances evidencing the belief that uttering violent, blasphemous oaths resulted in some kind of monstrous birth. The incident took place in Mears Ashby. In those deeply religious times a heavily pregnant woman called Mary Wilmore asked the advice of the Revd Locke as to whether her baby's head ought to be blessed with the sign of the cross. Locke ordered her husband John (a 'rough mason') to go to Hardwick and ask advice of the minister there, who informed him that it was an ancient necessity and ought to be performed upon the baby's birth. However, Mrs Wilmore had serious misgivings and saw the ceremony as an outdated remnant of Catholicism and swore that she would rather give birth to a baby with no head than submit to such a thing. In due course she went on to give birth to a monstrous infant, headless and with a mark that looked like a cross scarred into its chest. The pamphlet, entitled *A Strange And Lamentable Accident That Happened Lately At Mears Ashby In Northamptonshire. 1642*, is now in the possession of the British Library in London. Its frontispiece displays an image of Mrs Wilmore lying in bed, with her monstrous offspring on the covers before her, while three midwives look on in panic.

Joad Raymond's *Making The news: An Anthology Of The Newsbooks Of Revolutionary England 1641-1660* (1993) makes reference to yet another horrific birth that occurred in Rothwell around the same time. A Royalist pamphlet entitled *Mercurius Aulicus* (1654) brought to the attention of its readers the fact that a decade earlier a woman had given birth to a monstrous babe, whose lower part was not unlike an old woman's and whose upper part was black. Its mouth was lopsided and it had no eyes; it had ears that resembled those of a pig, and its back was like that of a fish. There seems, then, to have been a cluster of such incidences around this time. It reminds me of a story that I recall being told which concerned a man in Spratton who tried to trick his pregnant wife into thinking she had given birth to a cat. This was around the time of the English Civil War, and the idea was to engineer a charge of witchcraft against the poor woman. Quite how she was duped into this charade is unclear, but after the 'birth' the man presented his wife with a cat wrapped in a blanket, much to her horror. However, for once the law saw sense and it was the cruel husband who ended up being thrown in gaol.

There are modern echoes within this theme. Recently I was told a grim story by Fay B (a lady who grew up in Wellingborough but now lives in Lincoln). Fay was told that around '150 years ago' a 14 or 15-year-old girl had died during childbirth at Bedford County Lunatic Asylum, and the infant, although alive, was horrifically malformed. It had only one eye in its forehead and hair on its back. The dead girl's brother assumed responsibility for the tragic child. However, the brother – himself only 18 – supposedly took the child away and buried it alive somewhere in either Sywell Wood or Hardwick Wood, west of Wellingborough. Apparently the whole incident horrified the staff at the asylum and the birth was covered up. Fay was told this around 20 years ago by an aunt, and I cannot help but wonder if this was a veiled warning designed to scare her against teenage pregnancy.

QUEEN MARY'S TEARS

In 1854 Baker's *Glossary Of Northamptonshire Words And Phrases* noted the current rural superstition that the 'seed vessels' of the ash were known as 'keys', and if there were to be '...a scarcity of *ash-keys*...' then it meant that some member of the royal line would die within a year. One wonders whether this superstition was around – or perhaps even observed – in the year 1587.

There are vague stories of ill luck and misfortune linked to the execution of Mary Stuart, Queen of Scots, in Northamptonshire that persist to this day. The death of Mary within the great hall of Fotheringhay Castle at about 10 o'clock on 8 February 1587 brought to an end her tragic and turbulent life at the age of 44. Some 300 guests – mostly foreign dignitaries – had assembled at Fotheringhay to watch the spectacle of her beheading. She was in the 19th year of her English captivity, having abdicated the throne of Scotland in July 1567: fleeing imprisonment and rebellion at home she travelled south hoping for sanctuary with her cousin, Queen Elizabeth I of England. However, Mary's 'refuge' in England was merely another form of imprisonment, and here she became the hopeful focus of numerous Catholic plotters looking to remove the Protestant Elizabeth from the throne of England. Events reached a head in 1586 when letters passed between the dethroned Scottish queen and a Catholic militant from Derbyshire named Anthony Babington exposed a plan to assassinate Queen Elizabeth and rescue Mary from imprisonment, while a foreign force of Catholic sympathisers invaded England. The correspondence was smuggled into Chartley Castle, Staffordshire (where Mary was confined at that time), by a brewer's drayman, but intercepted by agents working for Elizabeth's zealous Protestant spymaster Sir Francis Walsingham. On 20 September Babington and his co-conspirators were brutally executed in London, and on the 26th of that month Mary was transferred to the castle at Fotheringhay to face trial.

Mary went on trial in October, accused of complicity in Babington's plot. Dressed entirely in black velvet, she told those assembled in the castle's great hall, 'Can I be responsible for the criminal projects of a few desperate men, which they planned without my knowledge or participation?' Mary knew her chances of acquittal were slim, and at one stage she dramatically pointed at a throne bearing the English coat of arms and defiantly stated, 'I am queen by right of birth, and my place should be there!' On 11 October she was convicted of treason.

However, there was a delay, as in London Elizabeth stalled signing her cousin's death warrant. Although she was certain of Mary's involvement in the plot, she dreaded being portrayed in the eyes of the people of England and the royal houses of Europe as a monarch who would sacrifice another queen to ensure her own position. Such a move would, she feared, create a dangerous precedent and arouse foreign Catholic sympathies; her willingness to have her cousin killed might come back to haunt her. Elizabeth apparently even mooted the possibility of having Mary murdered in a staged assassination to avoid appearing to have blood on her hands. When she finally realised there was no way out of it, Elizabeth signed Mary's death warrant and then asked to hear no more of it.

On the evening of 7 February 1587 the Earl of Shrewsbury sombrely informed Mary that she was to be executed at Fotheringhay Castle the following morning. Mary took the news calmly, her reaction being to place her hand upon a New Testament and declare herself innocent of any crime.

Mary rose at six the following morning and prayed for some lengthy time before walking in procession (a groom at the head of the line carrying a large crucifix) down the grand staircase at Fotheringhay and into the great hall to see the three-foot-tall scaffold, draped in black, upon which she was about to die in sight of hundreds of notaries from Europe. Clutching a crucifix, rosary beads and a prayer book before her, she endured a lengthy harangue from Doctor Fletcher, the Dean of Peterborough, who attempted to get her to renounce Catholicism – she firmly refused. Mary wore a white, lace-edged veil and regal black outer garments as she approached the scaffold. These were removed by weeping maids and servants, who were in a state of near collapse at the dignity their mistress was displaying, to reveal a dark red petticoat and bodice underneath. Thus, dressed entirely in dark red – the sign of a Catholic martyr – she was blindfolded and helped up the five steps to the scaffold, where she knelt on a cushion and placed her head upon the block. She commented to her executioners, 'I forgive you with all my heart, for now, I hope, you shall make an end of all my troubles.'

Among those present that day was one Robert Wynkfield, whose famous first-hand account noted the horrific details of Mary's execution. In two strokes of the axe Mary was dead, and the executioner finished cutting off her head with a pocketknife. Wynkfield wrote that Mary had died bravely, 'making very small noise or none at all, and not stirring any part of her from the place where she lay.' The executioner held aloft the head and shouted to those assembled 'God save the queen.' At this point the head fell out of the auburn wig that Mary had been wearing and hit the floor, and all saw that her hair '…appeared as grey as one of threescore and 10 years old, polled very short, her face in a moment being so much altered from the form she had when she was alive, as few could remember her by her dead face. Her lips stirred up and down a quarter of an hour after her head was cut off.' The Dean of Peterborough's shouted words echoed round the great hall: 'So perish all the Queen's enemies.' Gradually those assembled made their way out of the great hall, and the sheriff and his men carried the remains upstairs into a chamber where surgeons waited to embalm her. The body was left at Fotheringhay Castle in a lead coffin for a year before being transferred to Peterborough Cathedral in 1588.

The remains of Fotheringhay Castle.

There is much folklore attached to this sad, violent episode. Sydney Oldall Addy's *The Household Tales & Other Remains Collected In The Counties Of York, Lincoln, Derby & Nottingham* (1895) refers to a belief that one of those present at the execution hit Mary's decapitated head with his fist, at which she rolled her eyes and blushed. This is probably a variation on the documented observation that her lips continued to move after she was beheaded, but one or two of the tales surrounding the event fall into the realm of curses.

In 1603 England and Scotland were united when Mary's son, King James VI of Scotland, was also crowned King of England. In 1612 he ordered that Mary's body be exhumed from Peterborough Cathedral and reburied in Westminster Abbey. Turner's *History Of Remarkable Providences* (1677) recalled that there was a long-held belief in Northamptonshire that to exhume a corpse in this manner '...bodes death or some terrible calamity to the surviving members of the deceased's family.' King James chose to ignore the warning given to him by a Kentish man named Thomas Fludd, despite being told that it always 'bodes ill to the family when bodies are removed from their graves. For some of the family will die shortly after, as did Prince Henry, and, I think, Queen Anne.' Of course, the king's son Charles would be executed in 1649.

It is often said that James had Fotheringhay Castle razed to the ground upon his ascension to the English throne in 1603. He believed that the castle was jinxed, and as long as it stood it served as an ever-present physical reminder of what could happen to him if his fortunes changed. Some said that it was a symbolic revenge for his mother's beheading, but this is pure fiction: James had no direct memory of his mother, and his feelings towards her appear to have been somewhat detached. When news of his mother's execution at Fotheringhay was carried to him in Scotland, it is written that he either retired to bed early without any supper in a melancholic mood – or else gleefully remarked, 'I am now sole king [of Scotland]'. At any rate, Fotheringhay outlived King

James. It was actually pulled down around 1627 during the reign of his son Charles, after falling into disrepair. Perhaps there is some truth in a curse being responsible for the castle's demise though; there had been a castle at the site for some 600 years, and yet within 40 years of Mary's execution it had fallen into a state of such disrepair that it had to be destroyed. Perhaps the subsequent owners simply were not comfortable with the castle's grim past; maybe they genuinely believed that it *was* cursed. Stonework, elegant windowpanes and, famously, the staircase down which Mary walked to her execution were all transported to the Talbot Hotel at Oundle around this time. Strangely, there are no reports that Mary's ghost haunts the ruins of Fotheringhay – perhaps because the common belief that King James had it razed to the ground meant that somehow her ghost had been laid to rest.

Today there remains just one tiny portion of the masonry of the old Fotheringhay Castle, which stands before the mighty motte-and-bailey earth mound that formed its earliest foundations. The site is surrounded and adorned by huge thistles, the emblem of Scotland, which are supposed to have begun blooming the very summer after Mary's execution and have continued to do so every summer since. Here they are known as 'Queen Mary's tears.' Iron railings protect the remaining masonry of the castle, upon which is a plaque erected by the Stuart History Society in 1964, which declares 'In Memory Of Mary Stuart, Queen Of Scots, Beheaded In The Great Hall Of Fotheringhay Castle 8th February 1586/7.'

CURSED TO DEATH

The fondly remembered county author Denys (B.B.) Watkins-Pitchford laid the death of his own son, Robin, at the door of a curse. His 1978 memoirs *A Child Alone* explains that B.B.'s father, the Revd Walter Watkins-Pitchford, made a pilgrimage to Jerusalem in the early 1900s and there refused to give alms to a beggar, who cursed his family line. The reverend's eldest son would die, as would the eldest son of his youngest son, none of whom had been born yet. This is precisely what happened – with Denys's son Robin dying, possibly at Welford, aged only eight years.

However, aside from the numerous charges of death by curse levelled at Northamptonshire's witches, there is also the strange story of the death of Sir Augustine Nicholls.

Faxton is a tiny remnant village south west of Kettering, and Sir Augustine was its most famous resident. Born in 1559 in Ecton, Nicholls was a respected man from a distinguished family who studied law at the Middle Temple in London. He went on to become a judge of the court of common pleas and Knight of the Bath and was also entrusted as Keeper of the Great Seal to the young Prince Charles. While thus employed, Nicholls had a clerk working for him, a young kinsman named Thomas Dudley who went on to become Governor of Massachusetts.

Put simply, it is often repeated that Faxton village was the victim of a curse. Edward Foss's *The Judges Of England* (1857) tells us that Judge Nicholls died in Kendal, Cumbria, while on a summer circuit of the north: 'He is buried there, and has a fair monument in the church.' The popular version of the story is that the area around Kendal was the haunt of a bandit and murderer who found himself before the judge. At the arraignment (which took place in Carlisle) four women turned up and began to scream abuse in court. It turned out that they were relatives of the brigand on trial, and the spectacle ended with the women threatening spells and casting curses on the judge. The judge's line would never prosper, they yelled, and he himself would soon be dead.

Judge Nicholls died soon afterwards, at the age of 57, on 3 August 1616 of 'the new ague', and for such an important man the details of his death are a little obscure. If there is any truth in this story it might be speculated that he was a victim of his own fear, but this would seem unlikely superstition from such an educated man. *Northamptonshire Notes & Queries* (1896) asserts that Nicholls was poisoned to death at a Kendal tavern by the four women, who hoped somehow to save their relation facing the death sentence.

Whatever the truth, it is curious to note that back in Northamptonshire Sir Augustine Nicholls's line did indeed die out after his own death. He had married a widow named Mary Bagshaw but the couple had no children. So the estate at Faxton passed to his brother's eldest son, Francis, who was created a baronet in 1641. However, his grandson was the last of *that* line: he died without heir in 1717.

In Faxton the parish church that once stood also had a monument to Sir Augustine. The place — not even a hamlet now — has clearly seen better days. A ferocious outbreak of the plague in the 1660s killed nearly everyone who lived there, and this was another thing laid at the door of the 'curse', along with the general decline of the village. If a curse *was* to blame, it took a long time to work: the dwindling population and general relocation saw it only very recently fully abandoned. The last villager left in 1960 following the completion of the demolition of the parish church of St Denis. Within that parish church there was perhaps a partial explanation for the story. *The Gentleman's Magazine* noted in 1818 that 'In Faxton church is a handsome monument of Sir Augustin Nicholls, Judge, 1616.' The body of the judge was supported by four female figures which represented Justice, Prudence, Temperance and Fortitude. It is perhaps the case that these four figures represent the judge's murderers. During the demolition of the church in 1958 this monument was smashed, although the pieces of it were recovered and it now resides (fully restored) in the Victoria and Albert Museum in London.

The rest of the story can probably be traced back to the fact that Sir Augustine Nicholls was a judge, that he resided in Faxton, and over the centuries the village — which had stood since the ninth century — declined in both fortune and population. As a sad postscript to the story of the village, it is said that following the destruction of the church and the smashing of his monument the melancholic apparition of Sir Augustine Nicholls was to be seen at the site, his ghost mournful as if the death of his family home weighed heavily on his mind.

Alfred T. Story's *Historical Legends Of Northamptonshire* (1883) notes another instance of a fatal 'curse' in the mid-1600s. An arranged marriage was agreed between Bryan Cokayne, the eldest son of Charles, Viscount Cullen, and the heiress Elizabeth, daughter of Sir Francis Trentham. Both were at that time minors, and Bryan was sent abroad to Italy to further his education. It seems that young Bryan entered into many romances before returning to Northamptonshire as an adult to commit to his previously arranged marriage to Elizabeth Trentham. On the day of the wedding at Rushton Hall an uninvited woman turned up — one of Bryan's former dalliances — who after confronting him seemed to calm down and asked for a glass of wine to toast the wedding. She was given one, but, holding up the glass, she cursed Bryan and his new bride before all present.

Alfred Story found that there was a general belief in Rushton that after the wedding the curse had had its desired effect. Elizabeth, Lady Viscountess Dowager Cullen, had proved quite a hit at the court of King Charles II. She had become a lady of the bedchamber to Queen Catherine and had later allegedly embarked on an affair with the Duke of Monmouth (d.1685). Unfortunately, though, she ultimately died in near-poverty in Kettering almshouse on 30 November 1713. Bryan, second Lord Viscount Cullen, had already died abroad, 'a ruined and broken-hearted man' in absolute despair around mid-1687.

The Edwardian poet C.H.M.D. Scott based much of his prose on folk tales that he heard as a child in Northamptonshire, including a curious story from Deene, north east of Corby. 'Lord Brudenell' (that is, one of the Brudenell family who had been residents of gothic Deene House since 1514) was said to have been toasting in the New Year with distinguished company. Outside, the weather was dismal, but mingled with the howling wind was another sound: the unearthly moaning of a strange woman that guests could glimpse at the gate of the property outside. This strange 'darke lady' stood in the fierce weather and wailed as she looked at Deene House from afar, and the spectacle so unnerved one guest that he went to tell Brudenell about her. The lord, however, was too busy toasting in the New Year; as the clock struck midnight he promptly collapsed back in his chair and died before all present.

It is unclear whether the story concerns an actual woman, or whether she was supposed to be a ghost. Either way, the implication is that she was a sad and tragic figure that Brudenell had somehow wronged. Joan Wake's *The Brudenells Of Deene* (1954) notes that Deene House was long said to be haunted, only by a man, an 'unhappy ghost' of an ancestor who wandered in spectral form about the ancient corridors until he reached a 'certain bedchamber' where he vanished. Perhaps the story of the mysterious 'darke lady' was already well-known to the small village by the time the eccentric Lady Adeline Brudenell donned a nun's habit and 'drifted' about the hall pretending to be the place's resident ghost in Victorian times.

The link between ghosts and fatality in Northamptonshire appears rather more widespread than in other parts of Britain, as evidenced in the following tales.

GHOSTS AS PORTENTS OF DOOM

Sightings and manifestations of ghosts were often regarded as omens of impending death, and the phenomenon is a wide-ranging one. In some instances it was the mere glimpse of a supernatural entity from afar that was fatal (there are numerous instances of this in Northamptonshire, some of which are noted elsewhere).

Sometimes it was even possible to make sure you saw these ghosts. In common with many other parts of Britain it was often said that if you hid in a church porch on St Mark's Eve (24 April) you would be able to see a spectral procession of those doomed to die the following year make their way through the sturdy church door. Clearly, then, in some instances the phenomenon was more direct and involved actual interaction. At Helpston (in the mid-1800s when *Helpstone* was part of Northamptonshire) a village eccentric named Ben Barr would hide by St Botolph's Church and wait until midnight to see this procession of the damned. Thus, he claimed to know the fate of everyone in the village. Around the county at large, there was great fear of something called the 'death-coach', which doomed all who saw it. By the mid-19th century, although it was no longer seen, it '…is still *heard* rumbling along the old lanes.'

In the 19th century one such phantom coach was steered by a gaunt, white coachman and drawn by great, black horses. It was held to sweep up the gravel approach to Boughton House. Boughton is a former monastic house that was converted into a mansion by Sir Edward Montagu *c*.1528, and the 'Boughton Coach', as it was known, is likely to have been regarded as a death omen; many stately homes harbour such portents. It is perhaps linked to the story that Lady Elizabeth Cavendish (d.11 September 1734) cursed the building and its inhabitants after going insane. The 'Mad Duchess' had declared that she would marry none but royalty upon the death of her husband, the Duke of Albemarle; she became convinced that a Chinese Emperor wanted her hand in marriage, and so Ralph, Duke of Montagu, wooed and wed her in 1692 – disguised as an emperor of the Qing Dynasty. Ralph immediately placed her in confinement as a lunatic in the north-west wing of Boughton, during which time she spent her days screaming and cursing the Montagu line from the windows of her cell.

Does a phantom coach haunt the approach to Boughton House?

There is a curious anecdote noted in John Aubrey's *Miscellanies Upon Various Subjects* (1696) concerning the appearance of a phantom that, with hindsight, was seen as a spectral warning of death. Some 25 years previously it had been widely said in London society that the Countess of Thanet – Earl John's wife – had awoken one night while in bed with her husband; by the dim glow of the candlelight the countess had seen what appeared to be a ghostly figure in the bedchamber who resembled her daughter, Cecely, Lady Hatton, whom she knew with certainty was at that time far away residing in Kirby Hall, north east of Corby. The figure gradually faded away and the countess took this as an ill omen that something dire had either happened to her daughter, or was about to happen.

Lady Hatton was the wife of Christopher, the second Lord Hatton, who between 1670 and 1680 was the Governor of Guernsey. In 1675 the island was assaulted by a ferocious storm, during which lightning struck a gunpowder magazine in the grounds of Cornet Castle. In the resulting fiery explosion Lady Hatton was killed, as was Hatton's mother and several other women. Hatton barely escaped with his life himself, being blown in his nightshirt out of bed and through a window onto the castle wall.

The story is a curious one, as when the apparition of Lady Hatton appeared, she was at that time still alive. A more famous story with this theme was recorded by the Revd John Mastin, the vicar of Naseby, in his work *The History And Antiquities Of Naseby In The County Of Northampton* (1792). He had dug the strange story up from the archive work *Rastall's History of Southwell*, who had in turn recorded it as heard from 'a person off Newark att that time in his majestie's horse.' However, in this instance the apparition was of a deceased person and was held to have interacted with King Charles I, no less, but all the same the wraith represented a portent of forthcoming disaster, although its manner of delivering the message was different to the tale noted earlier.

The story runs as follows. In May 1645 the king's army halted at 'Daintree' (Daventry) and made camp. They had been on an expedition 'to attempt the recovery of the north' after successfully storming the Parliamentary garrison at Leicester. However, after receiving intelligence that Sir Thomas Fairfax and his Parliamentary forces had raised a siege at Oxford, it was decided to about-turn and return southwards. In Oxfordshire Fairfax received intelligence that the king's army was currently depleted and if his forces could intercept the Royalist army it might present an opportunity to end the war in one final stroke. It was possible: King Charles's army was fatigued and numbered less than five thousand after their campaigning. However, by the time he retired to bed in his chamber at the Wheatsheaf Inn (just to the north west of Daventry, in Braunston) Charles had formed a thorough and determined resolution to fight there and then, and face the armies of Sir Thomas Fairfax, who was by now marching on Northampton to look out for the king.

About two hours after Charles had retired to rest, some of his attendants were alerted to an 'uncommon noise' from the king's bedchamber. Rushing in they found him sat upright in terror in his bed, but as they looked about for intruders they saw none, 'nor nothing that could have produced the noise they fancied they heard.' This appears to indicate the commotion from the bedchamber was a kind of supernatural noise. Nonetheless, King Charles, in a trembling voice, confided that he had been visited by an apparition of his old friend and advisor Thomas Wentworth, first Earl of Strafford, who four years earlier had been executed in London – a victim of the growing power struggle between the king and Parliament. The king had been manoeuvred and finally forced to sign Strafford's death warrant – his most competent advisor, but a man whom Parliament saw as their biggest threat and a man hated by the people of London who knew him as 'Black Tom the Tyrant.' Strafford's execution was in essence a sacrifice to stop a civil war, or revolution; in fact it merely delayed one.

The implication is that Strafford appeared to the king as if in a dream, but whether Charles was supposed to be asleep or to have been woken by the wraith is unclear. Nonetheless, Strafford (after apparently insulting the king 'with unkindness') then proceeded to warn him that despite the fact that

Kirby Hall, linked to a strage precognitive event in the 1600s.

Charles had signed his death warrant, he was there to assist. The spectral visitor warned that on no account must the king face the Parliamentary army that was currently quartered at Northampton. He must turn about and lead his forces northwards as had originally been planned. Fairfax's army, he was warned, was one that could not be conquered by arms. At this point the attendants had rushed into the bedchamber to find King Charles in a state of distress.

The following day, the king decided – much to the surprise of his nephew, Prince Rupert, and the entire regiment – to do as the ghost advised. It is a testament to the chaotic state of the king's mind that Prince Rupert was able to talk him out of this and convince him once again to engage the Parliamentary army. That night Charles's slumber was once again disturbed by the ghost of his old colleague, the Earl of Strafford: 'The apparition appeared to him a second time, but with looks of anger' and warned him that if he engaged Fairfax he was lost; the wraith furiously scolded the king and said this would be the last time that he would warn him, before fading from view once more.

Whether this was a ghostly visitation or a result of Charles's troubled, indecisive subconsciousness is not specified. The ghost of Strafford visited him in the night to warn him, and there is a clear parallel with the equally famous instance of the seer warning Julius Caesar to 'Beware the Ides of March', upon which he would face great peril. The king, after remaining another day at Daventry in a state of complete indecisiveness, finally decided to heed the warning of the 'friendly ghost' and head north. By this time fate had conspired against him and he found that Fairfax was now too close and there was no avoiding the confrontation. As *The History And Antiquities Of Naseby* notes, 'This was called the Battle of Naseby, which put finishing stroke to the king's affairs…He was often heard to say, that he wished he had taken *the warning*, and not fought at Naseby; the meaning of which nobody knew, [only] those to whom he told this appearance at *Daintree*, and they were afterwards all of them charged to conceal it.'

(NB. A word of caution concerning this story: I was *told* by a drinker in the Wheatsheaf in Braunston in 2007 that 'King Charles saw a ghost here', and I have located the story here. Contemporary sources, however, indicate that it was in Daventry itself that events occurred. Future researchers may like to consider that there is a Wheatsheaf Court Nursing Home on Sheaf Street in Daventry, which I believe used to be an inn, and I suspect that this is possibly the building that the story relates to.)

THE OMINOUS DRUMMING FROM DOB'S YARD

The Revd Richard Baxter noted in his work *The Certainty Of The World Of Spirits* (1691) a remarkable phenomenon he had heard from a gentleman named Woodcocke, while the latter was a schoolboy in Oundle in the mid-1600s. Woodcocke '...heard about the Scots coming into England, [and he] heard a well in one Dob's yard, drum like any drum beating a march.' He had at first heard the ominous booming under the ground from a distance, and had sought out the well. He cautiously put his head into it, whereupon he heard the drumming clearer; he satisfied himself that there was no person hidden within its murky depths who could be playing some sort of trick. It drummed continuously for several days and nights and caused quite a furore in the village; many came to hear the noise for themselves and wondered what it portended. Although he does not say so, Woodcocke may have been referring to the invasion of northern England in late 1640 by the rebellious Scottish, resulting in a humiliating armistice allowing them to occupy six counties. More likely, the mysterious drumming was heard in the midst of the horrors of the civil war, perhaps when the Scots handed over King Charles I to the English Parliament at Newcastle in January 1647 after holding their 'guest' as a virtual bargaining chip in Edinburgh for months. The king was escorted to a parliamentary 'safe house' at Holdenby, Northamptonshire, before being arrested on 3 June that year by the soldiers of a man named Joyce, a coronet in Colonel Whalley's regiment. The king was then taken away from the relative security of his Northamptonshire confines to an altogether less secure future.

Woodcocke noted that the strange rumbling of the drum was reckoned to have been heard on numerous occasions afterwards, usually on the eve of some political upheaval: in 1685 he received a messenger at the Ram Inn, Smithfield, who had arrived from Oundle with the news that the well had been heard to drum upon the death of King Charles II on 6 February. Apparently, crowds of nervous villagers had stood about the well in fear, wondering what the subterranean thumping would herald. Woodcocke heard that after the king's death in 1685 it had 'drumm'd once since', but he does not elaborate in what year.

Revd Baxter, who first wrote of this mystery, died on 8 December 1691. A subsequent pamphlet entitled *Strange And Wonderful News From Northamptonshire* (1692) noted the well's *actual* name (before it was coined the Drumming Well) was Dobse's Well.

The drum continued to rumble on occasion afterwards. John Morton's *The Natural History Of Northamptonshire* (1712) recorded how the 'drumming' had begun once again on 4 June 1704 and that the rumbling could be heard from 60 yards away as it rose and fell. Ever the rationalist, he attempted to explain the phenomenon away in terms of fissures and underwater streams rising and falling, although in the common mind perhaps the noise was linked to the news in August of the British victory at Blenheim. Either way, the phenomenon was quite famous by the mid-18th century. By this time traveller Robert Dodsley found that, although most still believed that the well drummed, there were next to none who actually claimed to have heard it first-hand. By the time a contributor to *Notes And Queries* wrote of the well in 1853 it had become legend, and people did not seem too interested to know whether it was a geological curiosity or a true paranormal wonder.

Drumming Well Lane, to the rear of the Talbot Hotel.

The contributor had been taken to see the well as a small boy, and his fascination with the old legend had stayed with him into adulthood.

The *exact* location of the 'drumming well' is nowadays uncertain, although the well itself apparently survived into the 20th century – and was still ominously predicting periods of upheaval in Britain. Writing in 1930, George Long noted in his *Folklore Calendar* how many of England's 'holy wells' had disappeared in the last 20 years: 'A very tragic instance is the famous haunted drumming well at Oundle, which has now been built over; but I have met an old inhabitant who has heard the mysterious drumming which gave it its ghostly reputation.'

At the height of its fame the well is also reputed to have drummed to warn of the Great Fire of London (1666) and the death of Oliver Cromwell (1658), although there appears to be no evidence for this other than that these were two of the major events of the period and there is a local presumption that the well must have drummed to mark the coming of these events. These days the phenomenon is remembered by the street name of Drumming Well Lane, off West Street (A427), Oundle. The location of the sinister well was in the vicinity of the rear of the Talbot Hotel, to which Drumming Well Lane leads. If you are staying at the hotel, it might be worth keeping an ear out for the threatening, underground rumbling.

ANIMALS AS AGENTS OF MISFORTUNE

Among the more lingering of beliefs was that animal behaviour foretold bad luck, particularly where it involved unexpected or out-of-pattern animal behaviour. Typically, a correspondent to

Notes And Queries in 1850 explained that there was a belief prevalent in Northamptonshire that if a homestead hitherto free of mice was suddenly infested by the rodents then it meant that one of the occupants would soon die. Similarly it was thought that if a mouse was seen scurrying over a sleeping person, they were doomed. To witness one squeaking behind the bedstead of an invalid meant the invalid would soon pass on; and woe betide anyone who saw a pure white mouse scamper across the floor of the house, for that also meant someone who lived there would die very soon. Whether this was some subconscious connection to rats and the plague, or to witchcraft and their 'familiars' (sometimes said to resemble rodents) is unclear. Perhaps it says more about the filthy living conditions of the peasantry in 19th-century Northamptonshire, although the belief extended beyond the home. To meet with a 'shrew-mouse' while making a journey was reckoned to be extremely bad luck. Even insects formed part of these patterns of belief. If crickets were to desert the hearth it was thought to be the worst possible omen that a homestead could experience.

Why should this be? How could such seemingly random beliefs arise? What is even more curious, however, is that in some instances the animal's behaviour did not need to be particularly out of character; folklorist Thomas Sternberg noted in 1851 the belief that to see a hare bounding down the main street of the village meant that shortly after a fire would break out in the immediate vicinity. One can imagine that hares being spotted in the main thoroughfare of rural Northamptonshire villages was not *that* uncommon in those days…maybe fires were also more common in that era, leading to the supposition that one heralded the other. Perhaps the association started in Wellingborough. In 1837 the antiquarian John Cole noted how 'a few years ago' a rabbit caused much excitement in Market Street in the town. It darted out of reach of those who tried to capture it; it dashed into a barber's shop and when cornered became exceptionally aggressive. The rabbit actually leapt at one man's face scratching him badly before dashing off down Cheese Lane and disappearing into a drain. Wellingborough was, in Cole's time, evidently associated with fires, as his *History And Antiquities* indicates, although disastrous fires could strike anywhere at any time – the *Mercury* reported on 18 July 1785 that a fire had all but destroyed Kings Sutton, for example.

In line with other parts of the country, notably Lincolnshire, birds of all kinds were also considered as omens of doom well into the Victorian era. The robin in particular inspired reverence and even fear due to the belief that when someone lay ill within a house a robin would alight outside the window, then tap its beak three times on the pane, and to see such a thing meant without doubt that the person who witnessed it would shortly die. It was (or still is) presumably this ability that bred a terrified respect of the red-breasted bird into folk. Children were warned that it was a sacred bird, and generations grew up knowing that to kill one was next to sacrilege. Their nests were never troubled by egg-thieves, and this veneration also extended towards other members of the animal kingdom. Weasels and the (now-extinct) wild cat would not touch robins, even when they found them dead in the fields or on the roadside.

To see a crow by itself was thought to be extremely unlucky, and if you saw one perched in the middle of the road looking at you then that was indicative of some kind of wrath being visited upon you. It was even thought poultry could foretell death: the crowing of a hen meant that someone in the family would die very soon, and once heard the only way to avert this was to chop the hen's head off. If a farmer should chance to see his poultry regularly going to roost at noonday, instead of their usual time, it meant that he would shortly thereafter collapse and die. Who would have thought that the humble profession of poultry farmer could be so dangerous. (These beliefs are somewhat at odds with an incident in 2007 when I was unfortunately defecated on by a raven in Raunds while waiting to talk to someone about these superstitions; I was told – more than likely tongue in cheek – that this was lucky in that part of Northamptonshire.)

The historian John Cole noted examples of the sinister prophetic powers that certain birds were endowed with. In the aftermath of the Great Fire of Wellingborough in 1738, during which it had been common to hear the terrified exclamation 'Fire! Fire!', a caged magpie kept on the green by Mr Frank Gent had taken to mimicking this call. It would squawk, 'Fire! Fire!' and cause general alarm among the townsfolk who asked it where. The magpie would reply, 'At Frank Gent's!' Around 1797 a blackbird would alight at Gold Street in Wellingborough and caw 'Fire and murder! Fire and murder!' Townsfolk would gather daily to hear this, and they guessed it meant that the village idiot (who had recently disappeared) had been slain somewhere. An effort was made to capture this bird, but when it was trapped it promptly died, leading to further fear in Wellingborough. Cole thought that in all probability the bird had been trained and had then escaped – or been set free – allowing it to spread panic.

It is easy to see how the curious behaviour of birds aroused suspicion. In the 1830s a huge number of starlings would gather at 'Wheywell, between Ditchford and Higham Staunch' where they would perform amazing aerobatics and form 'definite shapes'. The most remarkable was one that looked like a balloon and basket, which would turn and sway in the evening dusk.

Perhaps the most extreme example of this concerns the case of the 'Seven Whistlers'. A contributor to *Notes And Queries* explained how he had been passing through Kettering in 1871 when his attention was drawn to a group of birds flying around in circles and uttering 'dismal cries'. The gentleman mentioned the incident to his servant, who promptly told him that the phenomenon was a well-known one and the birds were called the 'Seven Whistlers.' Whenever they started to act up like that it meant a pit disaster was imminent. The last time they had been seen and heard was in 1862, just before a tremendous explosion tore through New Hartley Colliery, Newcastle-upon-Tyne, killing 204 men. Curiously the appearance of the 'Seven Whistlers' did indeed presage another colliery disaster: the following morning the gentleman concerned picked up his newspaper over breakfast and saw that an explosion had ripped the Moss Colliery at Ince-in-Makerfield, Wigan, claiming 70 lives.

The diversity of the nature of omens seen in the natural world was neatly summed up in an article entitled *Folk Lore Of South Northamptonshire* in an 1851 edition of *Notes & Queries*: 'Omens of death and misfortune are also drawn from the howling of dogs; the sight of a trio of butterflies; the flying down the chimney of swallows or jackdaws; and swine are sometimes said to give their master warning of his death by giving utterance to a peculiar whine, known and understood only by the initiated in such matters.'

OMENS OF LUCK AND LOVE

It is not all doom and gloom, however. There were certain observances that were reckoned to bring good luck in Northamptonshire. When a spider was found upon one's clothes it meant that money would be coming your way. Similarly it was thought that if a cricket crossed the hearth of the home it was a sure sign of coming prosperity. To see two magpies playing together was likewise thought to be a very good sign. Anne Elizabeth Baker, a linguist who compiled the curiosities of the Northamptonshire dialect in 1854, noted how there was a common belief in the county that babies born with the caul, or kell – 'the thin membrane which sometimes covers the face of an infant at its birth' – were thought to be hugely lucky. Mothers would carefully preserve this membrane and their blessed children often carried this about with them throughout life; apparently it protected them from drowning. Incredibly, substantial sums of money were offered by those who worked near canals, rivers, swamps and the wider ocean for cauls in the hope that it would protect them.

Apparently these superstitions still prevailed well into the 20th century. On 15 November 1926 a woman by the name of Smith was charged in Higham Ferrers with fraudulently obtaining money from a widow. Smith had sold the widow 'charms to burn, wear and put under her pillow'. If the ones to be burned burnt brightly, the widow was told, £400 was coming her way. If they burnt dully it meant someone was holding the money back. The fortune-teller received one month's hard labour; the police superintendent in charge of the case noted that there were still many gullible people in rural Northamptonshire who relied upon such superstitions in their everyday lives, and the fortune-tellers who preyed on them 'are becoming a danger to the countryside.'

It was, perhaps not surprisingly, the area of love where there was the biggest amount of superstitious belief. According to Thomas Sternberg, compiling such superstitions in the mid-Victorian era, girls could be observed picking the leaves of a herb called the 'pick folly' one by one and chanting 'Rich man, poor man, beggar man, thief.' Whichever was spoken when the last leaf was pulled would be the occupation of their future partner. Since the odds are heavily in favour of a negative profession it might be thought that this was more an idle game of luck than a true way of divining the prosperity of one's future husband. But it is possible that there was an element of belief that the ritual worked, given that there are all manner of other superstitions that appear to have been genuinely believed and routinely practised. For example, 'young maidens' would carry with them the empty head of the 'knot-weed' in the firm belief that if they were to encounter their future spouse the plant would blossom again within an hour. The regional poet John Clare wrote of such practices, 'I've heard old women, who first told it me; vow that a truer token could not be.'

Christmas Eve was thought to be a time when such rituals were particularly successful. At midnight it was said that if a young woman went into the garden and plucked 12 sage-leaves without damaging the stalk she would see the ghostly shade of her future husband appear at the foot of the garden and make his way to the house. Another way to call up this ghost was a little more disgusting: the young woman needed to capture a live pigeon and stick it full of pins. Then – still alive – it was tossed onto the fire, at which point the image of her intended would become visible. One young woman told Sternberg that she had performed the ritual and had been promptly startled by the unaccountable noise of what she thought was a bag of nails falling heavily to the floor. She told the researcher that she was convinced she would become the bride of a blacksmith in later years. On the mystical date of St Marks Eve (24 April) it was the practice for three unmarried women to make a delicacy called the 'dumb cake' and perform yet another ritual which would allow them to see the shadowy wraith of their future spouses. The dumb cake was prepared and the women would break off a piece of the cake and eat it in silence as the clock chimed midnight. They were not allowed to say anything because if they did the spell would be broken. Those that were to be married would see the shadowy form of their sweethearts pursuing them as they retired to bed, and in order not to suffer spectral molestation the young women would already have unpinned their clothes so that they could get into bed quicker. It was believed that the shadowy spirit was attempting to get the young woman before she was able to get into bed, but if she managed to she had therefore 'controlled' the spirit. Other spirits announced their presence in the house by knocking or rustling, and the women would even go to the lengths of putting out pet cats or dogs so that any noise they made was not mistaken for that of the ghostly arrival. Those who were to remain unmarried would hear nothing and were sure to dream that night of newly dug graves, rotting corpses in winding sheets laid out on slabs in churches and wedding rings that would not fit upon fingers.

There was another ritual designed to conjure up spectral visions which involved eating the yolk of an egg in silence on 24 April and then filling the shell with salt. That evening, the young woman then had to make her way to the nearest church and lay a large branch or flower in the porch. As midnight approached she would make her way back to the church porch, accompanied by her friends,

It has always been thought that it is very unlucky to disturb graves in Northamptonshire. These curious 13th-century effigies were discovered accidentally in 1981 on the tower roof of Rothwell Church during renovations.

who had to wait at the church gate. The would-be bride then retrieved her flower from the porch, and if she was to be married in the next year she would see a ghostly wedding procession make its way into the church. She would see herself and her husband-to-be, arms linked, at its head and a procession of wedding guests following. The number of those following the bride and groom was the number of months the woman would have to wait before her marriage. If the woman was destined to die unmarried 'then the expected procession is to be a funeral, consisting of a coffin covered with a white sheet, borne on the shoulders of shadows that seem without heads.'

Sternberg wrote that in his time – the mid-1800s – this spectacle utilising eggs, salt, giggling girls, church porches and ghostly apparitions was still regularly performed. However, the older dumb cake ritual, he acknowledged, was seldom practised any more. These days, the exact recipe of the dumb cake has surely been lost to the ages, although perhaps in some Northamptonshire family it has been passed down through generations? Maybe somewhere in the county there are still those fond of old family recipes who perhaps unwittingly possess the means to conjure up the ghosts of the living and thus foretell who they will marry in later years.

CHAPTER 5

FAIRY AND GOBLIN LORE

INTRODUCTION

Folklorist Thomas Sternberg was essentially Northamptonshire's equivalent of the Brothers Grimm in Germany. He was endlessly fascinated by the stories that circulated among the peasantry of the county concerning fairy folk and goblin-like entities and avidly collected them. However, he was also quick to point out that these were not mere bedtime stories. *The Dialect And Folk-Lore Of Northamptonshire* (1851) points out that 'The belief in fairies, that most poetical of popular superstitions, still lingers among the rural population of Northamptonshire and South Warwickshire.' This mirrors the diehard belief from almost every other part of Great Britain that the human race once shared (or still does share) their environment with a much smaller race of elemental beings, a state of affairs that has sadly been overtaken by progress and scepticism. Mitchell and Rickard's *Phenomena: A Book Of Wonders* (1977) perhaps outlines the scenario best: '...part of the general pattern of events would be that from the earliest time there was intimate contact between our race and another, more diminutive and less material; that the link between the two peoples gradually weakened; and the smaller race retreated from areas of human habitation into the wilder regions, finally retiring into the upper atmosphere from which they now and then descend on brief visits.' Some, then, clearly link the demise of the fairy folk with the emergence of the UFO phenomenon.

However, this chapter is concerned with the time when the fairy folk were still our earthly companions. In Northamptonshire there were various types: Queen Mab and her lieges, bogies, bogles, Jinny-Buntail, Robin Goodfellow, the Shagfoal, the Redman. The patterns are the same across much of the English midlands, and it is interesting to note the similarities in tales of the elementals that are repeated in different locations.

For example in *Notes And Queries* (30 July 1853) Sternberg retold the story of an encounter between a farmer and a 'bogie' that took place and was commonly repeated around the county. The exact location is not specified, but Sternberg describes the bogie as 'a household spirit' of 'dwarfish stature', much like an elf, who was given over to mischief that extended to terrorising farmsteads in the manner of a poltergeist. The bogie was also tremendously strong, and it was said that one of these spirits entered into a dispute with the farmer over a field they both claimed a right to. (NB. Sternberg continually referred to this particular elemental as a spirit, despite it possessing the characteristics of a flesh-and-blood creature at times.) After much feuding the farmer and the bogie agreed to divide its produce between them. The farmer asked the bogie what he wanted: that which grew above ground, or that which grew below. 'Bottoms', replied the creature, meaning that which grew below the earth. So the farmer sowed the field with wheat and at harvest time reaped it all for himself, while the bogie had to settle for the stubble in the earth. Next, the bogie chose 'Tops' – he wanted that which grew above the ground. So the farmer planted turnips, and once again at harvest time reaped the whole crop for himself, while the stupid bogie fumed in frustration. Tiring of being outwitted, the bogie proposed a mowing match with scythes – with the very field as the prize for the winner, confident his superior strength would see him win. However, the night before the farmer laid scores of iron bars in the part of the field the bogie would be scything. During the competition the goblin quickly fell behind, as the iron rods in the earth blunted his scythe. Since the rules dictated that both the farmer and the bogie had to sharpen their scythe at the same time, the bogie shouted at his opponent: 'When d'ye wiffle waffle, mate?' The farmer, whose instrument was still as sharp as when he started, replied that it would be noon when they sharpened, and at this the frustrated bogie shouted, 'Then I've lost my land!' At this he disappeared.

This story has more famously attached itself to Mumby, a village on the east coast of Lincolnshire, but the original version would *appear* to have sprung up in Northamptonshire – at least, it seems to have been first recorded in connection with our county. The Mumby version is exact in almost every detail except that the elemental there is a boggart, a creature more like a troll than an elf. If nothing else, it indicates that stories of such creatures were popular fare and travelled widely. Sternberg noted in 1851 that there was a body of evidence to show that they were not merely fairy stories – these bogies and the like were actually *believed in* by former generations.

Researching in the early Victorian era, he noted the widely held belief that in former days bogies were thought to attach themselves to a specific farmhouse or grange, from where they would relentlessly torment the owners with mischief. They would set up residence in the cellars, helping themselves to ale and reigning supreme as king of the residence. Terrified servant girls would blame everything, from lost items to unexplained noises, on the resident bogie. His name was used as a threat to frighten unruly children in nurseries, and in days gone by householders would leave a 'creame-bowl' out to appease such creatures. This practice was repeated in other parts of the midlands, particularly in marshy, wet areas. It was also a truism that the 'fairy folk' did not take on today's familiar image of a gentle, winged sprite. In Northamptonshire they were more akin to elves or hobgoblins.

So did our near ancestors know of something we have now forgotten? Of course, belief in elves, bogies, fairies and goblins is a personal matter: Sir Charles Isham of Lamport Hall, Lamport, is

Lamport Hall and Gardens are open to tourists in August.

famously credited with introducing garden gnomes, not just to Northamptonshire but to Great Britain as a nation. In 1847 he arrived at Lamport Hall with 21 terracotta garden gnomes purchased in Germany, which he placed about the caves and plants of the rock gardens. Only one survives, a chubby little fellow in green overalls called 'Lampy' who is insured for one million pounds. This was, however, more than folly. Sir Charles passionately believed in the existence of gnomes, and remarked in his *Notes On Gnomes* that 'Seeing and hearing gnomes is not mental delusion, but extension of faculty.' He went on to say that each porcelain gnome in the gardens of the hall had a real, invisible gnome friend alongside it whom he had occasionally managed to snatch glimpses of.

This aside, apart from the unsubstantiated folklore of the Northamptonshire peasantry and the difficult-to-come-by first-hand accounts of encounters with the little people, the lingering rituals in the region aimed at appeasing the elementals suggest a superstitious belief that was perhaps based on something physical. Minute tools, as if fashioned by miniature people, have purportedly been unearthed in such diverse places as Suffolk and Devon. In the late 19th century was made the perplexing discovery of hundreds of tiny flint tools – scrapers, borers and knives – in the Pennine Hills. Curious, controversial photographs occasionally turn up to stoke the debate and offer 'proof' of the little people, such as the notorious Cottingley fairy photographs.

However, true belief in these various types of otherworldly folk for the most part died out long ago. Thomas Sternberg could find little in the way of first-hand accounts of these elementals, and was left with merely a wealth of anecdotal evidence (much of it which bordered on fairy tales) – but also a sensation that there once was a deep and true belief in these types of creatures. He enquired with a rustic as to why they were not seen so often and received the reply that the little folk had taken to causing so much trouble that a group of parsons had performed a ritual and banished them to the Red Sea. Apparently this event was common knowledge in rural circles, although the details were scant. Much folklore has a *basis* in genuine belief, if not even a little fact, and although the little people are seldom seen these days perhaps they are still there: the Helpston poet John Clare (d.1864) wrote:

> 'Now in the corn-fields, now in the new-mown hay.
> One almost fancies that such happy things,
> With coloured hoods and richly burnished wings,
> Are fairy folk, in splendid masquerade
> Disguised, as if of mortal folk afraid,
> Keeping their joyous pranks a mystery still,
> Lest glaring day should do their secrets ill.'

NORTHAMPTONSHIRE FAIRY TALES

Some might be interested to know that, much in the manner of the Brothers Grimm, Northamptonshire also produced its own folk tales concerning little people and elementals. In a similar vein to the German stories, some of the Northamptonshire ones are dark – disturbingly so. One can only hope that the story of Little Elly was designed to scare unruly children. Little Elly was a girl who realised her schoolteacher was an ogre who was kidnapping men and eating their flesh; the schoolteacher then kidnapped her, whipped her to death and buried her underneath a rose bush. Soon her tiny ghost-like spirit found its way into her parents' bedroom where it sang in a mournful voice: 'Dark, weary, and cold am I; Little knoweth Gammie where am I...' She was destined to sing this until her parents heard her and found her body – but they could not hear her, and she was never seen again.

This grim story, collected by Thomas Sternberg, appeared in *Notes And Queries* in 1853 and was told along the banks of the River Avon, which rises near Naseby and flows in a southwesterly direction via Stanford Reservoir along the Northamptonshire–Leicestershire border. However, one of the fables that particularly stands out as typical is the story of *Fairy Jip And Witch One-Eye*, first outlined by Sternberg in *Notes And Queries* in June 1852.

Centuries before, there had lived a malicious one-eyed witch who nursed an all-consuming desire to capture, cook and eat an elf. So she went to the top of the hill where she knew the fairies lived and rapped at the door, saying as sweetly as she could manage, 'Pretty little Jip, come and see the sack of cherries I have bought thee, so large, so red, so sweet.' Jip was a young elf who loved cherries, and he quickly came out into the daylight – whereupon the witch grabbed him and thrust him into a sack. Cackling and taunting the struggling elf, she set off home.

At some point the witch left the sack in the charge of a man cutting wood while she went on another errand. From inside the sack Jip pleaded that the man let him go; in the end the man relented and they both filled the sack with thistles so the witch would not notice. She returned, collected her 'dinner' and made off once more, commenting to the sack on her back: 'Ay, ay! My lad! I'll trounce thee when I get home for stinging me with thy pins and needles.' Once home she grabbed a huge stick and beat the bag until she thought she had smashed all of Jip's bones – but upon opening the mouth of the sack she found he had escaped and flew into a horrendous rage.

In a fury the witch stormed back up the fairy hill and using the same trick once again managed to snare Jip in the sack. The same pattern of events was repeated, Jip managing to escape this time with the help of a man breaking stones by the roadside. The witch screamed, 'Thou little rogue! I'll soften thy bones nigh-hand!'

Knowing the trick would not work a third time, the witch assumed the shape of a peddler with a churn on his back. She waylaid Jip in the woods and said to him, 'Ah Master Redcap [another term for fairy], look alive my little man! The fox is after thee!' The witch invited Jip to hide in the milk churn and then sealed it, assumed the shape of a witch once more and went straight home.

Once back at her hovel, the witch gave her daughter strict instructions to release the elf and immediately chop his head off. She then whisked out of the kitchen to prepare for her meal of elf. The old hag's daughter freed the elf and ordered him to put his head on the chopping block; at this, Jip pleaded stupidity and asked her to show him how he was to position himself. So the witch's daughter lay down and rested her head on the block – and of course Jip grabbed the hatchet and severed the woman's head. He then grabbed a huge pebble and disappeared up the chimney.

In due course the witch entered the room and made her way to the cooking pot which stood at the base of the chimney. She lifted up the lid of the pot, an action that involved her putting her head into the chimney – then Jip threw the pebble down the chimney chute, it smashed into her head and she lost the sight in her one eye. In other versions the pebble killed the witch.

It is interesting that in telling the story the names 'elf', 'fairy', 'spirit' etc are used interchangeably to describe Jip, indicating that centuries ago there was a blurring of the lines in names and descriptions of the 'little people'. The influence of the Brothers Grimm is clear in Sternberg's narrative and, indeed, in the story itself. Sternberg himself noted that in some instances such stories were, '…so extremely like the German ones, that, with very slight alterations, they would serve as translations.' Is it possible that such folk tales were common currency in Northamptonshire at the same time as similar stories were circulating in Germany? If versions of the same folk tales were circulating independently of each other in different parts of Europe, such an instance would be quite remarkable.

Stanford Reservoir is fed by the Avon, where long ago they told a grim fairy tale.

It has often been speculated upon how much of the Brothers Grimm's fairy tales was truth, or folklore based on truth, or pure fabrication on the part of the brothers. One might wonder the same about the story of Fairy Jip; Sternberg gives no clues, merely commenting, 'This story is from Northamptonshire...No sneers, therefore, gentle readers, but listen to the simple strain of Fairy Jip and Witch One-eye.'

BOGIE BEASTS

John Clare, the famous 'Northamptonshire Peasant Poet', was born on 13 July 1793 at Helpston – actually a village in the Soke of Peterborough, which was at the time part of Northamptonshire. His poems depicted images of rural England that showed a loving appreciation of nature; some, such as *The Village Minstrel, and Other Poems* (1820) focused upon the folklore he had grown up with in the early 1800s. In particular is his reference to '...offsprings of 'Old Ball'...a shagg'd foal [which] would fright the early-rising swain.'

Clare explained this cryptic reference for the benefit of his readership. An 'Old Ball', he said, merely meant the foal of a mare. The 'shagg'd foal' was something entirely different – a sinister, supernatural entity widely thought to haunt the country lanes and primitive highways and byways of rural Northamptonshire: 'It's a common tradition in villages that the devil often appears in the form of a shagg'd foal; and a man in our parish [Helpston?] firmly believes that he saw him in that character one morning early in harvest.'

Despite the assumption by Clare that the shagg'd foal was a demon in disguise, the creature's true nature was something of a supernatural mystery. Across the region there was more of a consensus of opinion that this scruffy looking young horse with blazing eyes was some form of trickster spirit: a goblin, boggart or a bogie beast which had taken the form of an animal to commit the kind of mischievous trickery on the road that the farm-dwelling bogie played from the safety of the cellar.

Folklorist Thomas Sternberg, three decades later, understood that the Northamptonshire Shag Foal was a 'mischievous goblin who prowls about the county in the guise of a shaggy foal.' In watery areas to the north of the county the tricks of the Shag Foal were potentially lethal. It would lure lost travellers into watery marshland using its soft whinny and glowing eyes. When the traveller found himself waist-deep in filthy water and lost in the undergrowth in the dead of night, the Shag Foal would drift away through the woodland, its whinny replaced by a horrific, distorted half-human laugh. Sternberg noted that in Northamptonshire this creature was reckoned to delude people into mounting it, '...and then vanishing with a shout of fiendish laughter' presumably after depositing the unfortunate traveller somewhere dank, wet and inhospitable.

This creature was one of the most famous rural supernatural entities of the 18th and 19th centuries, although belief in it was on the wane by the end of the 19th century – perhaps because improved transport facilities, road systems and bigger towns had robbed it of its playground. Nonetheless, belief in the creature lingered on in the Midlands into the 20th century – although seemingly only in the form of an entity that children's grandparents used to be fearful of. As late as 1902 natural historian George A. Morton was told stories of a Shag Foal that supposedly haunted the region around Barnack (near Cambridgeshire's border with Northamptonshire and Lincolnshire) by a woman whose family had lived there for generations. In days gone by this entity took the form of a large, black, scruffy looking bear-like animal.

The Shag Foal's behaviour was reminiscent of another 'dwarfish spirit', much like a goblin, who played the same trick. This creature was referred to as the Jinny-Buntail, and took the form of a strange light effect that misled drunks and 'night-faring clowns' on a confusing trek through dense undergrowth until they stumbled, lost, into a riverbank or muddy pond. In Sternberg's time the Jinny-Buntail was still an entity to be feared after dark during lonely, tipsy journeys home from the local public house.

CAPTURING THE LITTLE REDMAN

Sternberg, apart from being an avid collector of what were undoubtedly fairy tales, is often credited with being the first researcher in Britain to coin the word 'folklore' in the title of a publication – folklore being set apart somewhat from a fairy tale in that it was often sincerely *believed in* as opposed to being just a 'good story'.

In 1851 he found there was a lingering belief in a variety of fairy folk called the Redman, or Redcap. It was thought to be 'a small hairy dwarf', something like an elf, and wore a red bonnet. Although they lived in sizeable communities they were still solitary creatures who kept to themselves, hiding away in caves and old wells.

Sternberg found that the following anecdote was widely repeated as a 'real event'. It was said to have taken place during a time of great hardship when three brothers were 'reduced by the badness of the times' to take refuge in one of Northamptonshire's royal forests, where they built a dismal shelter and hunted the king's deer. (Since Rockingham Forest was the earliest to be made a royal domain, and one of the largest such forests in England, it is likely that the story was often set here.)

Remnants of Rockingham Forest, near Cotterstock: once home to the little Redman?

Hunting in the royal forests was a risky business. Successive lines of nobles and royals made these vast areas their own personal playgrounds, and the chase was taken seriously. It was reckoned that King James I took the right of the king to hunt deer here so seriously in fact, that '…one man in his reign might with more safety have killed another than a rascal deer.'

One day the eldest brother remained in the wooden shack to cook the ill-gotten meat while his siblings went out again to hunt. Suddenly a little Redman appeared next to his feet and pathetically pleaded, 'Plaze gie me a few broth.' The startled brother grabbed a hatchet to fend off the fairy-fellow (as one would have done a hungry animal) but while he did so the Redman grabbed the pot from the fire and dashed out the hut and into the forest. The eldest brother lost the agile sprite among the trees and ferns.

The following day the middle sibling was left to perform the cooking and fell victim to the same trick while his elder and younger brothers were out hunting. On the third day it fell to the youngest brother – a youth treated with contempt by the other two – to cook, but by now the lad was wise to what the Redman was doing. So that day, while his elder brothers were roaming Rockingham Forest looking for game, he idly stirred the pot, waiting patiently for the Redman to show up and say, 'Plaze gie me a few broth.' At this the lad made as though to give him the pot and then slammed it down on the Redman (for it was empty) trapping him. The Redman cried, squealed and attempted to escape but could not, and was finally forced to conduct the lad to his home: 'an old well, in a retire part of the forest.' Here the Redcap villagers were forced to pay a ransom for their captured brother and the lad was given a huge stash of gold in return for his captive. He was, as Sternberg was told, '…made a mon on for life [a man for life].'

FAIRIES AND FORTUNE

In line with the previous story, Sternberg avidly collected tales that involved interaction between county folk and the little people. There are familiar themes which (as before) are perhaps metaphors for rustic fears of sudden ruination, or the dreamy optimism of unexpected wealth.

In the 19th century a tale was still told of a vigilant farmer named Hodge busily engaged in threshing (a process of beating cereal plants to obtain the grains or seeds, but not the straw, using an implement called a flail). However, the cereal grain and wheat sheaves were vanishing from the secure yard in which they were being stored; so Hodge, believing an employee was robbing him, placed extra bolts on the doors and posted a sentry to keep watch all the time. However, each morning the guards swore that no one had passed them by, and the bolts remained untouched – and yet the grain was always missing from the yard.

Farmer Hodge was not sure what was going on, so one night he snuck into the yard and hid himself among the sheaves of wheat. At midnight he did a double take at the sight of two tiny elves who appeared in the yard by sneaking through the pike-hole. They began to work away at the sheaves, pulling out the straws and harvesting the grain into little bundles. Hodge watched silently, biding his time, waiting until the two little fairy folk sat down, worn out from their work. One said to the other, 'I twit; do you twit?', meaning, 'I sweat, do you sweat?' At this farmer Hodge rushed out and screamed at them, 'I'll twit ye if ye bent off!' ('I'll sweat you, if you be not off!') The two sprites vanished instantly and never again reappeared.

Conversely, another tale (which must have generated much hopeful thinking among the peasants of Northamptonshire) concerned the legend of three gifts presented to an old woodsman by a fairy, who appeared just as the man was about to take his axe to a particular tree: the fairy's home. The fairy granted the woodsman his next three desires so that he might spare the tree, and he relented. Before the day was out, however, the peasant had forgotten that he had been granted three wishes (Sternberg thought this was due to the surreal 'illusion' state that meeting fairies was thought to bring about, rather than stupidity) and he settled down before a roaring fire with his wife.

Presently he grew hungry and wished aloud for a 'link of hog's pudding'. At this, a tremendous rustling from the chimney announced the sudden appearance in the room of the meal. It comprised a great spread, and the event brought to mind the woodsman's earlier encounter. His memory refreshed, he told his wife what had happened earlier that day. She at once flew into a fury and told him to be careful what he wished for with his last two wishes.

For some reason, the woodsman flew back at his wife, 'I wish em wer atte noase', which presumably meant he made some ridiculously stupid wish in order to spite his nagging wife. The food flew and hit him in the face, attaching itself to his nose so tightly that force could not move it. In order to rid himself of his clownish appearance, the woodsman was forced to use his third wish to clean his face off.

It is unclear whether this is supposed to be a comment on rustic stupidity, nagging wives or a warning not to dabble with fairy magic, but in any event the story appears to be a joke – unlike the earlier story of farmer Hodge which reads like it was told as a *real* event, and mirrors modern poltergeist encounters in its sheer mundaneness. It was only occasionally, unfortunately, that Sternberg noted whom had told him the story, and in what part of Northamptonshire it was supposed to have occurred. What he did get across was the rustic *belief* in the realism of the fairy folk, and by association, the tales. One is left wondering whether the aforementioned farmer Hodge was a real person, and what event befell him to make his whimsical story capture the popular imagination.

BELIEF, BUT NO EVIDENCE?

Thomas Sternberg did his best to get past the unsubstantiated fairy stories and try to procure evidence of genuine belief – if not quite actual evidence itself – in the little people.

His investigations turned up some interesting pointers. Thirty years before, the poet John Clare had drawn upon Northamptonshire folklore to write one of his best-known poems, the darkly atmospheric *Village Minstrel*. In one part he describes the fairies thus:

'And tales of fairy-land he lov'd to hear,
Those mites of human forms, like skimming bees,
That fly and flirt about but every-where;
The mystic tribes of night's unnerving breeze,
That through a lock-hole even creep with ease.'

This sounds like the 'literary' depiction of the traditional fairy that is so familiar nowadays, but it does little more than illustrate that 'fairies' were common fare in traditional tales. Sternberg, much in line with folklorists in other parts of the midlands later that century, however, found that fairies in Northamptonshire took on the form of what sounds like elves, although they were frequently referred to as 'spirits' or 'goblins' (as noted earlier). An old woman of the county told him that two or three generations earlier she recalled the 'good women' of the cottages performing a peculiar ritual. Before bed the womenfolk would sweep the hearth thoroughly and place a bowl of water before it. This odd behaviour was to 'assist in the ablutions' of the fairy folk, which was a main reason for their visits. Presumably this meant that they visited a human dwelling to, among other things, use the toilet facilities! Children were warned that if they awoke in the night to the sounds of little footsteps gambolling across the hearth they were on no account to go and see what was causing them, for two reasons: firstly, if the little folk were left to their own devices, prosperity could attach itself to the house or farmstead, and secondly if their curiosity got the better of them and they went to spy on their night-time visitor, they would be struck blind.

Apart from recording this belief in his poem, Clare also noted the common supposition that fairy dances left marks in the grass called 'fairy rings'. It was in the south of Northamptonshire that Sternberg found the greatest evidence of genuine belief, including a 'green sour ringlet' in pasture land in the parish of Brington which was proudly claimed by the locals to be '*the* fairies' ring'. The parish contains three villages, Great Brington, Little Brington and Nobottle, and it is not clear exactly whereabouts the phenomenon lay, but it was considered quite a wonder locally.

The fairy ring was thought to have existed for centuries, and it was commonly suspected that a fairy dwelling 'existed under the area bordered by the dark circle.' It withheld all attempts to plough it, still somehow continuing to be visible, and locally there were dark rumours that disaster would afflict anyone who succeeded in this task. Running around the outside of the circle nine times on the first night of the full moon was supposed to enable one to hear sounds of mirth and partying from beneath the ground at this spot.

Not everyone was convinced though. The Revd Dr Joseph Wasse of Aynho (d.1738), during correspondence with one Dr Mead, considered that such fairy circles were the work of lightning, although he conceded that the effects could be visible for upwards of half a century. However, Northamptonshire folklorist Ann Elizabeth Baker noted in her *Glossary* (1854) that 'In whatever way this phenomena may be explained by philosophers, a poetical charm will always be connected with the popular superstition that the moonlight fairies there tripped their merry roundelays.'

The little folk were also thought, when in a playful mood, to lark and splash about lonely ponds or leafy brooks in the south of the county, and there were places referred to as 'fairy pools' on account of this belief. The aforementioned Jinny-Buntail (the mischievous spirit that led tipsy travellers into the rivers) was rationalised as 'the ignis fatuus, or Will with the wisp', although the exact nature of this phenomenon is still the subject of much debate among natural historians. Wells were often thought to be another haunt of the fairy folk, and locals were still known to avoid these spots after dark. In the village of Aynho there was a spring referred to as the Puck-well, 'puck' being a name for a mischievous nature spirit.

One tall tale from southern Northamptonshire (which has variants across the whole of Britain) went thus. A young man was making his way home from a neighbouring village, where he had been indulging all day at a fete. Drunk, he fell into a 'vast o' fairy folk' who were engaged in a football competition. Emboldened by dutch courage, he dashed into them and gave the ball an almighty kick: whereupon all the fairies vanished in a flash and he himself passed out. When he awoke, he was not sure whether he had dreamed his adventure at first – but then he saw the burst football with golden coins spilling out of it. He gathered up his riches and fled the scene. So it seems that in rare instances an encounter with the elementals could be advantageous.

In 1800 the poet Robert Bloomfield heard that in the enchanting woodland to the west of Silverstone, '…where human foot had seldom stray'd', fairies were supposed to dance and play around 'Wake's huge oak, their favourite tree.' Sternberg wrote, 'Near the village of Brington is (a fairy pool) so designated, where, I have been assured, a few years ago they might be seen rollicking on the surface, and gambolling among the water plants that lined the edges.'

Such creatures were all around us, apparently, at one time. However, this is as close as we get to 'proving' the existence of fairies in Northamptonshire. Belief, but no evidence? I happen to think that many of these types of stories have some basis in fact; perhaps the story of the farmer and the bogie, for example, is a mis-remembering of a competition between antagonistic landowners centuries ago. Or perhaps Farmer Hodge was being robbed by his employees, not elves.

A 'fairy ring' discovered by the author in grassland near the banks of the Welland, Marston Trussell.

This should not detract from the fact that these elementals were *believed in* until a time not so many generations ago.

You will have to make up your own mind. However, it may please some to know that the possibility of the little people still greatly fascinates. The fondly remembered local author Denys 'B.B.' Watkins-Pitchford (d.1990) was born at Lamport, and he would have grown up with the legends of the Lamport Hall 'gnomes'. In his memoirs, *A Child Alone*, he wrote very definitely that as a child he had seen a little 'being' with 'a round, very red bearded face…It wasn't a dream; I can still see the little red astonished face.' With these childhood experiences in mind, he later wrote a children's book in 1942 entitled *The Little Grey Men: A Story For The Young In Heart* about the last four gnomes in Britain who lived by a Warwickshire brook – one of the last regions 'where one might meet with a fairy.'

In July 2007 the BB Little Grey Men Trail opened in Brixworth Country Park, north of Northampton – a charming attraction for imaginative children and adults brought up on the adventures of Watkins-Pitchford's gnomes. As the *Northampton Chronicle & Echo* remarked, 'Who knows, someone might just spot a little grey man running under the bushes!'

Chapter 6

Ghost Stories of Northamptonshire

Introduction

It is just possible that Guilsborough in Northamptonshire boasts Britain's oldest spectre; at any rate it appears to be bizarrely unique. In 1818 a book on topography described Guilsborough as '…supposed to derive the appellation from a large Roman encampment in this parish, situated between the sources of the *Nen* and Avon. It is supposed to have been a camp of the Propraetor Ostorius: and at present is known under the appellation of borough hill, but often called the Burrows.' The Renton Sisters, Ethel and Eleanor, in compiling their *Records Of Guilsborough, Nortoft And Hollowell* in 1929, noted that when the southern embankment of this Roman encampment was dug away in the 19th century a great number of skeletons were unearthed, although what became of them is unclear.

Edwardian spiritualist Elliott O'Donnell, who lived for a time in Guilsborough, perhaps interpreted such finds differently. He noted that there was an 'unused burial mound' in the village – and that the spectral apparition of a savage-looking 'nude man' was said to have been frequently seen beside it. Some 250 yards from this spot, O'Donnell noted, was a 'barrow, close to which a sacrificial stone had been unearthed.' He speculated that the nude spectre was possibly someone who had been interred in the barrow in pre-history (which would surely make it one of the oldest ghostly apparitions ever).

This one instance highlights the eternal dilemma of what 'ghosts' are. The phenomenon of ghosts is a strange one; it takes many forms, and the supposition that they are related to tragic or sudden deaths is a curious one. Over the centuries there have been innumerable battles, murders, disasters, suicides, road accidents and people who died in the greatest despair resisting death – one would suppose that if this were the case then the land would be more populated by ghosts than by living people and there would be more concrete evidence.

It also begs the question of why there are so many different 'types' of ghosts. If the 'nude ghost' of Guilsborough was indeed that of a buried body then why did it appear to be a 'phantom echo' of the person as they were when they were alive – *but yet still be unclothed?*

Perhaps the simple answer to this is that in the 19th century, when this rumour was circulating, it might make sense to the superstitious that when a skeleton was uncovered and its ghost disturbed, it would appear in the manner in which it was buried. There are countless ghostly anecdotes from Northamptonshire that clearly belong to the realm of folklore, like this one, which have – these days – sadly little to evidence them other than the local assurance that these entities were at one time commonly seen.

For example, the village of Ashby St Ledgers was reckoned to be haunted in the early 20th century by the ghost of Squire Arnold, who sat atop a phantom horse in a certain lonely lane. The squire held his severed head underneath his arm. When Nortoft was a distinct hamlet (before being swallowed up by an expanding Guilsborough) it was reckoned that a lady in white drifted her way over Nortoft Hill and into one of the adjoining farmer's fields. Then again, around the county at large, phantom coach and horses were thought to sweep past travellers on lonely country roads at night.

Indeed, the majority of the time it seems there is an assumption that if a place *looks* haunted then it *must be* haunted, and one can imagine that a lot of stories are 'engineered' to fit this supposition.

This perhaps accounts for the lack of corroborative evidence in some of Northamptonshire's established ghost stories. For example, a ghostly white lady that is *rumoured* to drift the rooms of 17th-century Brockhall Hall (now a number of residential flats) is *assumed* to be that of a former owner's wife, Mary Hope, who killed herself in 1767 aged just 25. Likewise places such as Naseby and Fotheringhay are now well-known locally to be haunted... a supposition brought about down the centuries perhaps based on the belief they *ought* to be haunted. It is also a curious feature of Northamptonshire's traditional ghost stories that some of them appear to revolve around money, perhaps a reflection of the many stately homes and royal connections. In addition there were the urban legends, the scare stories to frighten children. In Victorian times children were told that if they did not behave then 'Black Parr' would get them. Who this was is not known, but Thomas Sternberg thought he might have been a demonised member of the family of Parr, the Marquis of Northampton, who served as sheriff during the reign of Henry VIII.

The belief in ghosts (and especially the accompanying exorcisms) prompted this comment from Sternberg in an 1852 edition of *Notes And Queries*: 'I must here remark that scenes of this fearfully ludicrous nature are far from unfrequent in our country districts. The besotted state of ignorance in which a great portion of our rural are still enrapt, renders them peculiarly open to the fleecing of these fanatics [exorcists], who, marvellous to relate, are almost everywhere.' I understand an exorcism is supposed to have been performed within the vicarage grounds at Easton Maudit, upon the death of the incumbent vicar, the Revd Francis Tolson, on 1 March 1746. This was after rumours got out that his ghost would not depart his beloved residence of 12 years. I was told that the exorcism was arranged by Tolson's wife Catherine, to quell the upsetting stories that her husband's ghost still haunted the gardens.

It might be thought, then, that all Northamptonshire's ghost stories which circulated before we had such a sophisticated media are of this folklore type, but this is not the case. Some were reliably recorded as contemporary events. For example, within Joseph Glanvill's *Saducismus Triumphatus* (1681) can be found the details of a bizarre poltergeist incident reported in 1658 to Sir Justinian Isham of Lamport, a scholar and politician who fought the Royalist cause in the civil war. He was told by a clergyman of events at a home in Daventry that, among other phenomena, involved furniture moving by itself, bedclothes being thrown off the bed by invisible hands and various small objects – including stones – being thrown about. This is clearly what we would interpret as a poltergeist outbreak. In the 17th century, however, it was interpreted as witchcraft, and is now a good illustration of the differing ways that supernatural phenomena can be viewed depending on the era. In another incident, Isham's son, Sir Thomas, received a letter in 1678 from one Gilbert Clerk of Loddington, who described a disturbing spirit which had invaded the home of two widows in Brixworth and which '...roots like an evil hogg.'

Around 1834 a curious discovery was made within the walls of Rushton Hall. Tucked inside a bundle of books and family papers (which had been walled up since 1605) was a letter written by Sir Thomas Tresham *c.*1584 in which he explained a possible reason for his building the famous late-Elizabethan folly Rushton Triangular Lodge, which is situated about half a mile from the old hall. The reason, he wrote, why he laboured so much in the construction of the lodge, with its emblems of the Trinity everywhere within and without, was that one night his servant had been reading the 'Christian Resolution' aloud to him when a strange thing happened. 'There was upon a wainscot table at that instant three loud knocks given (as if it had been with an iron hammer); to the great amazement of me and my two servants, Fulcis and Nilkton.' In accordance with Tresham's Catholic beliefs it was interpreted as the word of the Lord, and hence it has been speculated the lodge was subsequently built as a testament to his faith.

In the 19th century spiritualism was big business, and organisations sprung up to investigate claims of ghostly phenomena: the Victorian equivalent of today's 'ghost-hunters.' For example, at

Rushton's mysterious Triangular Lodge.

Passenham Rectory – on the extreme south-east border of Northamptonshire, near Milton Keynes – the Society for Psychical Research investigated the claims of a Mrs Montague Crackanthrope that she and her nurse had become literally obsessed that someone invisible was stood in the dining room watching them silently. In 1874 the rector, G.M. Capell, unearthed seven buried skeletons during renovations there. A more sophisticated media was also latching on to these types of stories, which certainly made for good copy.

Some of the tales within this chapter are well-attested ghost stories from Northamptonshire folklore. However, there are some very notable instances of documented ghostly encounters from our past as well, and a selection of both categories are featured here for the reader to ponder.

THE TRAGEDY OF BARTON SEAGRAVE

The Edwardian poet C.H.M.D. Scott recalled hearing in his childhood of a tragedy that had occurred 'in the 13th or 14th century'. A certain Lady Isobel Latimer, daughter of Lord Latimer of Braybrooke Castle, eloped with Lord Seagrave of Barton Seagrave. Some, however, repeat that she was actually *abducted* by Lord Seagrave, and that she was in fact betrothed to Hugh Neville, of Burton Latimer (who we learn had holdings in Northamptonshire granted to him by the king *c.*1215. If this was the case, it gives an approximate date of the alleged events). The elopement, or abduction, took place under the cover of a truly immense thunderstorm. However, the brother of Lady Isobel took off in pursuit of the fleeing couple – presumably, then, to either rescue her from an abductor or to drag her back home to face the wrath of the Latimer family. He ran the pair to ground at the ford of the River Ise, near Kettering, where in the melee all crashed into the swollen river: young Latimer, Seagrave and poor Isobel all drowned. (Some have it that Seagrave escaped the disaster and the third person who drowned was in fact Hugh Neville, who had accompanied young Latimer on the rescue mission.)

Scott noted that following the tragedy the three bodies were interred at the site of Barton Seagrave Castle and that an oak tree was planted over each grave, '…the decayed trunks of which are still said to exist.' Barton Seagrave Castle is thought to have been established in the early 1300s and fell into ruination around 1433, which further confuses the date this is supposed to have happened, although a *History Of The County Of Northampton* (1930) does indicate it might have earlier foundations. Some say the events happened later than Scott believed, perhaps during the Wars of the Roses in the 15th century. The confusion notwithstanding, in August 2008 I visited the sad remains of the castle's moated enclosures in an effort to try and find any sign of the three oak trees that evidenced this obscure legend. Sadly I was unable to. They may have been there – the site is very overgrown, and populated only by a few horses – but I was struck by the coincidence of the name Barton *Sea-grave*. It would seem that the manor was at one time merely Barton, before becoming divided into Barton Hanred and Barton *Segrave*. This became in time Barton *Seagrave*, and I cannot but think this name is a curious coincidence given the story of the tragic watery deaths all those centuries ago.

Needless to say, for centuries they whispered that Lady Isobel's ghost, white and transparent, drifted above the surface of this stretch of the River Ise. Scott best puts the scene:

Two horses fed by the side of the way;
In the bend o' the river three corpses lay;
Two were of men in the pride of their race;
Were they friends that were locked in a last embrace?
…But the third was a maid with an angel's face.

GHOSTS OF ROYALS AND RULERS

There are many traditional ghost stories in Northamptonshire that have very little to substantiate them other than the theory that the place 'ought to be haunted'. Sometimes it is the shade of a famous person, perhaps royalty, who haunts the scene of a major event in their life. The ghost of Nell Gwyn, the actress and mistress of King Charles II, was for centuries said to inhabit the ancient woodland of Salcey Forest, according to writer Andrew Green. By the 20th century the county was littered with sites such as this, and had been since as long as anyone could remember. Cromwell is still 'known' to haunt the battlefield at Naseby. But there are other examples of this type in Northamptonshire folklore.

Mary, Queen of Scots, is perhaps one of the most famous women who ever lived, and predictably since her death at Fotheringhay on 8 February 1587 there have been many rumours surrounding her tormented spirit. Despite popular supposition, Fotheringhay Castle was not pulled down by Mary's son, James I. It passed through the ownership of two of his courtiers, and by the time it ended up in the possession of the Earl of Newport it still contained its vast dining room adorned with exquisite masterpieces. As a young man, the Northamptonshire historian Thomas Fuller (1608–61) visited the castle and noted that one of the windowpanes was scratched, a mark said to have been caused by Mary's ring finger during her incarceration. In 1635 a visitor described in his journal that, although many of the huge rooms could still be wandered through, the castle was 'sickly and dying', ever since the Earl of Newport had commenced pulling it down. The banqueting hall had been taken to Conington Castle, Cambridgeshire, while other portions were carried to the chapel at Fineshade and the Talbot Inn (now the Talbot Hotel) at Oundle. Here, the three-level oak staircase is said to be the

The imprint of Mary's ring is allegedly emblazoned onto the Talbot Hotel's banister.

one that Queen Mary actually walked down on the way to her execution. On the balustrade in the mid-part of the staircase there is emblazoned into the woodwork a strange mark, a crown-shaped imprint which is said to be that of Mary's ring (the same one that scratched the window pane), created when she gripped the banister on her last, fateful walk. It is even famously said that her ghost walks these very stairs, wearing the regal black velvet and satin outer garments that she wore on her last day on earth. A stiff collar is about her neck; she wears pearls and beads, and a crucifix hangs on her bosom. Her hair is tied back and kept in place with a small bonnet or skullcap. She is thought to walk out into the yard and towards the archway of the Talbot Hotel, on West Street, where she disappears. Apparently, sometimes her face can be seen staring sadly out of one of the upper windows of the Talbot.

At times, usually on the anniversary of Mary's death, phantom sobbing supposedly resonates pitifully through the Talbot Hotel, appearing to emanate from room number five. Joan Forman's *Haunted East Anglia* (1974) also raised the question as to whether Mary haunted the nearby mediaeval manor Southwick Hall as well. Southwick, some three miles to the west of Fotheringhay, was certainly haunted, and there was a long-standing rumour that an underground tunnel had linked it to Fotheringhay. The passage (as I was told) 'might have' emerged in the crypt, which was an addition to the original manor house around 1320. Local lore has it that Mary would escape the Protestant confines of Fotheringhay to Southwick Hall, which was owned by the Catholic Lynne family. Here she could say Mass in their private chapel (in the so-called Gothic Room, where there can be found an altar recess). It is this spot which is said to be haunted by the wraith of a woman dressed in the garb of a well-to-do Elizabethan lady. Although it is not clear if this ghostly lady *is* Mary, it is popularly assumed today that the ghost must be that of the Queen of Scots.

Southwick Hall.

Within the village of Fotheringhay itself, the sombre strains of early mediaeval funeral music have been heard emanating from within the walls of the empty St Mary and All Saints' Church, a fantastic 15th-century building far too big for the village that it stands in – until you remember that the castle once existed here. Who these mournful tunes still echo is unknown: several members of mediaeval royalty were interred here. Among them were Richard Plantagenet, third Duke of York, and his wife Cecily Neville, in whose honour Elizabeth I had the present monuments created about the church altar and the pair interred in opposite tombs. The couple's youngest son, Richard, was born at Fotheringhay Castle on 2 October 1452: this was the future King Richard III, and he, like his father, was destined to die violently in battle. It is said locally that following his death Richard's mutilated corpse was buried at Grayfriars Church, Leicestershire, before being dug up in the 16th century and thrown into the River Soar at the spot known as King Richard's Bridge. Perhaps this unseemly treatment is why, according to tradition, the spectre of the ill-fated king wanders about the forlorn remains of Fotheringhay Castle to this day: he is seeking a proper burial, in the village of his birth and beside the tombs of his parents.

'STEADY! STEADY! I AM NOT READY!'

Close by the border of Buckinghamshire, in the south of the county of Northamptonshire, can be found the tiny village of Passenham. A crown official from Shropshire, Sir Robert Banastre, appears to have left a strange legacy here in the early 17th century.

Sir Robert's coat of arms adorns Passenham's church.

Around 1626 he rebuilt the manor and re-edified the church, St Guthlac's, although an 1849 survey of the church's architecture was less than complimentary: 'The whole of this structure displays marks of a fervent desire rather than a successful attempt to revert to the ancient principles of ecclesiastical architecture.' Sir Robert died on 13 December 1649, and St Guthlac's contains a fine monumental bust within the chancel installed in Sir Robert's memory.

It appears that despite his endeavours his enclosure of much of the village land left ill feeling in Passenham. Brown and Roberts noted in *Passenham: The History Of A Forest Village* (1973) that is was unfortunate that '…his memory is not a happy one; perhaps that he was there to keep a tight reign on the running of affairs made him unpopular among [the] tenantry.' In a chapter entitled *The Passenham Ghost* it is also noted that for decades his ghost had allegedly roamed the village: over the years this spectre has become familiarised as 'Bobby Bannister, the Demon Landlord.'

Banastre may not entirely deserve this moniker as he was a benefactor in certain areas, but nonetheless the familiar legend runs thus: following his death, during which he had attempted to confess his sins on Passenham, rumours spread throughout the village that a strange, armour-clad figure could be seen walking the green late at night, howling and moaning. This was thought to be Sir Robert's ghost, and on the day of his funeral the cortège was halted on the porch of St Guthlac's by a ghostly voice that bemoaned, 'Steady! Steady! I am not ready!' The coffin was opened, but the corpse within appeared just that – a corpse. So the service proceeded. Unfortunately it was plagued by accidents, and all the while those assembled could hear a familiar voice saying again, 'Steady! Steady! I am not ready!'

It was thought that this dismal state of affairs had occurred because Sir Robert had not been able to finish his deathbed recantation, and it was said that ever after a phantom coach and four horses thundered along the lanes after darkness had fallen, the unseen occupant of the coach crying out, 'Steady! Steady! I am not ready!' Legend has it that the bishop (of where is not said) led a group of clergy in an attempt to exorcise the spirit that was frightening the villagers. During the service of exorcism the ghost of Sir Robert Banastre materialised and beseeched them to stop, at least until he had finished his penance. Apparently the ghost was no more heard of after his wishes were adhered to.

This legend was drawn upon by author T. H. White (d.1964) in his collection *The Maharajah & Other Stories*, which contains a ghostly anecdote entitled *Soft Voices At Passenham*. He paints an atmospheric picture of the nearby River Ouse: 'Silent, green and slimy, it goes slow and cold through the flooded winter landscape: bearing with it the bodies of drowned maidens, goggle-eyed in mid-water…even the mill wheels no longer turn, mill wheels which used to collect their harvest of suicides…There was Nancy Webb, for instance, at Passenham Mill. She goes through it *once a year* with a dreadful shriek, carrying her baby in her arms, and her bones crackle in the great wheel like a firework squibs. The river makes nothing of this.'

This was the haunt of Sir Robert Banastre, or 'Bobby Bannister'. He had, according to White, broke his neck while hunting, and now his ghost rode atop a galloping horse, the pair accompanied by a pack of baying spectral hounds. On the day of the accident Sir Robert had fallen from his horse and it had bolted, dragging him all the way home. The skeletal figure now atop the horse was reckoned to have its neck out of joint, and the horse snorted fire from its nostrils.

THE REST-LESS GHOST: WONDERFUL NEWS FROM NORTHAMPTON-SHIRE…

The following story is alleged to have been a real ghostly encounter. The event was sung about in the form of a ballad, and the truth of the incident was recorded in a 17th-century pamphlet entitled *The Rest-less Ghost; OR Wonderful News From Northampton-shire, and Southwark. Being A Most True And Perfect Account Of A Person's Appearance That Was Murdered Above Two-Hundred-And-Fifty Years Ago.*

William Clark (or Clarke) was a malt-maker who lived in a farmstead called Old Pell's House at Hannington, west of Wellingborough. For a year his property had been subjected to violent poltergeist activity, which much troubled the cattle, but in the week between Christmas and New Year 1674 the cause of the trouble physically manifested itself before the startled Clark. The poltergeist 'turned the 'malt o'th' flowre', which drew Clark out to see what was happening. In the orchard the ghost then gave Clark an almighty shove and suddenly appeared before the startled farmer, who yelled, 'In the name of Jesus Christ!' In response to Clark's stammered questions the apparition remarked, 'I am the disturbed spirit of a person long since dead, I was murdered near this place two hundred sixty and seven years, nine weeks, and two days ago, to this very time, and come along with me and I will show you where it was done.' The ghost explained that in life he had lived in Southwark, south London, and his violent death while travelling through Northamptonshire had meant that all his monies and papers – hidden away at home – still remained hidden. Until they were dug up and disposed of, he could never rest. Since his death he had been unable to appear on earth because of the 'magical art of a certain friar' but as time went on the spell receded in power until he found he was able to manifest as an invisible entity at the farmhouse, and now as a fully fledged ghost.

Clark agreed to help, and on 10 January 1675 he duly travelled to Southwark. The ghost greeted him at London Bridge 'in the common habit of a man' and together they went to the former residence of the ghost. The current owners of the house must have been very shocked to open the door to a man and a ghostly apparition, but nevertheless they heard the ghost tell once again its pitiful story. The phantasm then led them to the cellar and told them to dig there; eight feet down they found a pot full of gold coins and some old papers which crumbled to dust as soon as they were touched. However, some were parchment that stayed complete and were dated to the early 1400s, proving that what the ghost was saying was true. The spirit gave Clark specific instructions on how to dispose of what had been found, and this he did; the money that had not rusted away and the deeds to some land were given to a female descendent of the murdered man.

When the money and documents had been distributed or destroyed accordingly, the ghost appeared one last time before Clark, smiling broadly, and said, 'Thou hast done well, and henceforth I shall be at rest, so as never more to trouble thee.' On 14 January 1675 Clark returned home to Northamptonshire 'very well satisfied.' The pamphlet adds that it is based on a first-hand account from William Clark himself which could be attested to by 'Will Stubbins, John Charlton, and John Stevens, to be spoken with any day, at the Castle Inn without Smith-Field Barrs.' Who these people are is not clear, although perhaps they lived at the house in Southwark and were maybe witness to the search for the money and papers.

The ballad was also contemporary, and adds the detail that in life the ghost was killed while passing via Hannington by a servant then employed at the farmstead. The servant hacked off his victim's head and buried the corpse somewhere nearby. It is not explained why; presumably it was an attempted robbery. In fact, with this story there are no half measures. The event either happened as described (and is, as such, a true account of a ghost), or it did not. In the words of the ballad of the time:

'So to conclude what here is penned;
And is laid open to your view;
Although it be a story strange;
Yet hundreds knows it to be true.'

HANGED HE'LL BE WHO STEALS ME, 1745

In 1764 a horrific murder case shocked the inhabitants of Guilsborough; however, it was the events after the crime which took on an eerie, supernatural theme, and which – if true – presents written testimony of an actual encounter with a 'real' ghost.

That year three men, Croxford, Seamark and Gee, and a boy by the name of Butlin, appeared at the assizes of Northampton accused of murdering a travelling peddler from Scotland who happened to stop at the home of Seamark, a shepherd in the parish of Guilsborough. The party of four ne'er-do-wells would often gather at this small dwelling, and the court heard how they had waylaid the peddler before robbing him and then attacking him. Finding that they had killed their unfortunate victim (whose name was not even known since he was a passing stranger) they dragged the body to a kiln where it was consumed in flames. Unfortunately, Seamark's nine-year-old son spied the four men cramming the body into the oven through the crevices in the floor of the room above, and ran to tell his mother, Ann Seamark, who reported the incident to the authorities.

All four were found guilty and hanged on 4 August 1764. The corpse of John Croxford was suspended in an iron gibbet cage on Hollowell Heath, north of the village of Hollowell, so that all who approached Guilsborough would see the treatment meted out to convicted murderers in this part of the world.

Shortly hereafter there appeared in print a pamphlet entitled *The Guilsborough Ghost, Or A Minute Account Of The Appearance Of The Ghost Of John Croxford, Executed At Northampton, August 4th 1764, For The Murder Of A Stranger In The Parish Of Guilsborough*. The author of this piece had held the position of prison chaplain at Northampton gaol, and it had been his misfortune to note that during their incarceration not one of the condemned men ever admitted their guilt. Even as they stood on the scaffold they denied any wrongdoing very vocally before the crowd that had gathered to watch them hang; in fact, so convincing were their pleas of innocence that many of those assembled – including the chaplain himself – began to doubt that the four accused had actually committed the crime. The executions, it seems, left a deep sense of unease in the parish of Guilsborough.

The case seems to have played on the mind of the chaplain. On 12 August 1764 (the Sabbath) he retired as usual to his study (it is not specified where this was; it may have been at Northampton gaol) and prepared himself for an evening of studying the New Testament. At the part where Saint Paul proposes, maintains and proves the resurrection of the body, the chaplain stopped to muse at the weight and wisdom of this argument – when he was struck to see out of the corner of his eye that a man was stood slightly to his right. This was remarkable: the chaplain had bolted the room from the inside so there was no way anyone could get in. Surprise turned to abject fear, and as the chaplain studied his uninvited guest he formed the impression that something was unnatural about him and quickly decided that he was locked in a room with a ghost. Falteringly, he demanded to know, with as much authority as he could muster, what the apparition wanted. It simply stood looking mournfully at him: 'When it spoke in a voice rather more hollow and intense, perhaps, than that of an ordinary human being, my fears were instantly dissipated. I was now able to take close stock of it, and observe that in features, general appearance and clothes, it closely resembled any labouring man; it was in expression and colouring, only, it differed – its eyes were lurid, its cheeks livid. Raising one extremely white and emaciated hand it desired me to compose myself...'

Gradually recovering from his initial fear, the chaplain sat and listened as the manifestation explained in 'clear and solemn tones' that it was the spirit of John Croxford, lately hanged and gibbeted for murder. The chaplain's expression registered complete awe as he recognised his ethereal visitor: it *was* the hanged man!

The apparition hung its head as it explained that it had been sent by Providence to remove any doubts that the four hanged men had been guilty. They were, he said, all of them criminals and miscreants to a man – including himself. The reason that their guilt had been so consistently denied is that all four sincerely believed they would never hang and that ultimately they would be pardoned. This was because once they realised they had been spotted attempting to dispose of the victim's corpse they supposed that the nine-year-old witness, Seamark's son, would be considered too young to be taken seriously. Besides, his wife would never betray Seamark. Butlin, the youngest of the accused, had only recently joined the gang, and they all considered that a court would find it hard to believe the young lad's first criminal endeavour was a murder. All four had wiped their hands in the blood of the victim, and then tasted it, entering into a pact there and then never to admit any sort of guilt whatsoever. They then proceeded to cram the body into the oven. While facing the court, all of the accused had managed to obtain liquor, and when Mrs Ann Seamark testified against her husband, drunk and fuelled by bravado they had made veiled threats against her, hoping to intimidate her into changing her story or totally withdrawing it. Even with the ropes round their necks they had expected the young Butlin to be reprieved and doubt cast upon the whole case, perhaps with transportation being their only punishment.

The ghost admitted that every word Mrs Seamark had spoken in court was the truth. They had, he said, never known who the man was they had killed. Gee and Croxford himself had encountered the Scottish peddler at Seamark's house and deliberately entered into an argument with him. They had not even needed to rob him, since they were not particularly broke – it was a crime borne out of boredom and bravado. However, the Scotsman proved to be stouter than they had reckoned for he argued back and the group came to blows. At this, Seamark and Butlin joined the affray after running from behind a hedge, and all four dragged the peddler out of sight into Seamark's yard where they killed him.

The ghost of Croxford went on, shaking its head. Their bloody pact and their offences to God as they stood on the scaffold now meant that they were in Purgatory: '…their souls were in darkness, under all the dreadful apprehension of remaining there for eternity…language, it [the ghost] added, was too weak to describe, and mortality incapable of conceiving a ten-thousandth part of their anguish and despair at present…' The chaplain told him that he wished to help and would like to record the details in depth as a kind of cautionary tale, but without proof of this extraordinary encounter people would think him either a lunatic or a drunkard, to which the ghost agreed. He told the chaplain that, in order to help people believe this spiritual encounter had really taken place, he would tell him a piece of information he could not possibly have otherwise known. He explained that not too far from the scene of the crime was the peddler's ring, which he, Croxford, had buried because he feared an inscription engraved on it was a portent: the inscription had read '*Hanged he'll be, he who steals me. 1745.*' After describing in detail the location of this stolen item, the spirit stopped talking.

A strange silence followed, and the chaplain became aware of the lateness of the hour. He glanced out of the window to see if any lights still shone from the windows of the neighbouring houses, and when he looked back the apparition had disappeared.

The following day the chaplain set off for Guilsborough and found the ring, with its grim engraving, exactly where the ghost had said it could be dug up. He ends his account with the observation that he 'hastened back to Northampton, resolved to make the whole matter public, and so dissipate the doubts certain folk still entertained regarding the guilt of the executed man.'

This pamphlet was printed in 1764 and again in 1819 and 1848. In 1908 the author Elliott O'Donnell was shown a copy of it by a friend who lived locally. The story amazed O'Donnell, especially when he found that some of the villagers could still point to the spot where the chaplain had discovered the ring. Indeed, this story truly is amazing; in fact, it is almost too good to be true, and the chaplain concerned appears unwilling to divulge his name. It is, then, either a complete fabrication, an outright lie if you like; or perhaps it is a fabrication with good, moral intentions. Could it be that the incident is based on the dreams of a sleepy chaplain who, troubled by the controversial executions and having just read of the Resurrection, fell asleep and dreamt the whole episode. If so, how would he have known where to locate the ring? Could it just be that this event actually happened as described? Could it be a full, true and sincere recording of an actual ghostly encounter? If so, although such a pamphlet does fall short of actually *proving* the existence of ghosts in Northamptonshire, it is perhaps nonetheless still among the most compelling evidence there is.

The Ghost of the Faithful Groom

The haunting of stately homes is a cultural phenomenon. There is scarcely a historic mansion or manor house the length and breadth of the British Isles that does not harbour an attendant ghostly anecdote, and as we have already seen at Boughton House, for example, Northamptonshire is no exception. North east of Corby can be found Kirby Hall, its present semi-ruined state still nonetheless evidencing the great classical country house that it must have once presented in the Elizabethan era. The poet Scott reflected how in Victorian times these roofless ruins were reckoned to glow, the premises ablaze with light and the sounds of ancient music, as though a Tudor party was in full swing. However, the prize for the 'classic' ghostly anecdote goes to Althorp House.

Althorp is the seat of the Spencer family, a country estate and stately home some five miles west of Northampton. It has been their long-term ancestral residence since the first incarnation of Althorp House as a red-bricked Tudor building built in the early 16th century. It has been the Spencer home ever since 1508, when John Spencer of Wormleighton, Warwickshire, purchased the site of the abandoned Norman village of Althorp – of which only forlorn earthworks remain now within the grounds of the park. The appearance of the original Tudor building was dramatically altered in the 18th century when Henry Holland, the famed Georgian-era architect, was brought in to oversee renovations.

The Victorian antiquarian John H. Ingram wrote that, 'The simplicity of its exterior is fully compensated by the attractions within; its magnificent library is one of the wonders of England, and superb collection of paintings another. Since Althorp has been in the possession of the Spencers it has been honoured by two royal visits; the first was paid by the Queen and elder son of James the First, and the second by William the Third in 1695, when a large gathering of the nobility and gentry of the county took place in honour of the event.' That was written in the late 1800s; of course Althorp is perhaps now more famously associated with Princess Diana, who is buried on a small island in the middle of the ornamental lake called the Round Oval in Althorp Park.

Ingram's *Haunted Homes And Family Traditions Of Great Britain* (1888) notes a classic ghostly encounter: a believable tale that generations of the Spencer line have now grown up with. In the 19th century Henry Drury was invited by Lord and Lady Lyttleton to visit Althorp with them, where Lady Lyttleton's father – Earl Spencer – was in residence. Sarah Spencer had married Henry, Lord Lyttleton, in 1813, while Mr Drury had been born in 1812; Mr Drury was later consecrated Archdeacon of Wiltshire in 1862, so this presumably dates the ghostly anecdote to around the mid-1800s – 30-or-so years before Ingram wrote of it in 1888.

After supper Mr Drury and Lord Lyttleton played billiards until a servant approached and politely noted that when the pair retired would they extinguish the lights themselves? He asked them to take care in doing so as Earl Spencer was very cautious about fire breaking out due to lit candles. It was two in the morning, and taking the hint the two men put down their cues and retired to bed.

Henry Drury found himself unaccountably awake during the night, a strange light falling across his face. Raising his head from the pillow, he saw '…at the foot of his bed a man dressed as a stable-man, in striped shirt and flat cap, and carrying a lantern with the bull's-eye turned full upon the disturbed sleeper.'

Drury sleepily enquired as to what was going on. Was the house on fire? The man with the lantern, half in shadow behind the light, simply stood and said nothing. Drury, getting angry, demanded, 'What do you mean by coming into a gentleman's room in the middle of the night? What business have you here?' The silent groom slowly lowered the lamp and then walked purposefully into the adjoining dressing room, while Drury shouted, 'You won't be able to get out that way', and threatened to report him to the earl.

There was no other exit from the dressing room, but the stable man did not walk out again; Drury, very tired, simply fell asleep. The following morning he mentioned the fellow's conduct at breakfast, adding, 'I suppose the man was drunk but did not look so.' After describing the groom's features and outfit, Lady Lyttleton turned very pale and said that Mr Drury had just described her father's favourite groom – who had died only two weeks earlier. It had been his duty '…to go round the house after everyone had gone to bed, to see that the lights were extinguished, and with strict orders to enter any room where one was seen burning.' Henry Drury, shocked by what Lady Lyttleton had said, refused to ever sleep in that bedchamber again.

Writer John H. Ingram stated that he was unable to find any other instances of this phantom groom appearing at Althorp; however, the story (or versions of it) is such a part of Althorp's folklore that on 30 July 2007 the *Northampton Chronicle & Echo* noted that a parallel version of the exact same story was still repeated in the 21st century, only retold as having happened *c*.1994. The haunted bedroom was 'known' to be the oak bedroom, a magnificent spacious room adorned with vivid portraits of folk from bygone eras. Following a party the current earl (Charles, the ninth Earl Spencer and Princess Diana's brother) was waving off his guests. As he helped a young lady carry her luggage from the oak bedroom, she – a little flustered – told him that her sleep had been interrupted by the sight of what she thought was a shadowy man at the end of her bed – who held a lantern and wore the cloak and general garb of a 19th-century groom.

Joan Forman's *Haunted Royal Homes* (1987) also notes that the corridors and halls of Althorp have been haunted by the ghost of the seventh Earl Spencer, Albert Edward John, since his death on 9 June 1975. The earl was an antiquarian and local politician, who was so immensely proud of his ancestral home that he opened it to the public. The story goes that members of the Spencer clan and their servants have occasionally glimpsed him. On one occasion a shocked female employee even remarked, 'How nice to see you my lord!' to his ghost. The gentlemanly spook is said to have smiled benignly, but did not reply to the woman.

GHOSTS AND WEALTH

Perhaps reflecting the perception of Northamptonshire with its many stately homes and royal connections as being a 'rich' county, there are numerous accounts of ghost stories linked to money. The Revd Frederick George Lee noted a fascinating story in his *Glimpses Of The Supernatural* (1875) based on such a theme.

The incident occurred in Barby, a village in the west of the county just shy of the Warwickshire border. On 3 March 1851 a 67-year-old woman named Mrs Webb had died at two in the morning in a house that had been willed to her by her late husband. In the final days of her illness she had been nursed by two neighbouring women named Griffin and Holding, and a nephew called Hart, to whom she bequeathed all her possessions. However, Mrs Webb was a notorious miser and there was much speculation in Barby that perhaps all her supposed riches had not been found.

Mrs Holding lived in the house next door to the one in which Mrs Webb had died. In early April 1851 she was unnerved upon hearing strange noises from next door: the sound of furniture being dragged and thumping against the wall. These sounds were repeated nightly at two in the morning, although the house had been vacant and boarded up since the old woman had died. Shortly after this a family named Accleton took up residence in the empty property.

The family of three slept in the same room that old Mrs Webb had died in and were regularly awoken at two in the morning by thumps, bumps and tremendous crashing noises from other parts of the house. One night the Accletons were awoken by the sound of their 10-year-old daughter screaming, 'Mother! Mother! There's a tall woman standing by my bed, shaking her head at me!' The parents could see nothing.

Shortly afterwards, while Mr Accleton was away, his wife and her mother were awoken at two in the morning by a curious light that enveloped the room: Mrs Accleton saw, '...quite plainly the spirit of Mrs Webb, who moved towards her with a gentle appealing manner.' Subsequently the wraith was seen by the two neighbouring women, Griffin and Holding, who stayed overnight. Some were saying that small, luminous balls of light could be seen moving up towards a trapdoor in the ceiling, and a strange, unearthly moaning sound – similar to the moans of a woman in her death agony – accompanied the lights. The rumour that Mrs Webb had hidden riches was recalled, and her nephew Mr Hart, a village farmer, was employed to go up into the roof through the trapdoor to see if anything was there. By candlelight he found old papers and deeds, and a bag full of gold sovereigns and bank notes. However, the spirit of Mrs Webb still moaned, groaned and thumped within the walls of the house – until Hart discovered that his aunt had left behind many unpaid debts. He discreetly paid them off and afterwards the noises in the house gradually died away.

The case was investigated by the ardent spiritualist and gnome-fancier Sir Charles Isham of Lamport Hall and all involved testified that this was precisely the way it happened.

There are variations on this theme. Apethorpe Hall, on the southern edge of the village of Apethorpe, has its construction dating back to the 15th century, but at the time of writing is uninhabited and stands dangerously close to complete decay and ruination, although restoration is planned. John Murray's *Handbook For Travellers In Northamptonshire And Rutland* (1878) notes the tradition that the ghost of Grace, Lady Mildmay, drifts about the property 'on certain nights' scattering silver pennies behind her as she goes. One wonders if the pennies are not themselves spectral, or whether some unaccountable discovery of silver coins gave rise to the tradition. Lady Mildmay died in 1620, and the legend is possibly based on memories of her charity when alive. She was something of a philanthropist and experimented with herbal remedies (allegedly including powdered skulls) to try and cure all sorts of ailments.

GHOSTS OF THE SLAIN

It is no surprise that when a heinous crime is committed the ghosts of those foully done away with are believed to still haunt the region. This is particularly the case in smaller villages, where the shock of a murder perhaps affects the community and is remembered long after a similar crime in a larger town has passed from memory. However, unlike documented 19th-century murders, it is sometimes the case that the original 'crime' is supposed to have happened so long ago that the details of it were not recorded and it has been remembered by word of mouth only. The details can be sketchy but nonetheless generation after generation knows that the ghosts of those brutally slain centuries ago still haunt certain localities in spectral form.

Apethorpe Hall's northern façade.

Numerous Victorian urban legends were based around such themes. Just over the Northamptonshire border in Cambridgeshire can be found the village of Elton, and in the southern extremity of the huge Elton Park – some 3, 800 acres – is the hall. Elton Hall originally dates to the reign of King Henry VII (1457–1509), but additions and renovations in the 17th, 18th and 19th centuries have produced the effect of an extraordinarily romantic building, as much gothic castle in appearance as a stately home. Scott's poetic *Tales Of Northamptonshire* (1936) recalled a legend about the hall that he heard in his youth. One of the hall's earliest owners was Sir Guy Sapcote of Huntingdonshire. Sir Guy was certainly a real person but of whom there appear to be few facts beyond his marriage to Margaret Wolston and the birth of his daughter Anne around 1500. Anne married for the first time *c.*1525 and so events can be tentatively dated to sometime after this.

Sir Guy had, the story goes, in his old age fallen into drunkenness and in turn the hall was falling into disrepair. He had no male heir, and as such he often fell asleep surrounded by his deeds and paperwork, jealously guarding them in a paranoid fear that one of his servants would forge them and take the hall upon his death. His behaviour might have been on account of a young page, whom all thought bore a striking resemblance to Sapcote and who was whispered to be his illegitimate son. Certainly the foul-tempered and permanently paralytic Sir Guy let the lad get away with ignoring his chores and sleeping idly on the banks of the River Nene. However, one night the inevitable happened and all the deeds, papers and parchments went missing and everyone in the hall was a suspect.

Sir Guy employed a servant, a trusted man who had been at the place 40 years and remembered the very first Sapcote – Sir Robert, who had built Elton Hall and died in 1477. This elderly servant persuaded Sir Guy that the young page was the thief, and blinded by alcohol and rage at this betrayal by his illegitimate boy the drunken knight brutally murdered the lad. Then, overcome with remorse, he was persuaded to flee the country; upon which the elderly servant – the real thief – forged the deeds

The River Nene by Elton Hall on a gloomy day.

to declare that Sir Guy had willed the hall to him. Sir Guy himself died in poverty in Milan, begging and crying, 'Pray for him who slew his son.'

The murdered page had been a sensitive lad, and even some 400 years later it was still said that in the valley of the River Nene (which forms the border of Northamptonshire and the Elton estate in Cambridgeshire) there was a ghost. On summer evenings the apparition of a young boy in mediaeval clothes walked along the riverbanks, carrying flowers picked from the meadows and around whom birds fluttered.

The Edwardian poet Scott also noted a legend attached to Glendon Hall, a 17th-century manor house that has long outlived the now-defunct village of Glendon itself, of which only a single farmhouse now remains. Glendon, home to a tiny population of farmers for some 430 years, was finally eradicated by Robert Mallory, who had the land enclosed for sheep in the 16th century. However, the legend concerned Sir William Lane, who was of a Northamptonshire family prominent since the late mediaeval era. Glendon Hall itself dates from the Jacobean period and Scott dated the legend to this time, but the story is something of a jigsaw puzzle and it is unclear which of the Lane dynasty the anecdote is actually supposed to revolve around. At any rate, not long after the hall was built Dame Margaret, Sir William's wife, was awoken by noises from the stable and found her husband missing from the bed. It was before daybreak, and Sir William had stealthily led his grey mare from the stall before galloping off into the moonlight. He thundered along the empty lanes past Kettering as though on some insane quest and simply never returned home. Legend has it that he was subsequently found stabbed to death underneath a giant oak near Pytchley, but it was never established why Sir William had left Glendon Hall that night, or whom he had been going to see. This may have been in 1616. Ever since then there had clung to the hall a strange, sad atmosphere which by the early 1900s the locals attributed to the fact that Sir William Lane had haunted the grounds of Glendon for three centuries.

In the village of Walgrave, halfway between Northampton and Kettering, I was told that a spectral white lady, who drifted about in a bridal dress, haunted the region. Apparently the ghost had been spotted in the latter part of the 1800s and it was said to be the shade of Elizabeth, Sir William Langton's wife, who had died – or been murdered – on her wedding night. When her coffin was prised open (so I was told) the corpse was still in a mouldering wedding dress. I suspect that *Langton* was actually *Langham*; since the mediaeval manor of Walgrave was purchased by John Langham in 1657 for £760, and Walgrave Hall, '…an ancient stone building SE of the village', passed to his descendents. The younger son, William, born in 1631, later became Sir William Langham of Walgrave, Sheriff of Northamptonshire. In 1657, at the age of 26, he married Elizabeth Haselwood 'by whom he had no issue' according to *The Baronetage Of England* (1839). Within two years Elizabeth had died and Sir William had married a second time to Alice Chudleigh – who had herself died within five years, while Sir William lived until the year 1700. The sudden, mysterious death of both of Sir William's wives at such young ages is perhaps the basis for the old legend.

The mediaeval manor house is merely a forlorn example of moat and earthworks now to the north of the village. Walgrave Hall, to the south east, still stands but is now much reduced in size and is a privately owned farm.

Curiously, a sensational crime in the vicinity has been all but forgotten. One of the early under-tenants of the manor of Walgrave, Robert Malesoures, fell into an argument with the village pastor, William Brokedys, over pasture land. On 9 September 1274, as Robert was passing the parson's door at twilight, two villagers and a servant bundled him into the property. There, while a terrified servant girl held a flickering candle, the three knifed Robert Malesoures to death at the behest of one of the parson's relatives, Alan Brokedys, who looked on. For the time, the killing seems quite well documented.

Doubtless genealogists could ascertain the probable truth of these village legends, but not the *absolute* truth, which is often how these stories start. There are other legends, which are even less verifiable: I have heard of an incident in the 1600s that is supposed to have occurred at the Hind Hotel in Sheep Street, Wellingborough. This (nowadays) Grade II listed building was at the time of the Battle of Naseby a recently built inn. Following a series of small clashes near Daventry with Royalist outposts, on 12 June 1645 Sir Thomas Fairfax arrived in Wellingborough. Here he was joined by the recently appointed Lieutenant General Oliver Cromwell, who arrived with cavalry reinforcements. Former staff members at the Hind will relate that the council of war took place between these two warrior-politicians (building up to the decisive clash at Naseby on 14 June) in what is now known as the Cromwell Suite within the Hind Inn. The room itself hides a secretive 'priest hole', and after the meeting a servant girl was discovered hiding there. She was assumed to be a spy and ruthlessly had her throat cut. Her tormented spirit is held to be responsible *to this day* for a mysterious sobbing that has been heard in the middle of the night at the Hind, as well as poltergeist-type outbreaks and random electrical failures. The story is a good one, but has all the elements of classic folklore: secret plots, priest holes and a brutal killing behind closed doors. This is not to imply that such barbaric practices did not occur though. On 26 December 1642 Parliamentary soldiers under Captain John Sawyer were sent to arrest Francis Gray, a prominent Royalist in Wellingborough. Gray had been storing bullets ready for a conflict, but, even worse, he had erected a cross at Isham upon which 'superstitious engravings' were swaying the populace to the Royalist cause. As the soldiers rode into Wellingborough to arrest Gray, a mob formed and someone in the crowd fired, hitting Captain Sawyer in the head. As he slid from his horse a peasant rushed up and hit him several times with a heavy stick. *Mercurius Rusticus*, a contemporary Royalist news-sheet, reported how a crowd of village women then attacked the stricken Captain Sawyer. He died after two hours, and his enraged brother Francis – another captain who had sided with Parliament – gathered reinforcements to retaliate against the village uprising. In approaching Wellingborough, it seems the first victim of his fury was Mr Flint, the curate at Harrowden, Bedfordshire, who had his head cleft almost in half by Captain Francis Sawyer using a pole with an axe-head attached to the end. Francis Gray was subsequently arrested and thrown into gaol until 1645.

A somewhat similar legend to that at the Hind is told of the Red Pepper restaurant in Market Street, Kettering, as recalled by the *Evening Telegraph* on Halloween 2006. In the 18th century an inn called the Duke's Arms had stood opposite an alleyway in Market Street, and it is said that a party of soldiers passing through the town became drunk there and collectively murdered a colleague during an argument. The victim was knifed to death in the alleyway – where now stands the Red Pepper. There appears to be no actual evidence of this, but according to the paper the murder is the explanation why now (just as at the Hind in Wellingborough) 'several owners of the building have reported feeling uneasy in the premises and have noted strange occurrences, including mysterious noises, especially in the stock room, and sudden drops in temperature.'

It is noted in *Northamptonshire Past & Present* (1948) that in the mid-1800s there was a house in Syresham where no one would reside. This was on account of the place being badly haunted. Apparently a tallyman (an observer of ballot boxes during elections) had at some point been seen to enter the property; he promptly vanished off the face of the earth, and his tormented soul was now the only thing that resided at the property. However, just as in all the other cases, there is no conclusive proof of events either way. So it is left to the subsequent ghostly phenomena to prove that the old village rumours of secretive, violent death were true, just as everyone had always suspected...

The manorial earthworks at Harrington: beware the Grey Lady.

CLASHING OF SWORDS

For a time in the 19th century the parish of Wellingborough was the property of the Vivian family, thanks to a purchase made by John Vivian *c.*1805, a gentleman who later became lord of the manor. It subsequently passed down the line to Major Quintus Vivian in 1837; around this time a relative, the Revd Charles Pasley Vivian, was rector at All Hallows Church. The family's residence was the imposing, gothic, Tudor-style Hatton Hall, situated at Broad Green, Wellingborough. Some of the surrounding streets bear the name of Hatton in recognition of the late 18th-century building.

However, between 1914 and 1944 the hall became Hatton Home For Boys, where they were taught and competed in sports, charity events and scouting. The school catered for boys aged between eight and 15 and there are still those today who can recall that the building was supposed to be haunted. The hall itself was named after Sir Christopher Hatton, a Tudor politician from Holdenby, Northamptonshire, but the school's motto was in fact borrowed from the Vivian's time at Hatton Hall; it was the Vivian family motto, which was *Vive ut Vivas* – roughly translated as, 'Live to the fullest.' The story commonly told is that more than a century before the hall became the boys' school, two young brothers of the Vivian family had fought a duel with rapiers in the attic, during which one had been mortally wounded. The winning brother bundled the corpse of his sibling into an old chest, where it stayed hidden until a servant engaged in spring-cleaning uncovered it.

The anecdote was first heard and noted by Edwardian ghost-hunter Maude Ffoulkes, who recalled being sent to Wellingborough for tutoring in the Victorian era. Her biography explains how, as a young girl, she would stand in the sunlight before the great armorial window at the hall and bathe herself in its myriad colours. It was said locally that on some nights the frantic clash of swords and thumping of feet could be heard quite loudly, as though a violent confrontation was taking place somewhere in the upper reaches of Hatton Hall. An atmospheric place indeed then, and by the time Foulkes's famous *True Ghost Stories* (1936) was published the hall was a school for boys – at which point the legend got a fresh lease of life; so much so that the story is a familiar one even today.

THE MUMMIFIED FOOT OF LAMPORT

A 1930s survey of Lamport picturesquely describes the old rectory there thus: 'The rectory, east of the church, is a well-designed two-storey building, with plain parapets and slated hipped roof. The stone of which it was built in 1730, and its fine staircase and wainscoting, came from the dismantled manor house of Hanging Houghton. The rectory and church are at the western end of the park, the Home Farm at its northeastern. There are good springs and quarries of stone.' It was in this very place that the writer Denys James (B.B.) Watkins-Pitchford grew up in the early 20th century, when his father Walter was rector at All Hallows Church in the hamlet.

Watkins-Pitchford's memoirs recall a terrifying piece of family lore that he dated to his grandfather's time in the mid-to-late 1800s. His grandfather had also been rector at Lamport and one day he brought home a grim curiosity he had purchased while browsing an antique shop in Northampton. It was a small skeletal mummified foot, and he had it placed within a box in the confines of a locked room in the attic. One night shortly afterwards the rector's daughter Amy had a horrific nightmare in which she dreamt of a ceremony performed by priests that involved them holding down a young girl and sawing her foot off. This so disturbed young Amy that she got out of bed in order to find her mother, but upon opening her bedroom door she received a further shock as the box and its sinister contents were now no longer in the attic. It was right outside her bedroom door, and the mummified foot protruded from the packaging as though it were somehow trying to 'get out'. Following this, the family saw to it that the foot was buried in consecrated ground at All Hallows Church in Lamport.

As an anecdote, this story cannot be beaten, but a mummified foot is a strange thing to be purchased by anyone, let alone a rector, only for it to be locked away immediately afterwards. Perhaps Watkins-Pitchford was suggesting that his grandfather had somehow become 'possessed' by the relic, or maybe the good-natured man bought it with the sole intention of giving it a Christian burial.

GHOSTS AND DEATH

T.F. Thiselton-Dyer's *Ghost World* (1893) noted that in Northamptonshire it was commonly believed that on Christmas Eve the ghosts of those buried at crossroads, such as suicides and murderers, wandered the scene of their burial. These ghosts wreaked their evil designs upon defenceless villagers which Thiselton-Dyer thought a strange feature of the ghostly phenomenon. As we have seen, there was, or is, a broad belief in our county that to encounter a ghost would bring misfortune and even death upon the unlucky victim. This aspect of the supernatural appears to be more of a recurring theme here than in other parts of Britain and has provided some interesting county legends.

At Harrington, a small village west of Kettering, there can be found the lonely remains of the manorial earthworks. This grassed-over site is known locally as The Falls, and there remains today little evidence of the terraces, fishponds and ornamental gardens that are once said to have graced the grounds of the manor house. The manor had passed by marriage to the Stanhope family and the grand gardens were designed by Sir Lionel Tollemache who married into the family (to one Elizabeth Stanhope) in 1620. After this the manor passed to the Tollemache family. It lasted another 125 years before it was pulled down.

The local pub is the Tollemache Arms. Here I heard it vaguely repeated that in the days when the manor garden was the pride of the Stanhope family, one of the ladies of the line, Jane Stanhope (or Jeanne, or Janet), lost her temper with an elderly villager employed as a gardener. She bashed the man over the head with a garden implement and killed him, much to the dismay of the Stanhope family, who had liked the old man. Quite who this foul-tempered lady was is not clear. There are a number of Stanhope ladies of the era who were named Jane, and I would not like to speculate to which one folklore has ascribed these actions. However, it is said that a ghostly Grey Lady, full of remorse, haunts these earthworks, but despite the spectre's apparent regret at her actions she is still fatal to encounter, just as she was when alive. I was told that 'anyone who sees her is supposed to die pretty soon.' This comment was followed by the standard disclaimer of, 'Whether that's true or not I don't know!'

On Christmas Eve 2007 I spent an uncomfortable night at what is probably one of the most eerie and atmospheric sites in Northamptonshire, the ruins of St John the Baptist Church at Boughton, on the northern outskirts of Northampton. The vigil was uncomfortable, quite apart from the fact of the cold, the wind, the fatigue and the darkness; for this spot is held to be the haunt of a very well-known ghost that I understand is fatal to meet.

The church dates originally to the 14th century and appears at one time to have been a very popular place of pilgrimage. In 1364 Pope Urban V allowed 'an indulgence of one year and 40 days' to those who worked at Boughton. Many miracles of healing were said to have occurred

Three decaying headstones stand before the ruins of Boughton church.

there, perhaps linked to the 'healing well' called St John the Baptist's spring which rose on Boughton Green (and can still be sought out by the eastern wall). It was also highly sought after for baptisms. However, even as long ago as the early 1700s the building was observed to be a ruin and was without a roof. In certain places the walls had been knocked down and the masonry was missing – presumably looted. The tower and spire finally collapsed in 1785, and a gazetteer of the county of Northamptonshire recorded the church in 1849 as being little more than a 'picturesque fragment' of its former self. This it certainly is: a confused mass of rubble, the ground thickly overgrown with weeds and nettles, and great portions of the remaining stonework hidden by ivy. There are few that will not immediately concede that it is the epitome of a haunted location. Being so near to Northampton (with its population of 203,000) does not seem to make it feel any less remote or hidden either.

I was already familiar with a certain legend about this place from C.H.M.D. Scott's poems. The poet had grown up at Boughton village, and the place fascinated him greatly; it is easy to see why. Decades before Scott's time, at a spot on the site called Piper's Irons, a man had supposedly murdered his sweetheart and as punishment was hanged from the bough of a giant oak tree. Maybe he was hung in a gibbet cage, hence the 'irons', but at any rate, as his body disintegrated it suffered the usual macabre fate of crows pecking at its head and eyes, and a brown owl would perch on the branch as though watching over it.

However, the often-repeated legend about these ruins is that at midnight on Christmas Eve a beautiful young woman in a white, flowing dress emerges and manoeuvres among the remnants of the gravestones. She has bright blue eyes and flowing red hair, but she is not of this earth – although she captivates the unwary with her soft demure voice in the same way sirens lure and trap sailors with their singing. Getting to the bottom of this story is difficult, and anyone who I talked to merely knew the ghost as the 'red-headed girl of Boughton church.' The story appears to bear all the trappings of an urban legend that stems from Victorian times, but at any rate the strange woman is supposed to take the unlucky gentleman's hand, enigmatically arrange to meet him again in a month and then kiss him. She then sweeps off and vanishes. For her unfortunate suitor it is the kiss of death, for he will not live to see the month out. It is a very well-known legend in Northampton, and appears to have caught the public imagination.

Hence 24 December 2007 found me sitting in the cold and dark to see what would happen. As midnight passed, and the only signs of life were car headlights on Moulton Lane visible through the vegetation, I began to feel slightly cheated; then, I began to feel slightly worried as to how I would explain myself if someone else turned up. At this I decided to leave, but curiosity compelled me to return a few weeks later in daylight to look among the random tombstones for any chiselled evidence as to how this story arose. Trying to get to many of the tombstones is a challenge. They are hidden by great swathes of overgrown nettle patches, but in the end I had to settle for the somewhat unsatisfactory 'evidence' I had been told of initially: that one of the three tombstones standing prominently before the ruin belonged to a young man in the prime of life, and at one time it bore the barely readable death date of 24 January 18-something-or-other. However, the inscriptions on all three are impossible to decipher now thanks to the ravages of the elements, time and natural decay.

THE FIELD OF SCREAMS

There are many places like Boughton church scattered throughout Northamptonshire that have attendant ghostly legends. *Northamptonshire Notes And Queries* (1888) explains that, 'Close to the Kettering and Uppingham road, on top of the rise north of Barford Bridge, is a mound planted with trees.' This mound, which was some 12 feet high and stretched approximately 95 feet across, was called the Drummer's Mound, and 'numerous legends were associated with it'. These included the belief that at midnight a ghostly lad would alight the mound and proceed to beat a drum strapped to his chest. It is widely repeated that well into the 20th century children gave this hillock a wide berth after dark until it was flattened in the 1960s.

One of the strangest stories I was told is that there was a field south of Brackley that had at one time been haunted. The gentleman who told me this said that as a youth he had always had this particular field – between Evenley and Mixbury – pointed out to him as the 'screaming field', and the anecdote (as far as I can make out) appears to be at least based on a real event. In July 1725, during an immense thunderstorm, lightning had struck a flock of sheep here and killed five of them; the flash also killed the shepherd who had ventured out in the atrocious conditions. When he was found laid out, it was observed that there were two footprints by his boots; evidence that the lightning flash had been so severe it had blasted the very ground where the man stood, made holes in the earth where his feet were and turned the soil to stone underneath the ground. This caused quite a stir at the time, and there were rumours of diabolical involvement, happening as it did near the ancient burial mounds on Barrow Hill. For generations after, it was said that this stretch of the Northamptonshire–Oxfordshire border was haunted. During thunderstorms people caught up in the onslaught were believed to be further terrified by horrific screaming that whipped up out of nowhere and chased them from the area.

CHAPTER 7

MODERN GHOSTLY ENCOUNTERS

INTRODUCTION

Many classic ghostly stories have very little to substantiate them other than local assurance that a ghost is 'known' to haunt a certain location or building. Today in Northamptonshire (just as anywhere) there are those who will point out a particular haunted location but will be unable to state whether the ghost has been seen recently. Typical is the site of Blakesley Hall, near the village of Blakesley, where I was informed that it was common to see weird lights emanating from within the deserted 13th-century building prior to its demolition in the 1950s. Apparently, the hall was served by a miniature railway during World War One, when the hall functioned as a military hospital. It was vaguely rumoured that it was now sometimes possible to hear the chug-chugging of a seemingly invisible engine. I was similarly assured that the road between Brackley and Halse was supposedly haunted by 'a man covered in blood' on certain nights. Correspondence in the Northampton Archives shows that a debt collector named Webb, having collected all his due monies, was mysteriously murdered in Halse in March 1626, his body left in the position of a staged suicide by a tree.

In the 20th century the nature of ghosts appears to have gradually changed. For instance, it is difficult to imagine that some stories noted in the previous chapter will ever be heard of again in such a format: this is particularly so in cases where ghosts take on a semi-physical presence and interact with the living, helping or warning them. Ghostly encounters these days are much more likely to be random affairs, which do not conform themselves into miniature stories such as some of the old legends did. With such a sophisticated media these days, one cannot imagine that a 'perfect' ghost story like the one written of in the pamphlet *The Guilsborough Ghost* would stand up to close scrutiny for very long in this day and age.

However, although 'ghosts' do not seem to behave like this any more, there are still living witnesses to supernatural phenomena who are willing to talk to researchers and the local media to ensure that the subject of 'ghosts' is taken just as seriously as it always has been. Although some types of ghost appear to have been lost to us, they do have their modern equivalents. For instance, the phantom coach and horses have drifted into the realm of legend now, for they are never seen and seldom heard of – but they have been replaced by the modern phenomenon of phantom cyclists and/or other vehicles. The phantom coach was often linked to a certain local dynasty or house; encounters with phantom cyclists and the like are too random to be tied down to anything so specific as an ancient family line.

Peter Moss's *Ghosts Over Britain* (1977) boasts a classic modern(ish) example of a ghost sighting that manages to combine a 'phantom cyclist' with the traditional headless spectre of folklore. In the harsh winter of 1940 one George Dobbs was walking via the cemetery along (what is now) the A508, heading south to the Fox and Hounds pub at Kingsthorpe on the northern outskirts of Northampton. The conditions were atrocious, and in the freezing cold of night George saw a cyclist approaching him, struggling to retain control of his bicycle as the wheels slipped in and out of icy ruts in the snow. Behind the cyclist was a car, and as he moved to the side of the road George noted the curious detail that the cyclist appeared to be headless – although he put this down to an effect caused by the headlights of the car. The approaching car, however, did not slow down for the cyclist, and did not even appear to see him. It merely drove into him, and as it rattled away in the direction of Market Harborough George felt certain he had just witnessed a fatality. In the snowy weather he searched the road for the cyclist – and yet found neither corpse nor bicycle. By the time he reached the pub he was shaking with shock and beginning to entertain the idea that he might have just seen a ghost. The local gravedigger then dropped a bombshell, commenting that he recalled the death of a cyclist *c*.1915 who had been decapitated in a road accident in snowy weather near the cemetery. Stories like this reassure us somehow – the world has not changed *too* much in Northamptonshire, and perhaps the anecdote lends some small believability to the existence of ghosts by virtue of its sheer pointlessness.

Until I see a ghost myself I will sit on the fence about the matter, but modern technology in some ways has occasionally provided remarkable evidence in favour of their reality. Joan Forman's *The Mask Of Time* (1978) notes how an electrician working in a Nissen hut near the old airstrip of Silverstone motor racing circuit received complaints from nearby residents about the noise he was making at night. He knew he always clocked out at five, and so one evening he left a tape recorder running and then locked the hut up as normal. The machine tape-recorded silence, just as he expected, but still complaints came about the night-time noise. So the electrician had the tape analysed – when it was played at a different frequency, all manner of bangs, drilling and other noises could be detected. However, the best example of technology helping to substantiate the phenomenon of ghosts is possibly the ghostly, kneeling figure photographed at Woodford's church.

The incident at Woodford has been highly publicised for decades now. In this technological era, far from belief in the supernatural waning, and perhaps thanks to such incidents, ghosts are big business. 'Ghosts walks' function as popular entertainment in Northampton. But these atmospheric strolls through local legend also compete hand in glove with more serious study of the subject by regional ghost-hunting concerns that appear to be springing up all the time. Northampton, it seems, is an ideal place to investigate the paranormal.

The haunted pedigree of the Wig and Pen, in St Giles Street, Northampton, is now so well known that it even attracted the attention of celebrity ghost-hunter Derek Acorah in 2005. The Wig and Pen displays on its wall a framed newspaper clipping attesting to its status as Northampton's 'most haunted pub', due largely to ghostly activity reported in the mid-1970s when the pub went by the name of the Black Lion Inn. It was reported that poltergeist-like disturbances bedevilled the staff, notably in the cellar where beer barrels had their taps mysteriously turned off (very common at haunted pubs), or else they moved about of their own volition.

In the late 19th century that very cellar beneath the Wig and Pen had been used by a butcher, of adjacent Dychurch Lane, to cure bacon in a vat. The butcher's brother, one Andrew MacRae, was in 1892 convicted of murdering his mistress Annie Pritchard and their infant child. Although Annie's body was found in a sack in a ditch at East Haddon, the baby's body was never found; however, there was strong circumstantial evidence that led to the dreadful supposition that Andrew MacRae had disposed of it in the copper vat in the cellar of his brother's establishment.

Local ghost-hunting concerns have turned up evidence of phenomenal paranormal activity in the cellar, and on 9 August 2005 the *Chronicle & Echo* reported how Derek Acorah had conducted a séance in the main bar. Here the celebrity 'contacted' the spirit of an entity called George who still resided there, who was adamant that the place was 'his' bar. 'George' had been Andrew MacRae's middle name. However, other ghosts at the Wig and Pen – such as the famous ghostly man accompanied by a big black phantom mastiff that appears in a bedroom – are less easy to link to MacRae's killing spree.

Some stories in this chapter *are* rooted in folklore; and modern folklore is being generated all the time. In late 2007 I was told that in the early 1980s there was a strange rumour circulating among

Does 'Skulking Dudley' still haunt the hamlet of Clopton?

a group of young girls in Raunds. It was being said that some of the children were reckoned to have seen the ghost of a man in 17th-century clothes rise from a particular grave at St Peter's Church late one evening. The entity had looked at his tombstone before sadly fading away. This odd behaviour was explained by the supposition that the annoyed gentleman's name had been spelled incorrectly on his tombstone – and his midnight appearances were said to be frequent, rather than merely 'annual'. Unfortunately for my informant and her sister, hearing this as young girls meant several frightened nights peering from behind the bedroom curtains of their then home near Church Street, waiting in trepidation to see if the ghostly figure materialised in the nearby churchyard.

They never saw him, and this story appears to be a modern urban legend reminiscent of the older story told to me by an archivist at Northampton library concerning the churchyard at Irchester. In this instance, if one were to run round a particular tomb seven times the lid was supposed to rise.

However, some modern ghostly encounters take the form of the pointless, inexplicable, split-second experiences referred to earlier and are by their very virtue puzzling anecdotes without the benefit of a historical 'back story' – although I have done my best to suggest a possible 'solution' where applicable. What this chapter, which deals with the 20th and 21st centuries, really proves is that in Northamptonshire some things never change – and that is the love of ghostly stories...and even the belief in ghosts themselves.

SKULKING DUDLEY

In the tiny, isolated hamlet of Clopton, east of Thrapston and just shy of the Cambridgeshire border, they say that up until recently this little place of less than 100 souls was haunted; haunted by the prowling phantom known as 'Skulking Dudley', a mediaeval lord who had once owned Clopton Manor and was destined to pay for the crimes he had committed when alive.

These days the story is a famous, but confused, one. It is unclear which of the Dudley line Skulking Dudley is meant to have been, and as *A History Of The County Of Northampton: Vol III* (1930) points out the early origins of the manor itself following the *Domesday Book* are difficult to unravel. It would appear that the manor became the property of the Dudley line when it passed to them by marriage *c.*1390. This was the marriage between Richard Dudley of Barnwell and Joan Agnes de Hotot, the daughter (and heir to Clopton) of Robert de Hotot. Apart from the occasional leasing of the manor to trustees, the land stayed in the possession of the Dudley line until 1724.

Brutal but unsubstantiated stories concerning the Dudley line were the basis for the later legends of Skulking Dudley. There is believed to have been some congenital birth defect among the men, which rendered every second generation with a hunchback (a symbolic sign of a true villain ever since Shakespeare's *Richard III*). The *Reader's Digest's Folklore, Myths And Legends Of Britain* (1977) explains that a 15th-century Dudley is supposed to have been a local tyrant who insulted a neighbouring landowner. The young man challenged him to a duel, but Dudley was a coward and on the day of this clash of honour he took himself to bed pretending to be sick. His daughter, disgusted but determined to retain family pride, donned her father's battle armour to fight in his stead but was no match for the young landowner. However, just as he was about to run her through she lifted her visor and the young landowner realised what had happened. He later married the girl. If this has *any* truth, the Dudley family tree indicates that the Dudley in question *may* have been Richard's son John (b.1413), who seems to have sired two daughters, Joyce and Joan, who appear to have been the only daughters in the Dudley line who this story could possibly fit around. Then again, perhaps the Dudley in question was a hanger-on, a member of the extended family. At any rate, this cowardly man is supposed to have met his end when a peasant turned on him and hacked him to death with a scythe during harvest-time.

A History Of The County Of Northampton noted in 1930 there was a small piece of woodland called Skulking Dudley's coppice that 'presumably gained its name from one of the lords of the manor.' Indeed it did, but in an unconventional way. It is famously said that the phantom of Skulking Dudley could be seen drifting – distinct and hunchbacked – from the manor's moat on moonlit nights. Then he made his way past the old graveyard via the site of a church that had been left to fall into ruination after a lightning strike in the late 1700s. These ruins, incidentally, were where the current St Peter's Church has stood since 1863. Dudley would make his way, shadow-like, to the coppice named after him, darting in and out of hedges and the tree line as he went. All the time he wailed that he was doomed to suffer for a murder he had committed in the 14th century. Since Richard Dudley did not inherit Clopton until 1390, then it was either he that had been the murderer, or one of his ancestors who had killed someone in a squabble over Clopton Manor sometime before Richard himself obtained it through marriage. By the early 20th century it is said that the level of fear had gotten so bad in the village that in 1905 the Bishop of Peterborough, Edward Carr Glynn, led a retinue of two dozen bishops to the village. Here, they allegedly performed an exorcism, the secret ritual ending with all the clergymen throwing lighted candles into the moat of Clopton Manor.

As ghost stories go, it is a confusing one; the crimes of whichever one of the Dudleys named as 'skulking' vary in detail – even to the century they took place – depending on who you ask or what you read. Dynastic feuds in the Middle Ages over inheritance, endowment and property often led to violence and death, so there is likely to be some misremembered truth in the 'history' of Skulking Dudley. However, it is more likely that the 'ghost' is based on the memory of the misdeeds of the early Dudleys – which over time became a 'collective' single bogeyman figure in the minds of this isolated community.

HAUNTED PLACES OF WORSHIP

As we have already seen at Raunds, churches and other places of worship are fertile ground for allegations of ghostly activity. Delapre Abbey (or more properly the Abbey of St Mary de Pratis) on the southern outskirts of Northampton is well known to be haunted.

The building dates to the reign of King Stephen and was founded by Simon II de Senlis, the Anglo-Norman Earl of Huntingdon and Northampton, with the king's blessing. It remains one of only two Cluniac nunneries built in the British Isles, and was answerable to the Abbot of Cluny in Burgundy, France. The nuns were granted large estates in Hardingstone as well as the churches at Great Doddington, Barton and Fotheringhay. Later, King Edward III confirmed further churches upon the nuns, of which at any given time there were 15-20 at Delapre; however, by this time in the early 14th century it appears to have begun to fall into a state of neglect, although it was still inhabited. In 1460 it received an uninvited royal guest, the doomed King Henry VI, who was briefly incarcerated here following the Battle of Northampton on 10 July 1460. This clash was fought within the extended grounds of Delapre, south of the banks of the River Nene, with the Yorkist victor the Earl of Warwick taking the insane king captive. Some say that the nuns, hearing the clash of weapons and the screams of the dying men, used a secret underground tunnel to flee Delapre to a friary based in the middle of Northampton. Others say more practically that the nuns were forced to treat the battle injuries of the wounded Yorkists. Some of those they could not save are said to be interred in the same ancient burial ground as the nuns. (In fact, in September 1820 workmen at a house called Three Cups in nearby Bridge Street unearthed a mass grave containing the skulls and other bones of some 400 who died in the battle.)

Delapre Abbey, c.1818.

In 1538 King Henry VIII forced Delapre Abbey to surrender to the crown, and it was subsequently sold to the Tate family. On the main staircase within Delapre Abbey there has been seen a spectral woman descending the stairs, hands together before her, dressed in the dark-blue habit of a Cluniac nun and wearing a veil. She is familiarly known as the 'Blue Lady' (or Grey Lady) and I have been told she is 'still seen', although quite by whom is open to question. She is also supposed to wander the grounds of the former abbey and pause at the remains of the Eleanor Cross – which can be found at the southern Hardingstone edge of the estate (near the main A45 London Road). Perhaps she does this in veneration of Edward I, husband of Eleanor, who granted the abbey royal protection in 1294. He had had the Eleanor Cross at Delapre erected four years earlier because her body rested at Northampton Castle during her long, final journey back to London.

Open to question is the identity of this dignified holy lady. No one seems to know, but my money would be on either Abbess Katherine Knyvet, who died during a great plague outbreak in 1349, or more likely Delapre's last abbess, Clementina Stock. She was elected in the early 1500s but on 15 December 1538 she saw her abbey taken from her under the notorious Dissolution of the Monasteries. Despite a spirited battle she was forced to concede Delapre to 'John London, Clerk to the king's use', and although she was treated well her nuns were forced to survive in near-poverty on insultingly-low pensions.

These days Delapre Abbey is occasionally mentioned in the media as the site for a 'ghost sleepover' carried out in the name of charity, or else the subject of investigation by television ghost-hunters. I cannot find anyone who will admit to seeing the ghost, although all repeat that she is 'still seen'.

Perhaps more substantive is the ghostly encounter noted as taking place at St Mary the Virgin's Church in Dallington, on the western edge of Northampton. It is one of those brief, seemingly random moments when the natural and supernatural world collide: in 1907 two schoolgirls visited St Mary's following a walk about the area. One was a young local girl, who had led the pair to the church, and she entered first. Her friend stayed outside and watched bemused as the other entered…and then shortly thereafter fled from the building in extreme distress. So she herself bravely entered the empty church, and was confronted by the semi-transparent vision of what *looked* to be a crowd of people kneeling before the altar. Afterwards she said, '…they appeared to be made of a substance similar to soap bubbles.' This comment is curious: perhaps the incident was nothing more than the imagination of two young girls who saw dust caught in the strange light of the mighty stained-glass windows; or perhaps it was the only way that these two young Edwardian girls could describe the translucent appearance of these phantoms (which were perhaps accompanied by the small 'orbs' often photographed at haunted sites) in their bafflement.

THE GHOST OF AN EVIL MAN

Writing in the mid-19th century folklorist Thomas Sternberg noted this of ghosts: 'The popular belief in ghosts, too, distinctly recognises the existence of a middle state, to which the soul of the good man goes, while that of the evil-doer rests in its "wormy bed" till the day of resurrection.'

It seems that phantom echoes of awful events still linger within the grounds of Barnwell Manor, an historic estate in the village of Barnwell (two miles south of Oundle) that also houses the ruins of mediaeval Barnwell Castle. Of the original owners of this estate – the le Moyne family – very little evidence survives. The *Hundred Rolls* indicate that one Reginald le Moyne, or Moygne, built the original motte-and-bailey castle at Barnwell around 1132, but that one of his descendents, Berengarius (or Berengar), was responsible for Barnwell Castle as it can be viewed today.

Berengarius le Moyne is an enigmatic character; he succeeded to the estate in 1270, during the reign of King Henry III, but by this time work on the 'lofty and massive walls, the loopholes in its strong

Whose skeleton lies buried in the foundations of Barnwell?

towers, the entrance gate with its portcullis' had, apparently been long ongoing. Berengarius, as lord of the manor, succeeded in obtaining a market day in Barnwell twice a week, and an eight-day fair to be held once a year. A huge 'market cross' was erected and Barnwell, for a while, seems to have enjoyed great prosperity – until the Abbot of Peterborough, Richard of London, successfully lobbied to have the annual market and fair done away with, as it took business away from one in nearby Oundle that he had a vested interest in. In 1276, after a mere six years at Barnwell (much of it spent in legal squabbling with the local clergy), Berengarius sold the estate and the castle to the Abbott and Convent of Ramsey – who mysteriously succeeded in getting the Barnwell fair reinstated in 1278.

It seems that Berengarius le Moyne may have been manoeuvred out, but he left a strange legacy in the area, and for generations went by the name of 'Black Berengarius', apparently a reference to his dark features. In subsequent centuries it was whispered among the peasants that the now-decaying Barnwell Castle was cursed; deep within the walls, they said, lay the bricked-up skeleton of Berengarius's younger brother – who had suffered the wrath of Black Berengarius following an argument over which of them would marry their cousin, Beatrice. This unhappy lady, preferring the murdered brother, had thrown herself into the River Nene and drowned. It was even whispered that Berengarius himself had come to a sticky end. A later ballad speculated that he had been killed by the greedy monks of Ramsey, his body tipped into a ditch – and it was his own skeleton which lay mouldering in the foundations of the castle: 'Between his ribs the nettles grew; And hid the skeleton from view; That had been lord of Barnwell.'

Berengarius's descendents made a failed attempt to recover the castle in 1330, and by the year 1540 the traveller and historian John Leland noted of it as a ruin: 'At the village remain four strong towers, part of Berengarius' *Castel* after belonging to Ramsey Abbey and now to *Monteacute*.' The castle interior had been all but stripped of its innards and there now only remained a small hut within which was a groundskeeper's residence. However, 1540 was also the year that King Henry VIII granted Barnwell to the Montagu family, who had the adjacent distinctive, grey-stone manor house built. This went on to become the principal living quarters on the estate as the castle fell further into disrepair. The Montagu line owned the estate until 1913. In 1938 the whole estate was purchased as a residence by Prince Henry, the Duke of Gloucester, two years after he had married Lady Alice Montagu-Douglas Scott.

In 1948, during their residency, an unnerving incident occurred during a séance at the castle, as outlined in Joan Forman's *Haunted Royal Homes*. Prompted by persistent rumours that the castle and its grounds were haunted, a local historian named Tom Lichfield and a friend who possessed the psychic gift undertook a series of séances (the first two at Lichfield's own home) to glean more information. On 20 September 1948, at the first séance, the two men assembled and apparently 'contacted' the spirit of a former abbot of Ramsey Abbey who told them that in the days following the le Moyne family's ownership of the castle it had been used as a court and place of execution. Later on one of the le Moyne clan themselves was contacted at the séance: one Marie le Moyne, who bemoaned through the spirit board her message that she had died a horrific and untimely death while the castle was being built *c*.1266, after what appeared to be a long period of confinement. She could not – or would not – say who had imprisoned her, but evidence of her torment could be found in a chest that was buried in the dungeons.

Lichfield believed that Marie was likely to have been a wife of one of the le Moyne clan, and apparently found archived evidence of her existence; subsequently he believed her death during the building of the castle was the basis for all the subsequent stories of Black Berengarius, crimes of passion and walled-up skeletons.

At a second séance on the evening of 30 September 1948 Black Berengarius himself came through and blamed his 'excesses' on his mind becoming unbalanced due to the constant pressure wrought upon him by his foe Abbot William de Gurmecestre of Ramsey Abbey. However, when the third séance was held on 9 November 1948 in the north east tower of Barnwell Castle itself, the event ended quickly following a frightening supernatural encounter. *Haunted Royal Homes* explains how the séance attempted to again make contact with Berengarius le Moyne, to try and find out what ailed him. Through the medium of the spirit board he apparently replied, 'I will fire to warn you.' Lichfield and his friend, already shaken, were further shocked by a sound like a flash of lightning above their heads which revealed the upper body of what looked like a monk in the doorway looking at them. This incident so frightened the two men that they pushed the table away and immediately left the room and fled the castle.

Lichfield later discovered that the insignia of the le Moyne line was supposed to have as an emblem the upper body of a monk carrying a folded whip in his hand.

Was the fantastical appearance during the séance at Barnwell a sign that Berengarius still bore his hatred of the abbots, even after nearly 700 years? Or that in displaying the emblem of his crest he was demanding that Barnwell Castle be recognised as the home of the le Moyne family for all time?

Either way, the mystery of who the unlucky member of the le Moyne clan is whose skeletal remains still allegedly lie immured within the ruinous shell of Barnwell Castle seems now a story that will never be told.

WOODFORD'S KNEELING MAN

The Church of St Mary the Virgin in Woodford is famous countywide for a remarkable curiosity discovered during restoration work in 1867 – a heart burial niche. Within a recess cut in the west face of the northern compound pier, now faced with glass, were found, wrapped in a coarse cloth, the remains of a human heart in a box. The historical riddle of who this mysterious organ once belonged to need not concern us here, but it is interesting to note the local legend which observes that its discovery in the 1860s was allegedly presaged by the appearance of the ghost of a former rector, Andrew Powlett. The story goes that the ghost supposedly appeared in the church hall, and an investigation of the panelling there revealed a secret hole in which was found a chalice and a letter: the letter directed the investigators to the pillar and its hidden relic.

This appears to be a legend, but the story is fascinating when taken in conjunction with a remarkable incident in the 1960s – when what is judged to be one of the best examples of a photograph of a 'true' ghost was taken. In July 1964 16-year-old Gordon Carroll and a friend were within St Mary's admiring the architecture of the ancient place, which has foundations dating back to the early 12th century. They were quite certain they were alone in the church, yet when a photograph of the 13th-century chancel was later developed Gordon was astounded to see what appeared to be a ghostly figure kneeling before the altar. The sepia-quality photograph was shown in the *Northamptonshire Evening Telegraph*, but over five decades it has now been reproduced innumerable times in various publications – and has generated an enormous amount of controversy.

Most of the church architecture is in focus; however, 'the photograph also appears to show a figure kneeling (viewed from the back) before the church's depiction of Christ on the cross. The room is illuminated by the three great stained-glass windows. The 'person's' feet are splayed outwards in the manner of one who is in the position of being on their knees before the cross (rather than sat) and the head is lost to sight, presumably bowed low. However, the figure is blurred, and it does not look as though it is praying; its shoulders are lopsidedly slumped, and its arms appear to be hanging limply at its sides. The garments this entity wears could be interpreted in any way: it could be dressed in the garb of a priest's smock, or the heavy long coat commonly worn in the 16th and 17th centuries. It could even be interpreted

Could the ghost be linked to this mummified human heart in Woodford's church?

as being clad in the tunic of a crusader knight. Or perhaps, the sceptical have pointed out, it could be a cleaning lady who wandered into shot and bent down to scrub the altar; the boys, however, were adamant that they were alone. A photograph taken at the same time immediately afterwards shows no figure at all.

A print of the photograph is now displayed within the church for the curious to decide for themselves. This incident has been the subject of much debate for decades…but this eerie photograph is still alleged to be one of the best of its kind.

ECHOES OF NASEBY

Northamptonshire was the setting for perhaps one of the most famous military clashes in British history, and to this day there are those who know of the phantom echoes of the Battle of Naseby.

Naseby is generally considered a turning point in the English Civil War. Until then King Charles's campaign in the Midlands had been going well. His nephew, Prince Rupert of the Rhine, had surrounded Leicester on 30 May 1645 and then stormed the town the next day when it refused to surrender. Leicester was sacked and looted, and here the first cracks in the Royalist army began to show; hundreds of troops fled after the attack with their stolen plunder.

Parliament was determined to stamp out the growing Royalist activity in the Midlands, and to this end had reorganised its army into a 22,000-strong force christened the New Model Army based along the disciplined lines of Oliver Cromwell's 'Ironsides'. Royalist outposts near Daventry carried the news to the king that their detachments had clashed with Fairfax's men on 12 June; the main body of the Royalist army was making for Newark when it halted and about-turned to engage the challenge.

On a foggy morning two days later the two sides squared up at Naseby Field (locally called the 'Broad Moor'), to the north of the village. The king's army had marched south from Market Harborough and positioned itself strategically near Great Oxendon. They waited in vain for the Parliamentary army to show itself, and so started southwards once again. By the time they spotted the Parliamentary forces positioned about a mile north of the village of Naseby, the king perhaps felt the gut-wrenching tension of the hopelessly indecisive: stopping at Dust Hill it would have been clear that he was vastly outnumbered. His forces comprised 7,400 men, of which 4,100 were on horseback – while the Parliamentary army just to the south consisted of some 14,000 men, 6,000 of which were on horseback, and they presented a front about a mile-and-a-half wide. Not only that, but the Parliamentary army occupied the strategic high ground.

Cromwell, at this point in the war a lieutenant general, convinced Sir Thomas Fairfax to pull the Parliamentary army back somewhat, so as to provoke a Royalist advance, and this simple strategy worked. At first the roundhead cavalry was swept aside by Prince Rupert's Royalist cavalry, but the weight of numbers soon began to become the decisive factor. Many members of the undisciplined Royalist cavalry attacked a roundhead baggage train, looted it and then fled the battlefield. Oliver Cromwell bided his time for upwards of an hour before letting his Ironsides loose on the Royalist cavalry on the far side of the battlefield. The Royalist cavalry, forced by circumstance to fight uphill, were quickly routed even before the Ironsides smashed their way into the king's untried Welsh infantry.

Seeing his forces falter, Charles spurred his horse onwards to lead a morale-boosting charge to their rescue, but at this point the decisive moment in the battle occurred. A Scottish nobleman, the Earl of Carnwath, seeing that this manoeuvre was probably suicidal, grasped the reins of the king's horse, swore at him and led the horse in the other direction away from danger. The Royalist soldiery saw this, terror swept through their ranks as they witnessed what appeared to be the king fleeing the field of conflict and so they themselves fled. Prince Rupert's cavalry bravely covered the king's retreat as he fled to Leicester, but for all intents and purposes the day was lost and King Charles must have known that, almost certainly, he had lost the war.

How the sides squared up at Naseby; from the plaque at the monument.

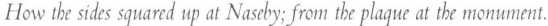

133

That date was 14 June 1645. Some 6,000 people died in the encounter, and Broad Moor was littered with thousands of corpses of men and horses, but the evidence of the brutal carnage became most obvious the nearer to Dust Hill one was. Horror followed upon horror; many defeated Royalists fled northwards in the direction that the king had taken towards Leicester, but got lost and followed a route that led them into the grounds of St Nicholas's Church at Marston Trussell. Here, just shy of the border with Leicestershire, they found themselves trapped between the church and the swollen River Welland. Sir Thomas Fairfax's men hunted them down in the marshy ground and butchered them in an act of merciless savagery. (Even as late as 1830 there was a field between here and Lubenham, Leicestershire, referred to locally as Slaughter Field, or Slawford.) Local lore has it that an oak within the grounds of Marston Trussell Hall hid King Charles, even as his pursuers searched below for the remnants of the Royalist army. No one was spared: 100-or-so women in the Royalist camp, probably related to the Welsh infantry, were brutally hacked to death by celebrating Parliamentary troops.

Like numerous other famous battles, it was said for generations afterwards that phantom armies could sometimes be seen clashing above the valley. Even later, however, the Revd John Mastin was told a more whimsical ghost story, which appeared in his *History And Antiquities Of Naseby* (1792). When he first came to Naseby, one Charles Wilford, who owned the Bell Inn on Church Street (demolished in the 1850s and now the site of the FitzGerald Arms), told him a very strange ghostly anecdote. Some years after the battle of 1645 two women had gotten into an argument in the churchyard of All Saints and come to blows. They were stopped by the ghost of a man who had been shot down at Naseby, who had risen from a grave and parted them!

In fact, Mastin supposed, it had not been a ghost at all. The event had really happened, but not as it was now remembered well over a century later. In fact, a Royalist soldier called Humphrey Thompson had been wounded in the battle and returned to his home parish of Naseby, where he became parish clerk and sexton of the church. He had, in fact, been digging a grave in All Saints when the fight erupted between the two women.

Nonetheless, it is very easy to see how such ghostly anecdotes attach themselves to the site of the battle. It is still a very atmospheric, isolated site, and the immense deathly silent valley of Broad Moor quickly conjures up images of the utter carnage that changed the face of England all those generations ago. Weapons and other relics of the battle were still being discovered 200 years later, including occasional bone fragments. I remember hearing years ago that around 1950 two cyclists were supposed to have stopped in the lane that runs via Naseby Field for a rest; their breather was interrupted by the sudden appearance of several scruffy looking men wearing leather aprons who pulled great wooden carts along the road. These grim-looking men marched in silence and paid the cyclists no heed. There was something deeply unnatural about them that prompted the two fellows to quietly get back on their bicycles and take off. Later, they learned that it had actually been the date of the battle itself, and believed what they had encountered were the ghosts of local peasants making their way to the site to collect the remnants of the slaughtered casualties.

Remarkably, by sheer coincidence, while I was writing this piece there appeared in the *Northampton Chronicle & Echo* a weird photograph (which has since been flashed around the world via the internet) that was taken on the evening of the anniversary of the Battle of Naseby in 2008. Many people had gathered at the site in memory of the event, or to see if they could detect any paranormal activity. During the night some people present thought they could detect thumping sounds, or noises like cannonball firing. A member of the Northampton paranormal group took a gloomy photograph with a digital camera some time later, which *appears* to show a human form with a sash and a breastplate, striding along and apparently carrying something which could be a musket, pikestaff or perhaps something like a flag. There is room to speculate that it may have been another person that was present, who perhaps wandered into shot – except that it is tempting to view the 'person' as walking somewhat above the ground level…either way it goes a long way to ensuring that legends about the Battle of Naseby will be a long time dying out.

GHOSTLY THEATRICS

No theatre anywhere in Britain is complete without its age-old rituals and superstitions that must be performed to ensure a good show. Quite often an appearance of the famous ghostly Grey Lady of The Royal & Derngate Theatre, Northampton, is judged to be a positive omen – at least there is no suggestion that she is harmful in any way. The Royal Theatre itself opened in 1884, and is next-door to the ultra-modern Derngate Theatre, which opened in 1983 – an amalgamation which accounts for the theatre's odd name. The Grey Lady allegedly takes the form of a benevolent woman in late Victorian clothes and is sometimes glimpsed standing in box B in the older part of the building, as though watching the performance. In 2004 Beryl Whitney, a co-host of the famous Northampton Ghost Walk, told the *Northampton Chronicle & Echo* how a '…lady from the box office, when she had finished her duties, would often go and sit in a box overlooking the stage. Then one day one of the actors commented that it was nice that she had been able to bring a friend along with her – but she had been entirely alone all the time.' The Grey Lady seemingly particularly enjoys watching children perform on the stage, but who she is supposed to be is unknown. Like Delapre Abbey, Derngate Theatre has been known to host overnight 'ghost-hunts', and apparently the strongest presence can be felt in the dark rooms underneath the stage. Here it is reckoned an invisible, sinister aura can be felt, as though there is someone there in the darkened confines who is exceptionally malicious.

The foyer of the old Lyric Theatre, Wellingborough.

However, it was at the former Lyric Theatre, on Midland Road, Wellingborough, that the most unnerving reports came from. The place dated from the mid-1930s; prior to its incarnation as a bingo hall it had functioned as a leatherworks, a theatre and then a cinema. It allegedly stood on the site of a former congregational chapel burial ground, and I have heard that some of the graves were disturbed.

In 1969 it caught the attention of some of Britain's leading ghost-hunters. The last film had been screened in April, and there was an uncertain future facing the theatre. In his *A-Z Of British Ghosts* (1971) expert Peter Underwood wrote how a strange white figure was observed on the interior balcony of the palatial foyer. A witness described it as being '...like a white shadow or statue that had not been unveiled.' It had moved from one side of the balcony to the other and then disappeared from view. Another witness stated, 'It scared me so much that I ran out into the street.' This strange figure was seen so frequently that the vicar of All Saints' Church, the Revd Cyril D. Payne, visited the Lyric – but afterwards he refused to talk to the media about the whole thing. The Catholic Bishop of Northampton, Charles Alexander Grant, refused to allow a priest to conduct a service of exorcism, further fuelling the excited local speculation. So it was left to a group of local psychical researchers to conduct a number of all-night vigils at the Lyric in November. During these séances messages were 'tapped out' which were interpreted as 'Help!' and 'Bring back priest!' The whole story caused a minor sensation at the time after it was reported in the *Evening Telegraph*.

The investigators concluded that something supernatural was present in the foyer of the theatre. However, as the late ghost-hunter Andrew Green ruefully noted in *Ghosts Of Today* (1980), their theories as to who the ghost was were sadly confused: a soldier who had lived on the site who died in the Great War; a former manager who had hanged himself rather than face bankruptcy; a man named 'Daniel' who had been buried at the site in the 19th century.

The Lyric Cinema subsequently became the Lyric Theatre Bingo and Social Club. Andrew Green notes that by 1971 there were still reports of a mysterious white figure being fleetingly seen by bingo players moving across the balcony. Cleaners reported that they were frightened by an unaccountable tapping noise they could hear from up on the balcony. Green apparently thought the story of the suicidal manager most credible, perhaps the foyer being the site of his hanging. If this is true then it should not take much effort to turn up evidence of such an event in the local press of the last 80 years. Perhaps that would conclusively 'prove' who the strange white person was who watched the patrons enter the Lyric's foyer from the haunted balcony.

The Lyric Theatre was demolished in 1975 but a new building erected on the site now goes by the name of the Lyric Club, although there does not appear to have been any repetition of the events of almost 40 years ago.

THE DUTCH DOLL: A NORTHAMPTONSHIRE LEGEND

A survey of Northamptonshire in 1818 described the village of Finedon, south east of Kettering, as '...a pleasant and respectable village, in which is a large, handsome church, consisting of a nave, two aisles, a transept, chancel, large southern porch, and lofty tower, with a spire. Beneath the chancel is a family burying vault. West of the church is Finedon Hall, a large mansion, belonging to Sir William Dolben.' In Church Street, the charity school for girls could be located: a well-designed two-storey house with a slated roof erected in 1712 by one of Sir William's forebears, Sir Gilbert Dolben.

The charity school is now a private dwelling and is notorious for a classic piece of folklore which is perhaps one of the most well-known urban legends today in the county of Northamptonshire: the bizarre and somewhat unsettling story of the so-called Dutch Doll.

There is a feeling that there was something a little eccentric about the benefactor who had originally built the charity school in Finedon in the early 18th century. Sir Gilbert Dolben seems to have been old before his time, fascinated with the bore of regional Tory politics and Anglicanism. Nonetheless, he was reliable, stoic and efficient enough to be created the first Baronet Dolben in 1704. By the time he died in 1722 his charitable girls' school had graced Finedon for some 10 years. A near-contemporary record of parish workhouses recorded how 'at this place 20 poor girls are set to work, taught, lodg'd and wholly maintained.' It also noted how Finedon went by the dual spelling and pronunciation of either Findon or Thingdon. The girls cooked, cleaned, knitted, read, spun, said grace and visited nearby St Mary's Church every day, all the time watched by a stern mistress. They earned a small wage and at 17 left the place to enter domestic service. For the most part, Sir Gilbert had left a very successful legacy in the village.

At Christmastide 1823 rumours began to sweep the village community that the charity school had been invaded by some kind of supernatural entity. Thumps, bangs and furious hammering on the doors were beginning to frighten some of the girls out of their wits, and sometimes the noises were so thunderous it seemed that the very building itself shook. Doors slammed of their own accord in parts of the house, or flew open by themselves in other rooms. The poltergeist-like disturbances continued for weeks into the New Year, and generated much excitement in Finedon. Crowds would gather near the building hoping to see or hear for themselves the so-called 'Finedon Ghost', and events even generated a poem by a Thomas Dexter, part of which ran:

'The goods were moved from the house,
The children sleep away;
And some of old Saint Crispin's sons
Now labour there all day.
And if the spectre should appear
Their work they will let fall,
And dash their lapstones at its skull,
Or prick it with their awl.'

Clearly the rumour was that the girls had been evacuated so the clergy could perform an exorcism. However, the blame was ultimately laid on a human factor. The hubbub continued until there was a dramatic expulsion of three of the girls from the school. Sarah Durden, Maria Hacksley and Hannah Randall were all accused of 'playing tricks and persisting in telling lies about noises' in early 1824. (Northampton Archives contains the scrapbook of one William Horner, who collected cuttings of the strange events at the time.)

Nonetheless, the village rumour that the charity school had been, or was still, haunted persisted. As late as 1943 village historian Reginald Underwood wrote, 'Even today I know of old Finedon residents who still declare their unshakeable belief that the School House is haunted and that queer and inexplicable things still happen.'

By the time Underwood noted this, the 'haunting' at the charity school had become associated with a three-foot tall, six-inch wide solid wood effigy of a late Stuart-era (or early Hanoverian-era) charity schoolgirl. It is unclear at what time this doll came into the possession of the school, but in 1824 it supposedly graced the door of the place and was visible to all the girls. Beautifully moulded and coloured, the doll wore a laced bodice, blue dress and white bonnet, and held a book in its right hand and a scroll bearing the legend *Search ye the Scriptures* in its left. However, this so-called Dutch Doll (on account of its hard composition, not that it came from Holland) simply *looked* odd: it bore a strangely – almost disturbingly – expressionless face, and its soulless eyes somehow bore the mark of something living and haunted. This waist-high object was, according to legend, taken down from the school's entrance following the events of 1824 and confined to the depths of the cellar.

The 'haunted' girls' school at Finedon.

It is repeated that a Victorian school headmistress called Mrs Kay would drag unruly girls down to the cellar and throw them in there; the terrified girl would have enough time to see the sinister wooden doll in the corner of the room, apparently looking at her, before the cellar door was slammed behind her and she was trapped alone in the darkness with it. For any girl who knew the doll's association with the outbreak of poltergeist activity it must have been a terrifying experience. Among the other girls it was whispered that somehow the doll was able to free itself from the cellar and walk about the school premises of its own volition at night-time, its dainty little feet making 'clonking' noises as it walked up to the dormitory door thresholds and halted outside in the corridor. The general suggestion was that the doll was either empowered to walk the school by the supernatural entity that still resided there, or, even more disturbing, it was itself somehow *alive*. By 1943 it had become 'a sort of legend' according to Reginald Underwood: some girls declared they had actually seen it inside the school, but most boys in the village scoffed as to its actual existence and supposed supernatural powers. Underwood wrote, 'It is, of course, no myth. I have more than once seen and handled it', but he does not note where it was kept – merely that it was in the possession of the school at that time.

The Dutch Doll remained a presence within the girls' school until 1954 when the premises closed. The wooden effigy was then removed and put on display within the Church of St Mary's, where its notorious reputation preceded it despite its new holy sanctuary. People will recall today how they did not like sitting near it, and the rumours had also grown in stature by this time: it was said that at some point the stories about the doll walking the school – and even the village of Finedon itself – so alarmed people that unknown persons had sawed off her toes to stop her wandering. Some even said that blood ran from the mutilated wooden feet.

The stories cannot be proved one way or the other: for the Dutch Doll is lost, apparently stolen from the wall of the church on 24 January 1981. Two thieves simply abducted the Dutch Doll in the broad

Did the Dutch Doll march out of Finedon's church?

daylight of early afternoon, and she has not been seen since. This crime has spawned another village urban legend, the kind of scare story used to pacify misbehaving children at bedtime – that the doll simply walked out of the church of her own accord, and if they do not behave then she will come and get them…

Many details of the story appeared in Underwood's now difficult-to-locate *The Pageant Of Finedon* (1943), although I was lucky enough to be directed to a copy in an antique bookshop in Brackley. Much of it can be repeated almost word for word in Finedon these days. Many of the residents have grown up with the legend that this silent, strangely sad wooden girl at one time wandered the 'pleasant and respectable village'. In 2007 I was assured that the man who made the doll modelled it on his own daughter, and she subsequently drowned; this appears to be a new element to the story. Whatever the truth, it is now such a fixture in the popular imagination that it has even generated a novel. Although many in the area still retain memories of the curious fear they had of the doll during childhood, there is still a feeling that the village is actually a little *proud* of this unique and spooky piece of folklore. She is, after all, invaluably rare, and the people of Finedon – although having been unnerved by this curiosity for generations – would almost certainly, if not a little warily, now welcome her back home.

BLISWORTH'S HAUNTED TUNNEL

A write-up for Halloween 2002 by the *Northampton Chronicle & Echo* drew upon the well-known legend that Blisworth Tunnel is supposedly haunted. The tunnel is part of the Grand Union Canal, the north portal of which is entered south of the village of Blisworth. After 3,076 yards (2,813 metres) its south portal exits at Stoke Bruerne, where the canal winds in the south-easterly direction of Milton Keynes in Buckinghamshire. The tunnel is truly a wonder of the industrial era, and is an achievement

The south portal of the Blisworth Tunnel exits at Stoke Bruerne.

that Northamptonshire is justifiably proud of. The opening of the canal on 25 March 1805 was proudly celebrated by the *Northampton Mercury* at the time.

Such technological advancements come at a price, however, and it is reckoned that some 50 lives were lost from the beginning of the tunnel's construction in 1793 to its completion 12 years later. This allegedly included 14 navvies who died when part of the construction collapsed, engulfing them with quicksand in 1796. Following this disaster the direction of the tunnel was altered to avoid further accidents from the weak seam. Blisworth Tunnel was the last part of the whole canal project to be finished, and in the interim it became necessary for boats to transfer their wares to a horse-drawn tram at one portal. The animal would then be led to the other portal over the hilly land, pulling the tram along railway lines so as to aid the shifting of the heavy goods. On the other side those wares would then be transferred to another boat and the journey would start once more.

Sometime around 1990 it is famously repeated that a married couple were navigating their narrow boat southwards through the dank, gloomy confines of Blisworth Tunnel. In the southern part of the tunnel they suddenly became disoriented, noticing that they were faced with a fork in the canal. With a choice of right or left, they opted for the right tunnel: far away down the darkness of the left tunnel they could see it was lit by lanterns and could hear the sounds of construction and men conversing loudly. Eventually the couple exited the tunnel at Stoke Bruerne where they reported their confusion to a waterway official – who of course informed them that there is no fork in Blisworth Tunnel, there is only one way in and one way out.

The eerie supposition is that the couple had seen a spectral re-enactment of events 200 years previously, when work had just started on the tunnel, before the catastrophe in 1796. This story has caught the public imagination and has been repeated in the local media – perhaps because it has to be wondered if there is a worse place to encounter a ghost than when you are trapped and moving slowly within the claustrophobic stillness of a tunnel.

Charles Dickens described an atmospheric journey through the tunnel in 1859: 'The place felt delightfully cool, going in out of the full-glare of a fierce noon-day sun; and this effect was increased by the dripping of water from the roof, and the noise caused by the springs, which *broke in* at various parts of the tunnel.' Clearly the tunnel was not quite watertight, but there were other problems. There is a story relating to an accident in the tunnel just two years after Dickens passed this way. On 6 September 1861 a steamboat crewed by five was navigating the tunnel; two of the boatmen laid on planks on their sides using their feet to push against the tunnel walls – so as to 'walk' the steamboat through the tunnel. A lack of ventilation in the tunnel led to these two 'leggers', William Webb and Edward Broadbent, fatally succumbing to fumes; two of the engine drivers collapsed near the furnace and were horrifically burned, although they did survive. The fifth man collapsed into the water near the south portal at Stoke Bruerne, but the shock of the impact revived him. Not surprisingly, stories of people within the tunnel experiencing suffocation or even hearing crying and moaning echoing around the walls near the south portal are common.

MODERN HAUNTS

These days outbreaks of ghostly activity are still regularly reported, with the local newspapers taking a very keen interest. What is instantly noticeable is that the haunted spots tend to take the form of something more prosaic than a stately home, or less atmospheric than the ruins of a church. It is likely to be cinemas or shopping aisles in supermarkets that are haunted. Somewhat mundane, you might think – but if 'ghosts', in whatever form they take, are part of our shared existence then why would they just confine themselves to Tudor pubs, ruined castles and battlefields?

In April 2004 the *Evening Telegraph* reported the experiences of staff at Budgens supermarket on Gladstone Street, Desborough. The store had opened in 1995 but in a previous incarnation it had been a railway yard, and indeed railway tracks run adjacent to Gladstone Street. However, the poltergeist-like phenomena reported by the newspaper seemed much more extreme than the vibration effects of trains shooting by. Produce on shelves had been observed to shudder and rattle when there was no train passing, and similarly objects had been observed to whisk themselves off shelves as though an unseen hand had thrown them. Staff working the Sunday shift would report that for some reason, when they unlocked the store in the morning, four cans of bitter were always found on the floor. Perhaps the eeriest allegation is that a voice can regularly be heard saying, 'Good morning' by the stairs at the back of the store. One worker described it as '…this whispering over my shoulder. It was a lovely calm male voice. I turned around and nobody was there.' Speculation has it that the phantom inhabitant of Budgens is a man who threw himself off the Glendon north junction bridge to his death on the same stretch of track that bypasses Gladstone Street. This unfortunate man was reckoned to have become suicidally depressed after returning home to Desborough in the 1940s, having seen action in World War Two.

In July 2008 it was the turn of the Home Bargains store in the Newlands shopping centre, Kettering. Here staff reported that items moved along shelves by themselves and secure fire doors could be found open – all of which was blamed on the forced relocation, during development, of human remains buried at the site in Gold Street. Perhaps the most famously haunted 'modern' location in Northampton itself is the Grosvenor shopping centre, a modern shopping complex built on the site of the ancient Grey Friars Monastery. The monastery has not existed as such for centuries. As far back as 1857 historian John Brooke had described the site as a ruin, given over to other development: 'The Grey Friars Monastery was in the north-east quarter of the town, but is now demolished and most of its site is built upon; but it stood in that part of the town which now lies between Newland and Victoria Streets and to the eastward of the upper end of Grey Friars Street and of Lady's Lane; a small portion of an ancient wall, with buttresses, and some little remains of masonry, built up in the walls of adjoining houses, are now visible...Its site has also been identified by stone coffins discovered near there, in excavating the soil for building purposes.'

The Grey Friars, or Franciscans, had been established in Northampton in 1224. The order lasted until the Dissolution of the Monasteries in the 16th century and was often at the centre of local squabbles and drama. King Edward I granted the monastery a horse and cart in 1277, but this gift became the focus of a prolonged argument as to whether the friars should be allowed it following the mysterious killing of one Richard de Lilleford, '...lately slain by the said cart.' In 1308 the bishop excommunicated a band of men who had invaded the church and abducted certain members of the congregation.

On 28 October 1538 the monastery surrendered to the king and thereafter fell into a prolonged state of decay. Given the atmospheric and historic location of the modern Grosvenor shopping centre it is hardly surprising that it is reckoned to be haunted. I have heard it said that (famously during the 1970s) cleaning staff were terrified after hours by the spectral appearance within the shopping precinct of a bald-pated man wearing the rough, simple grey smock of a member of the order of Franciscans. This harmless ghost is very well known and he is simply called 'The Grey Friar', although it has to be wondered if perhaps in life he was John Wyndlowe, the warden of the monastery and the man who signed the deed of surrender to the king, which – as was so often the case – effectively closed the monastery down and ended its life.

GHOSTS OF THE ROAD

The *Northampton Chronicle & Echo* of 29 October 2004 makes reference to a classic example of a 'road ghost', which I have also heard once or twice repeated verbally as being 'fact'. Apparently at the level crossing west of Lamport a number of drivers have been shocked to encounter what appears to be a monk who walks out in front of their vehicle swinging a lantern. He vanishes as they run into him, and upon stopping they scour the road for a body, but are unable to find one. Perhaps he is linked to the demolished St Denis's Church, Faxton, which incorporated parts of an earlier 12th-century chapel.

In February 2008 at the World's End, the historic bar and hotel in Ecton, I was told that the area between the A4500-Wellingborough Road crossroads and Mears Ashby was similarly haunted. The public house can be found at the crossroads, and John Cole's *Hist. Of Ecton* (1825) notes that the building in its current incarnation was built c.1765, but prior to that it had been an inn called the Globe. Local legend has it that many Royalist soldiers captured after the battle of Naseby were incarcerated here in appalling conditions during the long march back to London. Many died of battle injuries, fatigue and mistreatment, and so when the pub was rebuilt in 1765 – in memory of this – it was renamed the World's End. However, surprisingly the haunting is not related to these events. The ghost was (or is) called the Grey Lady, and she takes the form of an elderly abbess who appears before fatigued drivers in the lonely connecting roads around Sywell Reservoir. Urban legend has it that beneath her wimple she displays the skeletal features of the long dead, or else no face at all, and that she appears to be trying to approach the vehicle. John Cole, writing in 1825, heard that locally there was supposed to have been a nunnery in or near Ecton at one time that fell under the sphere of nearby Delapre Abbey. In Ecton Hall itself, he found, was a yard still referred to as 'Nun's Court'. If so, then the ghostly nun has wandered the highways for some centuries; I was told that, apparently: 'On Halloween you can still see her at midnight. She puts her hand up to try and stop you.' Washbrook Lane is seemingly where she has been most frequently observed lately.

The Halloween 2006 copy of the *Evening Telegraph* reminded its readership of the stir caused in the mid-1980s by the famous 'bearded monk' that was supposed to have haunted Barford Bridge over the River Ise. The ghostly monk is reckoned to have appeared at this spot on the A6003 for centuries, but in 1984 it was reported that he had apparently moved with the times. As one heads northwards, just before the bridge, there is an unclassified road that leads to Geddington. On numerous occasions people driving along this minor road at night have been shocked to glance in their rear-view mirror and see the phantom face of the monk looking at them from the back seat. This again conforms to the modern urban legend of the 'phantom hitch-hiker'. Perhaps the monk is linked to nearby Pipewell Abbey, which was founded for Cistercian monks in 1143. Like so many others it fell victim to the Dissolution of the Monasteries on 5 November 1538 and was granted to Sir William Carre. When the men presented with overseeing this task forced the monks to grant Pipewell's interior fittings to them, the last abbot – Thomas Gyllam – was forced to undergo the indignity of sitting on a commission to confirm that, after 400 years as a monastic concern, Pipewell Abbey and its contents belonged to Sir William Carre. Pipewell soon fell into neglect, and villagers began to loot the property, including a tinker – whom the commission investigating the rape of Pipewell Abbey had hanged at Northampton. Perhaps this undignified end is the reason why the monk appears to be trying to attract the attention of road users these days?

There are also rumours of 'ghost vehicles' on out-of-the-way country roads, which are blamed for minor accidents: it seems they vanish from sight after forcing other road users onto verges, but I cannot seem to pin down where this is supposed to occur.

MODERN URBAN LEGENDS

My own theories about 'ghosts' are that in the first instance the phenomenon cannot be pinned down to a specific definition. From ghosts that are pure reflections of a hated or famous figure from a village's folklore, to entities that interact with humans and the phantom replay-type ghost, variations of which were mentioned in previous chapters, all of these display certain characteristics that place them in a particular category. Then there are poltergeists and other assorted totally random encounters, terrifying in their meaninglessness. These last type seem to pervade our modern world more frequently, and while I have time for folkloric headless cavaliers and phantom coaches it is the pointless, inexplicable encounters that impress me most; for their very banality or inexplicability somehow seems to lend more credence to their being real. After all, I have heard of people who have seen mysterious, crying little girls who simply faded away: or in one instance I have heard first-hand of a mobile phone call received by a young woman from a deceased relative's own mobile (a phone naturally switched off and shut away). Yet I have never met anyone who claimed to see a phantom coach and horses, or to have held a physical discussion with a ghost.

It was widely publicised, for example, that a pair of newlyweds had been 'attacked' in the bedroom of their flat in Raunds by an unseen entity. The incident had occurred in 1978 on the very night of the wedding. Apparently the pair had felt that 'something' invisible was watching them in the gloom of the bedroom – and then the presence had grabbed the man round the throat, throttled him and thrown him violently out of the bed. Naturally the couple fled the bedroom, and indeed the flat, but there the story appears to end. If the couple had been making love, then perhaps this entity was some kind of jealous or puritanical poltergeist that manifested its displeasure through violence. It is the completely terrifying inexplicability of the incident that captured the imagination locally, and the story is even remembered today. Why would any couple make up such a random story, let alone on their wedding night?

Then there are places that are assumed to be haunted because of a particular incident that happened – a disaster, a suicide, a murder – or because they simply *look* haunted. Under this umbrella are instances of alleged encounters that appear almost to conform to modern urban legends. This type of ghost story has always been with us – the type of tale that appears to have no substance, but still sounds spookily impressive.

One of the most peculiar anecdotes of this sort concerns the dismantled railway sidings to the south of Bradden. There is a rural bridge which crosses the old route of the line, by the River Tove, and in June 2008 I was told that a man had 'recently' parked his car near the bridge in order to relieve himself one evening around midnight. As he returned to the car his attention was drawn to the small valley beneath the bridge where a bright, circular light appeared to be growing nearer. A moment later he saw the solid-looking outline of what he took to be an impressive old-fashioned steam locomotive sweeping through the overgrown bracken, belching smoke, although its immense bright light at the front hid much of the detail. It swept silently and slowly underneath the bridge and out the other side, disappearing once more into the countryside darkness.

I was told this by a friend, who had in turn been told it by a work colleague whom she thought had heard it during an evening out...the old 'friend-of-a-friend' scenario. I suspect if I traced this story backwards I would probably not get anywhere, but it is an interesting anecdote nonetheless. Possibly it was some sort of bizarre weather phenomenon. However, it was repeated in all sincerity in the telling.

This same person also told me what would seem to be a classic example of a modern urban legend, a bizarre story that was doing the rounds in the mid-1980s among schoolchildren. Apparently a teenage boy had used a certain telephone box on the corner of a street in Northampton but had misdialled the number. After ringing a couple of times a voice came onto the other end of the line; it was a male voice, and, in between convulsing sobs, it said something like, 'Help me, I'm dying. They got me. Tell Elizabeth I love her' before the line simply went dead. The youth in question, after recovering from his initial shock, redialled the number once more and received the same tortured message. At this point I asked whether the plea was *exactly* the same, and was told that the mysterious voice at the other end of the line said the *same words* but she did not think it had been an *exact* repetition of what had been said before. Apparently there was shortly hereafter a small group of teenagers who knew this telephone number, and the exact telephone box from which the number had to be dialled – it did not seem to work at just *any* call box. How much truth there is in this story is impossible to tell, but maybe it will ring bells, so to speak, with today's adults who were schoolchildren at the time.

In these last two chapters we have seen that the phenomena of 'ghosts' encompass a wide-ranging spectrum, and the variety of stories range in credibility from the exceptionally impressive to the folkloric and barely believable. All, however, make good tales, and this selection is merely a small fraction of the hundreds of ghostly legends that are out there in Northamptonshire. What does this tell us about the 'reality' of ghosts in modern Northamptonshire? That is an unanswerable question; perhaps the real question should be what does the sincere persistence of belief in ghosts tell us about the nature of fascinated human superstition?

Whatever credence one gives to these stories, it is clear that the mystery of ghosts in their many forms is here to stay. Currently attracting the attention of the media and the curious alike is the Knight's Lodge public house on Tower Hill Road, Corby. The *Evening Telegraph* of 31 October 2008 reported that here the new landlady had been startled on her very first day (six weeks previously) by a brownish, hooded monk-like apparition that she caught sight of in an upstairs room; the figure appeared to be praying. Since then, she told the newspaper, she had also heard phantom sobbing and whispering on the stairs – which was linked to the locally held belief that a little girl had at some time been killed falling down the stairs at this sturdy looking, centuries-old pub. And so it goes on. One is left with the distinct feeling that it would be possible for this chapter to continue indefinitely.

CHAPTER 8

THE WEIRD ANIMAL KINGDOM

INTRODUCTION

Curious stories about animals always delight us, and there are many from Northamptonshire. Some are grounded in the real world; some conform to superstitious beliefs about animal behaviour (as noted in Chapter 4); and some even belong to the realm of the paranormal.

Among the former are the incidences of known animals displaying unusual physical characteristics. In the 1830s a rabbit shot at Ecton appeared to be 'sabre-toothed': two teeth of the lower jaw were observed to be of considerable length, bending upwards and back towards the face, almost to the eyes. The antiquarian John Cole commented, 'The wonder is how the little animal could obtain its food.' He also noted that around 1817 a *white* crow was captured at Mears Ashby and exhibited as a curiosity in Northampton. The 18th-century county naturalist John Morton managed to obtain and exhibit a four-legged quail. It had been found dead in its nest in a field in Middleton Cheney, and doubtless in his day such oddities were viewed with suspicion as portents. In 1942 great excitement was caused in north-eastern Northamptonshire following the birth of a duckling at Molesworth which had a second set of eyes and a beak on the back of its head. It also had four wings and four legs.

Surely the strangest discovery was noted in the *History, Gazetteer And Directory Of Northamptonshire* (1849). Around 1839 a baffling discovery was made '...while levelling a hill in front of Mrs Lovell's house' in Bugbrooke: several decapitated human skulls were found, together with numerous horseshoes, leading to the supposition that at some time there had been a violent skirmish. Accompanying these finds was the entirely random discovery of '...a crocodile in a petrified state'. There is little more to this enigma. Although crocodiles did inhabit the sub-tropical British Isles some two million years ago (before the Ice Age), to find one 'petrified' alongside human remains was very strange. In 1867 the *Gentleman's Magazine* discussed physical evidence pointing to the survival of a colony of small crocodiles in neighbouring Oxfordshire 10 years prior, and speculated that such beasts had lived on 'as native fauna' in small pockets in the Midlands.

Turtles, elephants, bison, hippopotami, sabre-toothed cats and woolly mammoths have also inhabited Northamptonshire (sometimes alongside early humans) throughout the millennia. The introduction of turnpike roads in the county threw up an interesting discovery around 1756 in a field south of Kettering. A tooth, vertebrae and jawbone of some mysterious animal of truly enormous size was unearthed and colourfully described at the time as coming from a creature '...living before the fountains of the great deep were broken up, when the whole earth and its inhabitants perished by water', that is to say the biblical flood of Noah's time. Similarly two tusks of an elephant had been unearthed in 'Bowden-parva Field' (on the Leicestershire border) in about 1757 according to Victorian naturalist C.C. Clarke. In 1832 the bizarre discovery of some bones and great antlers from a herd of elk were unearthed five feet below ground during the excavation of a new channel for the River Nene in meadows below Wellingborough bridge. The antlers were nearly a yard in length 'but not in a fossil state' and were found along with nuts, and – strangely – human artefacts, including an earthenware pot and a mysterious key. Elk roamed Britain towards the end of the last Ice Age, and the find was probably the remains of an abandoned camp. However, the observation that the antlers were *not* fossilised raises interesting questions for archaeologists.

Slightly nearer our time, a sad piece of folklore concerning one particular animal is likely to be true: the legend of how Mary, Queen of Scots's little black Skye terrier fought tragically to stay with its doomed mistress as she walked down the great staircase of Fotheringhay Castle on her way to her execution. From her bedchamber to the Great Hall it loyally trotted through the feet of her ladies-in-waiting and the guards, darting in and out of Mary's sweeping skirts as she made her solemn way. Stories of canine devotion to their owners are legendary the world over, even to the point of saving their lives. According to Robert Wynkfield, an eyewitness to the tragic spectacle in 1587, after Mary's beheading the dog crept underneath her petticoats and had to be removed forcibly. However, it could not be controlled, and would not leave the corpse, '…but came and lay between her head and shoulders' until it was removed once more and taken away to be washed: in its confusion it had become covered in Mary's blood. Historian Agnes Strickland writing in 1859 noted that during this scene some barbarous individual had fetched a plate and attempted to get the little dog to lap its mistress's blood up. 'With intelligence beyond that of its species' the dog would not touch the saucer, and, not only that, it refused to eat anything ever again, and eventually pined away to death.

Very possibly this sad story is wholly true, and says much about the indignity Mary suffered even after death. It bears some parallels with cases of aggressively protective pets; *The Times* reported in October 2003 how an elderly man who farmed llamas at Loddington had broken his hip after falling down a rabbit hole. He had crawled in agony to a nearby road to flag down help. However, by this time his four llamas had formed a protective ring around him, and when police and paramedics attempted to get anywhere near him they became exceptionally aggressive. They repeatedly drove off would-be rescuers and the farmer eventually had to be removed from the roadside by an air ambulance helicopter. Even then, as it flew away the llamas chased it on the ground as far as they could.

The list of animal oddities rooted in the natural world is seemingly endless. For instance, the early 18th-century natural historian and antiquary John Morton recorded a 'snail graveyard' at Mears Ashby. Upon coming across this curiosity while digging pasture land, an area 250 feet by 130 feet was roped off – and to a depth of three feet down were found the shells of snails of many kinds. A foot down in the peaty earth the carpet of snail shells became thicker; three feet down it was almost like wading through a quicksand of shells. No live ones were observed during the investigation.

In 1853 a contributor to *Notes And Queries* asked an enigmatic question: 'In Mr Jessie's *Life Of Beau Brummel* I met with a passage which spoke about the "well-known" fox of Whittlebury Forest. Can any of your readers kindly inform me what the celebrity of this consists, which Mr Jessie takes for granted is so well known?' I suppose that this is the fox referred to in *The Family Magazine* of 1843, which was allegedly captured and bagged four times in the same coppice in Whittlebury by the Duke of Grafton's hunting party before being taken to London on the venison cart. Each time it somehow got free and was recaptured time and again at the same spot. It was proven to be the same animal after it had escaped and returned a second time when its lip was cut and its ear had a hole clipped in it. Between Whittlebury and Silverstone there is today a piece of woodland called Foxhole Copse, which I assume is where the fox had its home and where it kept returning.

In 1920 it was reported that some 30 flocks of sheep across Northamptonshire and Cambridgeshire spontaneously stampeded in panic. This happened at widely separate locations, and thousands of the animals jumped their hurdles and broke free. What caused the great 'sheep stampede' was never resolved.

Some tales are classics. In April 2006 the two worlds of 'the one that got away' and the familiar US urban legend of 'monster catfish' came together when an angler at Ravensthorpe Reservoir caught a truly immense pike. The fish, dubbed the Beast of Ravensthorpe, weighing in at 42lb, broke the net during the titanic struggle to get it in the boat and was too heavy to be weighed on the scales. The angler had his photograph taken with the Beast – before throwing it back into the water. He commented, 'I held it up and it was almost as big as me . . . and I'm 6ft.' There was speculation that the enormous fish could grow even bigger – perhaps in time, if caught again, becoming the biggest pike ever known in the British Isles. For the time being, however, the pike has hidden itself once more in the freezing waters of the reservoir, no doubt to become an urban legend among the hundreds of anglers who descend here every year.

Notes And Queries related in 1850 the mysterious spectacle of many dead harvest mice lining the verges of rural footpaths in south Northamptonshire on summer evenings, none of which bore any external wounds or had any other apparent cause for their deaths. This gave rise to speculation that harvest mice were unable to cross paths that had been walked by man; those that tried were 'struck dead' on the verge.

Some animal oddities noted here are rooted in the real world, but some are more supernatural. A phantom white cockerel is said to strut its way about the strange-looking Jacobean building called Haunt Hill House on Kettering Road, Weldon, according to the *Northants Evening Telegraph*.

THE DUN COW

One of the most famous of English mythological 'animals' is the Dun Cow, a creature that features in the Anglo-Norman romances of the legendary warrior hero Guy of Warwick. Guy is first mentioned in the 13th century as *Gui de Warewic*, and scholars have tentatively placed the 'historical' context of his adventures as taking place during the reign of King Athelstan of England (d.AD 939) in the Warwickshire/Oxfordshire region of the Midlands. According to legend, Guy, in an attempt to win the hand of a lady of higher social standing than himself, endured all manner of trials and feats in order to prove his worth. He travelled widely and battled all kinds of dragons and giants – nearer to home he is said to have killed the animal known as the Dun Cow.

According to the story, the Dun Cow was a real, horned bovine animal of colossal size that belonged to a giant who lived at a Bronze Age stone circle on heathland in Shropshire. It produced an inexhaustible supply of milk for the region, until one day an old woman sought to trick it and asked it to fill a sieve. Of course, the mighty animal could never accomplish this, and after it eventually ran out of milk it broke free in a fury and made in the direction of Warwickshire.

The Dun Cow caused carnage and mayhem as it went. By this point Guy of Warwick is supposed to have won his lady's heart but had become restless for more adventures. He had intended to sail from England, but as his ship lay stuck in harbour during a thunderstorm he heard the tales that were circulating among the peasantry of the monstrous cow terrorising the Midlands: 'She [the animal] was beyond the ordinary size of other cattle, six yards in length, and four high, with large sharp horns and fiery eyes of a Dun colour.' The animal had made its home somewhere on Dunsmore Heath, between Coventry and Rugby. Here it resisted all attempts to capture or tame it; many died in their encounters with the animal, which also killed livestock as well. Things had gotten so bad that King Athelstan himself, in York at the time, ordered that the Dun Cow be killed, and whoever slew the beast would be awarded a knighthood.

Guy of Warwick ran the Dun Cow to ground and there ensued a titanic battle, with Guy's armour and the cow's tough hide preventing either from seriously injuring the other – until Guy managed to stab the beast behind its ear, its only vulnerable spot. Guy repeatedly struck the animal here until its knees buckled and it finally sank to the floor, dying in a pool of blood.

The tales of Guy of Warwick were popular until the 17th century, and, although the element of the Dun Cow appears to be a later addition to the saga, it nonetheless drew upon centuries-old folklore of the man and his deeds. Francis Warwick, author of the authoritative *Warwick Castle And Its*

Earls, wrote of the legend in 1903, 'It is difficult to believe that it is purely fabrication, or that Guy of Warwick was entirely a mythical character.' It is with this in mind that 'proof' of the clash with the Dun Cow crops up in Northamptonshire.

In this bizarre realm, where myth meets what is allegedly proof of reality, there supposedly existed numerous relics of the clash on Dunsmore Heath. A certain Dr Caius wrote in 1570 of how he had observed a huge, horned skull and massive vertebrae at Warwick Castle in 1552. He had been told they had belonged to the Dun Cow. Enormous rib and blade bones were also proudly displayed in Coventry and Warwick, and were alleged to belong to the creature.

At St Peter's Church in Stanion there can still be found what is said to be part of the beast's skeleton. *Murray's Handbook For Travellers In Northamptonshire & Rutland* (1878) noted that the bone was around 7ft long, and that it was said locally that the old woman who had played the trick on the animal had been a witch. It seemed that the village had also taken the Dun Cow to its heart (since they thought they had a piece of it in their church) for they ignored the legend that it had gone berserk and been brutally killed. In Stanion they said that it had died of a broken heart. However, church historian Thomas North contradicted this, in the same year writing that the Dun Cow had been an uncontrollable monster that ravaged Rockingham Forest in Warwick's time. Until very recently a large square riveted iron bell had been positioned next to the rib at Stanion: people were told that a local peasant had somehow managed to fasten it to the Dun Cow's neck to warn people of its approach. Whatever tale was told, however, it seems that there was a sincere belief that it was the rib of the creature, and many people came from miles around to see the wonder. Graffiti scratched on the rib dating back to the 1600s testifies to this.

It has been speculated that the remnants at Warwick Castle were relics of large animals from the Ice Age, and although an unlikely supposition it is tempting to idly speculate that the Dun Cow was more than a mere mythological creature; perhaps she was a remnant of some gigantic beast from prehistory that had survived until the 10th century in small pockets of England.

Could this really be the relic of a mythical creature?

In 1849 a bemused correspondent to *Notes & Queries* asked, 'Has any palaeontologist examined the bone of abnormal size kept in St Peter's Church, Stanion?' He described it as seven feet long, nine inches across, quite flat and of a great thickness. The Dun Cow rib is in fact likely to be a whalebone, which were sometimes procured for archways in churches. It was not entirely unheard of for whale bones to find their way into Northamptonshire: in 1837 John Cole was greatly puzzled by the spectacle of a whale's jaw bone that formed a gatepost on the Finedon road (A510) to Wellingborough. Either way, the immense bone at Stanion is still a curiosity of folklore, and has been for centuries. Apparently much of the carcass of the slain Dun Cow was buried in the Lincolnshire limestone between Kettering and Corby, at an unclear location designated Cowthick Pit somewhere along (what is now) the A43.

KILLING WOLVES AND BOARS

Wolves have long disappeared from the impenetrable woodlands and wilds of Britain, deliberately hunted into extinction as vermin. Strange, then, that one of Northamptonshire's oldest legends concerns a spectral wolf that saved the legendary 11th-century Fenland rebel Hereward the Wake. A near-contemporary version of events, the *Gesta Herewardi*, is the first to tell of Hereward and his outlaws becoming hopelessly lost in the impenetrable forest of the *Bruneswald*. Saint Peter took mercy upon them, and in thanks for Hereward's piety in returning stolen treasure to Peterborough Abbey he sent a gigantic white hound which led the warriors through the dense woodland of the midnight forest. Furthermore, Will o' the Wisps lit the tips of their spears to illuminate their passage. As dawn broke Hereward and his men recognised the path that they had been led to and at this noticed that the white hound was in fact a spectral white wolf, sent by Saint Peter, which promptly disappeared into the forest.

The *Bruneswald* forest is nowadays vastly reduced, its name remembered in the village of Newton Bromswold, Northamptonshire, just shy of the Bedfordshire border. It is this strategic locale that has led to general guesswork placing the incident with the white wolf in the immensity of Rockingham Forest, whose ash, oak and elms touched the great *Bruneswald* forest. Later authors drew upon this supposition. Although highly romanticised, Charles Kingsley's *Hereward The Last Of The English* (1866) essentially elaborated the original *Gesta* when he wrote, 'A huge wolf met them, wagging his tail like a tame dog, and went before them on a path.' Hereward and his men took the animal for a dog, and felt compelled to follow it, only realising at daybreak that it had in fact been a *wolf* that had saved them: 'And as they questioned among themselves what had happened, the wolf and the candles disappeared, and they came whither [realised] they had been minded, beyond Stamford town, thanking God, and wondering what had happened.'

There is evidence that wolves still roamed parts of Britain in the 14th century, notably in Northamptonshire. During the reign of King Edward I, Thomas de Engaine, Lord of Blatherwic, was charged by the king to employ, at his own cost, dogs to kill 'wolves, foxes, marten cats, wild cats and other vermine' within the counties of Northampton, Rutland, Oxford, Buckingham and Essex 'whensoever the king should command'. Although certain animals within the royal parks such as roe deer would be granted protection, in 1340 the wolf was considered a pest. De Egaine had overlordship of Laxton and *Pightesse* (Pytchley), but it would seem — according to legend — that the last wolf in England was actually slain in the county by one Jock of Badsaddle near Orlingbury.

The *History, Gazetteer And Directory Of Northamptonshire…*(1849) notes that it was common knowledge at the time of writing that the Church of the Blessed St Mary the Virgin in Orlingbury contained an ancient freestone tomb bearing the effigy of an armoured man. This was Jock (or Jack) of Badsaddle, who had resided at Badsaddle Lodge (a former manor house surrounded by a moat in the village) and who had killed a wolf *and* a ferocious wild boar in a meadow adjoining the manor during a titanic and bloody struggle. Following the 'dreadful encounter' Jock had partaken of the waters of a spring and subsequently died from its effects; this spring was by the mid-1800s referred to locally as *Jack Badsaddle's Spring*.

The tomb that bears the effigy is dated *c*.1375 and can be found hidden away in the chancel of St Mary's. There is a popular supposition that 'Jock' in fact killed the *last* wolf in England – and in doing so saved the life of the king who was also out hunting. All the dates seem to tie in, and if this is true then the king saved would have been King Edward III: the grandson of the very king who charged de Engaine with exterminating the wolf population which, a century earlier, had widely scavenged parts of Northamptonshire.

An 1836 directory of Northamptonshire describes Badsaddle as '...a hamlet and hundred in the parish of Orlingbury'. The moat at Badsaddle, west of Orlingbury, can still be pointed out. However, quite who 'Jock' of Badsaddle was is uncertain: the tomb of this heroic slayer of wild animals and defender of royalty in Orlingbury may in fact be that of John de Wythmale. However, tradition has now ascribed it as belonging to Jock of Badsaddle, although 'Jock' or 'Jack' was (supposedly) de Wythmale's nickname. The tomb is now cracked and worn, and almost hidden from view.

As with much of Northamptonshire folklore, the story is somewhat confused, although it probably contains some grain of truth. Some say that Jock slew England's last wolf, some say he killed a gigantic wild boar – and some even say that he killed *both* in the protection of his king. The English wolf population is thought to have actually died out in the north around 100 years *after* the alleged encounter in Northamptonshire, so maybe even Jock's fame as the slayer of England's 'last wolf' is incorrect.

The weathered tomb of the wolf slayer, tucked away in Orlingbury church.

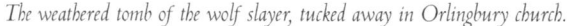

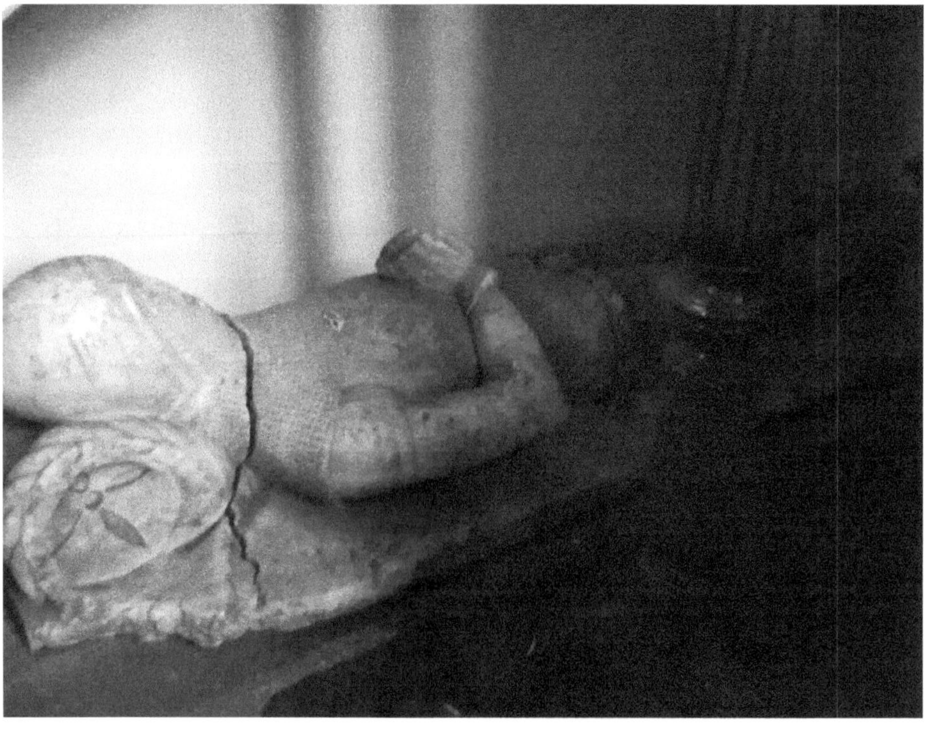

It is perhaps more likely that the animal Jock slew was a wild boar of monstrous proportions. Although the wild boar was becoming scarce by the 14th century, they were sighted until the mid-to-late 1600s in England. The poet C.H.M.D. Scott wrote of the encounter as having taken place in Rockingham Forest:

> The King stood under Langley Oak;
> That elder princely tree;
> And he brushed his cloak before he spoke;
> To Jock of Orlingb'rie;
> And the monstrous beast between them lay;
> A grisly sight to see.

It is interesting to note that the early 18th-century natural historian Revd John Morton recorded talk of a colony of wild boars still residing in Rockingham Forest in his time: a sow had escaped from Burghley House, where the boundaries of Lincolnshire, Cambridgeshire and Northamptonshire all join. This animal had mated with a wild boar and produced a race of feral pigs that were alleged to have been spotted in Rockingham Forest. They were wild and exceptionally aggressive, he noted.

STRANGE DEER OF SILVERSTONE

Old Oak: The Story Of A Forest Village, a book written in 1932 by John Linnell concerned much of the lore that he had grown up with as a child around Silverstone. One very strange story is recounted as follows.

An ancestor of Linnell's called Saywell had been a farmer who worked the land near what remained of Luffield Abbey in the mid-1700s. Luffield was a defunct parish that straddled the border between Northamptonshire and Buckinghamshire near Biddlesden, and by 1732 the ancient abbey no longer stood. Even the old church had fallen into such a state of disrepair that only part of the tower remained visible. All about was the great mediaeval hunting forest of Whittlewood which radiated out from Silverstone and crept over the border into Buckinghamshire. The original size of the forest (as with Rockingham) is now difficult to appreciate, shrinking as it has done to a thick scattering of woods and copses. Linnell wrote, 'The deer were all caught up to be killed or sent away to stock private demesnes; the oaks were felled in thousands...'

However, in the days before this a strange event is said to have occurred. In 1740 Saywell's farmlands were pestered by herds of deer which he would regularly have to chase off. Gradually he noticed that one buck appeared to be leading him in a certain direction into the woodland but would always escape him at exactly the same spot, vanishing from sight as though it were a ghost animal. Saywell became obsessed with capturing this deer because, as Linnell had heard it told, it had a *man's face*. Saywell could never capture it, however, and ultimately resolved to dig at the spot in the copse where it always managed to elude him. Here the farmer was aghast to uncover a hoard of treasure which Linnell, writing 200 years later, suggested had been hidden by the monks of Luffield Abbey during some conflict.

In 1943 the abbey's site became a World War Two bomber base, RAF Silverstone. The airfield's three runways later formed the basis for the world-famous Silverstone motor racing circuit – the home of the British Grand Prix since 1948.

'DANCER' THE DOG, THE LITTLEST HOBO

Dog owners will not be surprised by the following story, noted for posterity in William Lennox's *Recreations Of A Sportsman* (1862), which concerns a foxhound called Dancer kept at Winwick in the west of the county.

In 1793 Dancer was the favourite hound of huntsmen 'Old' Joe Smyth and Mr Taylor, who kept a pack of the animals at their premises in the village. Lately, Dancer had not been 'quite sound' so the huntsmen and the other dogs left for a fortnight's hunting at Lutterworth, Leicestershire, without old Dancer. The first day's hunting was so exhausting that the entire group, hounds and horses included, decided to stay the night in the town of Leicester itself.

The following day as the group were about to set to again in Lutterworth, they were told – much to their amazement – that shortly after they had dashed off into the woodland of Lutterworth the previous day, blaring their horns, a lone dog had soon arrived at the spot. Here it had simply sat there all day until nightfall, at which point it had begun to show signs of uneasiness. The following morning the hound had gone. From the exact description of the animal it was clear that it was Dancer and that she had somehow broken free of the enclosed kennels in Winwick and pursued the group all the way to Lutterworth, where she had apparently sat waiting for them to come out of the forest before giving up.

Old Joe Smyth was concerned for the welfare of his favourite pet, and the hunt was partially abandoned while Smyth made enquiries about the whereabouts of Dancer. Smyth figured that Dancer, having been on the hunt to Lutterworth many times, would have made her own way back to the Winwick kennels, and so he returned home. Here, he was amazed to find that Dancer *had* reappeared back at Winwick, but she had disappeared once more looking for her companions. It was ultimately found that the poor dog had made her lonely way into the county of Warwickshire to the home of a Mr Newcombe; months earlier Smyth had taken his pack there on a hunting expedition and Dancer had, apparently, remembered this and gone there next in search of her masters. Here she was reunited with an overjoyed Joe Smyth, who had finally tracked down his wandering pooch. At the time all were quite simply amazed by the 'reasoning faculty' that Dancer had employed in searching for her masters.

Such stories really do explain why dogs are man's best friend; however, as one who has never owned a dog I still find such behaviour intriguingly curious. *The Sporting Magazine* of 1804 notes a remarkable instance of the abilities of a bloodhound at Thrapston. The Thrapston Association for the Prosecution of Felons trained and presented the authorities with a bloodhound for the purposes of catching sheep-rustlers. The association was asked to prove the dog's abilities, and so the animal was given the quickest scent of a 'sheep stealer' hired for this performance. The man then dashed off into the woodland at 10 in the morning, watched by a great group of people.

An hour later the bloodhound was unleashed after him; '…when, after a chase of an hour and a half, notwithstanding a very indifferent scent, the hound found him hidden on a tree, at a distance of 15 miles, to the astonishment and satisfaction of all present.'

BELIEFS ABOUT ANIMALS

The fable of the trial of speed between the tortoise and the hare is a famous one which (although already around in one format or another) was popularised in 1840 by the Brothers Grimm. They explained that the race was between a hare and a hedgehog, but it may interest some to know that at the same time – possibly independently – a version of this story was repeated as having happened in southern Northamptonshire. In the county version it is a race between a *fox* and a hedgehog which took place in the woodland west of Silverstone. The fox could not understand why it could not beat the hedgehog in a race: in fact, the hedgehog's wife (who looked very similar to her husband) would repeatedly position herself at the finishing line. This led the fox to think that somehow the hedgehog was finding a quicker way through the forest. He challenged his adversary to one-too-many races and ultimately expired due to exhaustion. Fairy tales aside, this story may reflect the superstitious abilities attached to hedgehogs by farmers in the 19th century, who viewed them (strangely) as being more cunning than foxes or weasels. It was observed in 1850 that there was a widely held belief that cattle were absolutely terrified of hedgehogs because they would suck at a cow's udders as they slept in the night. I have heard this belief attached to hedgehogs elsewhere in the Midlands and can only wonder if it is still thought of as a truism in the county.

Also repeated in neighbouring counties were the stories of curious powers ascribed to bees in Northamptonshire. *Notes And Queries* mentions that in the south of the county it was thought that bees were exceptionally sensitive and would desert the premises of a quarrelsome family.

There was also a belief in Northamptonshire that snakes could not die until the sun had set. That is to say that if one were crushed or chopped at sunrise, it would somehow squirm and linger until sunset, even if its head were lopped off.

Even the humble frog has gained its place in the lore of Northamptonshire. The early 18th-century historian Revd John Morton, in his expansive *Natural History Of Northamptonshire*, noted that there was a four-week period every year around the month of August, when the weather was at its hottest, that a weird natural phenomenon was observed in the county. During this time frogs were observed to keep absolutely silent; that is to say, for some reason the innumerable little fellows who inhabited the wet and marshy banks of the county's lakes, rivers and streams were collectively never heard to croak during this time. Their bodies were also observed to be greatly swelled, and this time of year was whimsically referred to as *poddock-moon*. Morton commented, ''Tis a thing observ'd by almost every body here, and the matter of fact is indisputable; but 'tis generally looked upon as very strange and unaccountable.'

Toads were generally regarded for some reason with great abhorrence. In 1851 a correspondent to *Notes And Queries* reported that in the county districts of Northamptonshire there was a general belief that toads were *venomous* like snakes, and that they were empowered with some sort of supernatural ability. It was thought unwise to even *look* at them in certain districts. What bizarre combination of circumstances brought about this awed belief in toads can only be guessed at.

ANIMAL ATTACKS

Thomas Sternberg wrote of owls in 1851, 'The ominous screech of this, the most ominous of all birds, is still heard with alarm…when, as happens sometimes, he exchanges the darkness of his ivy-bush for the rays of the sun at noon-day, his presence is looked upon as indicative of bad luck to the beholder.'

Clearly the unusual daylight appearance of an owl was regarded as an ill omen, and it is with this in mind that a Mr Louis Linnett of Luton suffered an extraordinary assault. *The Daily News* reported on 31 October 1928 how Mr Linnett had been motorcycling between Grendon and Wollaston when, somewhere in the vicinity of Lower End, he was arbitrarily attacked by an owl. The bird pulled the unfortunate man's hair out and slashed his forehead, cheeks and eyes with its beak and talons. Mr Linnett stopped the motorcycle and dived into a hedge to escape the random attack; his eyes blinded by blood from his wounds. Still the owl kept coming at him, and as the hedge offered little protection Mr Linnett was forced to throw himself onto the wet grass, face-down, in order to protect himself. Twice he beat off the owl, but both times it continued to attack him, biting his fingers as he lay on the ground. At length the owl flew off and an exhausted Mr Linnett was spotted by a passing motorist who took him to Grendon. What it was that prompted the owl's exceptionally aggressive attack, the shocked Mr Linnett could only speculate.

An earlier chapter noted the equally aggressive behaviour of a cornered rabbit in Wellingborough, and I am indebted to Ms T who provided this piece of family lore for my benefit during a visit to the south of the county. Ms T is in her 60s and recalls that as a child in the early 1950s she was told a bizarre story by her grandfather, which he told as having happened to *his* father before him. This would place events as occurring perhaps in the late 1800s. As a young man Ms T's great grandfather had been making his way back from a pub in Abthorpe (presumably the 17th-century New Inn) and had followed a path which had taken him through fields towards the old mill and the murky, sluggish little river called the Tove. His route then took him westwards along the riverbank in the direction of a footbridge over the river, and thence in the direction of Slapton. It was night-time and raining heavily, and as the young man made his tipsy way via the riverbank he became aware of two or three sleek little heads in the reeds poking up and looking at him 'like meerkats'. The animals were, of course, stoats and they appeared to be following him in the darkness, their little eyes glowing in a fixed stare. As he stumbled along the gloom of the rural riverside he noticed that there were more and more of them, when all of a sudden they swarmed out and began to perform what could only be described as a dance. There were not more than 20 of them, but they appeared to intertwine and cross paths ahead of and behind the young man, forcing him to continually look over his shoulder or else turn around in the muddy track as he walked to check behind himself. Eventually they disappeared but then seemed to regroup behind him – at which point they launched an almighty charge in his direction, forcing him to run for the Slapton bridge. However, their speed forced the young man to lose direction and run towards the soaking embankment near the bridge, where he lost his footing and flew down into the water of the river. Now thoroughly soaked, he scrambled back up and out of the muddy water and onto the bridge, which he ran across into Slapton – and then he paused for breath. Looking back he could see that the group of stoats had halted, and they now formed a line at the bridge (on the Abthorpe side) where they stayed motionless, as if wondering what to do.

The young man beat a hasty retreat through the rain back to his home in Blakesley, where he was berated by his wife for turning up home soaked and coming up with a ridiculous story. His wife accused him of falling into the river while drunk, but his story is at least partially credible. The notion so fascinated me that I looked into the behaviour of stoats and found that there was a common belief across England that stoats hunted in packs and were reputed to be able to mesmerise their prey. They also had a reputation for being prepared to assault prey much bigger than themselves, and to kill without leaving any signs of violence on the carcass. Online, there are other alleged instances of 'stoat packs' attacking human beings during bad weather conditions.

The story is a fascinating one: by the 1850s stoats were considered vermin, with one Northamptonshire farmer commenting that all sorts of 'varmints' infested his woods. There were '...pole-cats, wizzles [weasels], stoats and such'. Farmers would resort to the magic of so-called 'white witches' to keep poultry safe from 'weasels and other farmyard marauders'. They would paint a small black cross on an egg and this apparently cast a supernatural spell over the weasel, ensuring that it would stay away from the property.

Animals such as the weasel and stoat were clearly regarded warily. Maybe, when the circumstances are correct, desperate stoats will group and attack humans? It is a strange and unnerving notion, perhaps, especially for those who dwell in isolated rural areas in Northamptonshire.

BIG GAME HUNTING IN NORTHAMPTONSHIRE

On 14 June 2008 the *Northampton Chronicle & Echo* reported that yet again an animal resembling a panther had been spotted in the county. A 41-year-old man had been out walking the family Labrador in a patch of woodland near Roche Way, Wellingborough, when a large black feline animal emerged from the bushes on the overgrown pathway. The animal was witnessed from a distance of 20 yards or so and upon seeing the dog-walker seemed surprised and quickly ran into the undergrowth near some cricket pitches. The witness was quite sure that it was larger than his pet dog, and it had a very long tail which almost touched the ground before curling upwards. The encounter apparently agitated the Labrador, which began barking at the big cat.

Such incidents are now part of modern Northamptonshire folklore and there can be few who live in the county that have not at least heard the rumours that ABCs – Alien Big Cats – lurk in the more wild and remote areas of the county, and indeed the region at large. The Wellingborough Panther – and animals like him – have been reported for years in Northamptonshire now, and as with all cryptozoological creatures this raises the notion that there is not one single big cat, but rather a colony – or colonies – of them. Sightings of the 'panther' appear to date back to 1994 when such a creature was spotted between Bulwick and Southwick, which is in itself notable: this is more or less the time when the phenomena 'escalated' across the Midlands at large, with Southwick being the place geographically where one would naturally expect the big cat to start putting in appearances, given its proximity to other 'cat-heavy' counties such as Lincolnshire.

By the time it was spotted in 1997 it was clear that the big cat was here to stay. At 8:30am on 2 January it was spotted by three Kettering refuse collectors, who claimed that against the white backdrop of the snow at Great Cransley they saw – from 100 feet – a jet-black panther-like animal that looked to be about 6.5 feet (2 metres) in length. They tracked it across a field before it evaded them near woodland.

Nowadays the cat is a firm favourite with the local media. By 2002 the number of big cat sightings in Northamptonshire had risen from one a year to eight. By December 2003 the creature was being taken so seriously that the National Farmers' Union began urging farmers to keep a lookout for the animal and to photograph it if possible, following five sightings that year in Northamptonshire alone, between Kettering and Corby.

It would be self-defeating and tedious to recount every sighting of the animal(s), but some encounters do stand out as being remarkable and provide some interesting pointers. For instance, on 13 April 2004 it was reported that there had been a hair-raising incident in Lings Wood, on the eastern edge of Northampton, two weeks earlier. A man was out walking a friend's Jack Russell along a popular dog-walking route at midnight when he saw '…a mass of black jump out and a paw trying to claw the dog.' The Jack Russell had been nosing around in some bushes, and the incident so agitated the small dog that it would not allow itself to be walked along the route for some considerable time afterwards. Indeed it also unnerved the dog-walker, who commented to the local paper, 'It was very, very scary. The hairs on the back of my neck just shot up.' For some reason it is 'people out walking their dogs' who seem to experience the big cat most frequently; perhaps it is the scent that draws the normally secretive cat out into the open, before it realises that either the dog is too big to attack or that it is accompanied by a human master.

The year 2004 was a 'bumper year' for big cat sightings. It was actually spotted twice in one day, on the 25 June. A man out walking his dog at 5:30am saw a large animal about two feet high and six feet long come out of the grass and bound along the side of the River Ise towards Cheyne Walk, on the eastern outskirts of Kettering. He commented, 'I am not usually one to believe this sort of thing, but I know what I saw. It was gone in seconds.' At 10:30pm the same day the big cat was spotted near Wicksteed Park. The description was the same – large, black and feline-looking – it darted out into the road and then into the park.

Around the same time in 2004 the *Evening Telegraph* began offering a reward to anyone who could provide solid evidence that the big cat existed following an unnerving incident when a woman passenger in a car driving along Rushton Road, Rothwell, claimed that a sleek panther-like animal had raced alongside the vehicle. It was around 12.30am and in the darkness a completely black animal with a short, shiny coat flew alongside the car at 'tremendous speed' before disappearing into undergrowth. The animal had been about four-feet high and four-feet long, and its eyes had glowed supernaturally; at first the woman had thought that it was people carrying torches. On 14 July it was reported that the animal had startled another motorist near West Haddon. Here it had emerged into the road, running in front of the car before the witness even had time to apply the brakes, and disappearing into hedgerows on the other side. He commented, 'It was at least three times the size of a domestic cat and it moved like a tiger or a panther. It was a bluey-grey colour I have never seen in a cat before.'

Occasionally the Northamptonshire big cat leaves 'proof' of its existence. There are said to be instances of its footprints being discovered in muddy ground where it has been spotted south of Corby, but more substantive evidence came to light in July 2004 near the farmland at Niden Manor, Moreton Pinkney. This is in the south of the county and a long way from the animal's usual stomping ground, but on 26 July it was reported that a lady who lived at the farm was alerted by the sound of her dogs barking at 'something out there'. She subsequently found that one of the sheep had been killed by a gash to the throat, and furthermore large claw marks had rent the bark of a tree nearby. It was speculated, however, that these marks were 12 months old. This means that if the same animal was responsible for both the sheep and the tree marks then it had been resident in the area for some time, and was presumably a *different* animal to the one spotted at Kettering the previous month. The death of the sheep was attributed by an investigator from the British Big Cat Society to either a person with a large knife or a big cat; the marks on the tree could have been caused by a 'puma or a leopard' sharpening its claws, as is the habit of domestic cats. On 29 July 2004 it was even claimed that someone had managed to get a photograph of the big cat: at 10.30am the manager of a go-carting track east of Daventry looked out of the office window and saw the animal just sitting in bushes. He described it thus: 'It was about four-feet long and two-feet high, with a massive head – it was completely awe-inspiring.' He claims that he managed to grab a digital camera and get a shot of the big cat; but the *Evening Telegraph* would not pay the reward as Daventry is outside its circulation area! One would have thought that £100 for the photograph was a small price to pay for what would potentially be the scoop of the decade, so it would seem that this enigmatic photograph is, for the moment, unsubstantiated evidence. Around the same time the paw prints of a large feline were found on the other side of the county at Oundle Golf Course – leading, once again, to the supposition that there is more than one big cat out there.

On 17 January 2006 it was announced that the first British Big Cats conference would be held in March at the Sun Inn, Marston Trussell, to be attended by anyone with a keen interest in the subject, from eyewitnesses to zoologists. This coincided with the mysterious discovery of panther-like paw prints in the snow of a back garden in Market Harborough, just across the border in Leicestershire. Experts descended on the property, including zoologists from Twycross Zoo. They determined that the prints were 15cm across, 28 inches from heel to toe, and indicated the animal had quite a long stride. However, there was general agreement that the prints did not come from a feline animal – further adding to the confusion of what these animals actually might be. Whatever this particular beast was, it had managed to scale a six foot fence to get into the property, as 'skidding' track marks indicated where it had landed. It had then meandered about the back garden before scrambling back up the fence and over the top.

Is a big cat haunting the picturesque countryside around Daventry?

Since then there have been multiple eyewitness accounts in Northamptonshire's countryside of a huge feline animal, between four-and-six feet in length. It is generally described as sleek-looking and having very powerful haunches as it moves stealthily along. It is often glimpsed at night at the side of the road from the security of a car interior, with the car headlights often giving the animal's eyes an eerie glow and making its coat shine supernaturally. Or else it is seen by startled dog-walkers, who briefly catch sight of it in the undergrowth. It *appears* to favour the north east of the county, but perhaps it is getting bolder; the aforementioned sighting at Roche Way, Wellingborough, in 2008 was (for the first time) an encounter slap bang in the middle of an urban area.

One cannot help but make some fascinating observations at this point. As elsewhere in Britain, the case of the Northamptonshire ABCs presents no coherent structure: a wealth of purported evidence and yet no *absolute* proof, with genuine uncertainty as to the number, location and even the species of the elusive beasts. Explanations for the sightings, such as they are, and possible alternative identifications of the animal are consistently trotted out nationwide with so much vague surmising as to make the ABC explanation, in some cases, more plausible. For example, the feline connection has led some to speculate that they are in fact remnants of the British wildcat population. There were wildcats in Northamptonshire at one time: however, the Revd John Morton noted that they were rarely heard of by the early 1700s, although the wildcat population lingered on into the mid-1800s. Thomas Sternberg noted that discordant wailing of the wildcat, or 'birder', could still allegedly be heard at night-time in the region of Whittlewood Forest, although by his time they were a mere rumour. He speculated that if there were any left, their species would have 'degenerated' by inter-breeding with the domestic cat.

If the Northamptonshire big cats *are* wildcats this does not really explain why they went for over 150 years without being seen in the county – before the glut of current sightings began *c*.1994. The explanation also does not account for the difference in appearance and size between the British wildcat and the county 'panthers'.

Some even link the big cats to the UFO phenomenon, claiming they are displaced animals that have been 'abducted' from their natural habitat only to be returned to the wrong country. Some things can be tentatively regarded as 'definite', however, which is that unless every single witness is either hallucinating, mistaken or lying then some kind of gigantic cat, or cats (for there are surely more than one) prowls the Northamptonshire countryside. As a counter argument to this, it has been suggested that if there *were* colonies of such animals living in the remote countryside of the British Isles then surely at some point more definitive proof would have emerged than merely 'circumstantial evidence'. However, as the late sci-fi writer Arthur C. Clarke observed, the most successful of all the beasts in the animal kingdom are those which we do not yet know of, or can even prove exist.

The lack of proof, however, raises an interesting point in folklore terms. The assumption is that Northamptonshire's 'Black Beast' is a flesh and blood animal. Yet, just like all the other panthers, he will never be caught or conclusively filmed or photographed. A few footprints may be found but these will prove contentious. There will, however, be much reliable witness testimony. After the cat 'flap' (no pun intended) has died away, the animal will reappear somewhere else in the county a couple of years later, and it cannot help but be noted that in this respect these animals are phantoms not too dissimilar to the phantom 'black dogs' of days gone by – seen and yet somehow invisible at the same time. Although the phantom dog, Black Shuck, is primarily an East Anglian apparition, it is nonetheless a truism that phantom hounds were a nationwide phenomenon. In Northamptonshire there is a tradition that the country lanes of north-eastern Northamptonshire were once the haunt of a *shuck*, and the phantom black panther of today also seems to patrol this region primarily. Although this generation lives by the internet, mobile phones and DVD players – and likes to think of itself as less superstitious than generations past – this is modern folklore in the making and would seem to be the most likely type of mysterious encounter that any one of us could experience these days. If Black Shuck were a phantom ethereal hound, could it be that these black felines are his modern equivalent? Until one of the big cats *is* caught, who can tell?

COLONIES OF WALLABIES

Apart from the mystery of the big cats there may also be a colony of wallabies living in rural Northamptonshire, if recent reports in the local media are to be believed. The commotion began in January 2007 when a motorist driving near the isolated village of Maidford caught sight of a mammalian pair of eyes at the side of the road. He slowed down in order to look at the animal, which he thought was a fox – and was amazed to see that it was a creature which resembled a wallaby, sitting by the roadside and apparently waiting to cross the road. Although the animal was seen in the winter gloom, caught in the car's high beam, the motorist was perfectly satisfied that he had not misidentified the animal. In the following days local residents reported that they were finding strange footprints in fields that were, '…a bit like a dog's, but were much bigger'. People out walking their dogs in Maidford Wood were also reporting that their pets were becoming agitated and putting their noses to the ground as if they had picked up an unusual scent. Following this report, the *Northampton Chronicle & Echo* received numerous other accounts from people claiming to have seen a wallaby in the county. Many appeared to have been glimpses of the animal from drivers who shot past it in rural locations, but one woman claimed to have looked out of the kitchen window of her home in Wootton, south of Northampton, and actually seen a wallaby hopping through a field on 14 January. If this was the same animal, then it was covering quite a lot of ground in its search for food; it also, apparently, managed to successfully navigate the M1.

It should be noted that there *are* a handful of feral wallaby populations in the British Isles. In fact there have been since the late 19th century, although always in tiny numbers. Today the feral wallaby population in Britain is estimated to number less than 50. All of them presumably stem from escapees from zoos and private collections, but there has never been any confirmation of such a colony in Northamptonshire. Like the big cat scare, the whole story has the feel of a modern urban legend about it: were it not for the fact that the witnesses are always very definite about what they have seen.

Prior to the January 2007 sightings there had been another flap of wallaby sightings two and a half years previously. Where this animal came from was also unexplained, but the sincerity with which witnesses report the animal is evidenced by a story in the *Chronicle & Echo* of 12 August 2004. Duston is on the western edge of Northampton and it was here on the afternoon of 6 August that a woman spotted a wallaby bounding through her garden. It was beige, about three-feet tall and had a 'slim, whippet-like face'. It bounded like a kangaroo. A woman who was hanging out her washing the following week saw the same animal.

Northamptonshire does indeed appear to occasionally produce non-native animals and birds from its depths. On 10 May 2007 a giant, graceful peacock alighted in Cottingham Road, Corby, at seven o'clock in the morning. The royal-looking bird appeared quite tame, allowing itself to be fed, but both Rockingham Castle and Kirby Hall said it was not one of theirs that had escaped. Kirby Hall, nonetheless, agreed to give the peacock a new home. However, the mystery became compounded when, after the peacock had been captured in Oakley Vale about 10 days later and securely locked up in a rescue van, *another* peacock appeared from somewhere to strut about the gardens of the bewildered residents of Corby.

Such sightings are never really properly explained. It is as though the animals or birds have simply 'turned up' in the county. Although domesticated wallabies have briefly escaped into the Northamptonshire countryside from private collections before, there is no clue as to where the one(s) spotted in 2004 and 2007 came from. Do they perhaps form a very small feral colony, hidden away for the most part in the wilds of Northamptonshire? At the time of writing the wallaby has not been spotted for a year and a half, and perhaps it has died, although I would put money on it that, just like the Northamptonshire panther, one is spotted somewhere else in the county before too long.

THE WOMAN WHO SWALLOWED AN H'ALLIGATOR

Finally, the following story appeared in *Northamptonshire Past And Present V.4 (1969–1970)*. The story dates from the early 1900s and concerned a 'carrier' called Sarah Ann Smith who regularly undertook a journey to Northampton with a 'horse van'. On one trip she was forced to stop at an inn, suffering from sickness and complaining to the landlady that there was something in her stomach moving about. At Northampton Hospital Sarah was given an emetic that made her vomit up a live newt; how it got there was a mystery, but the doctors theorised that she may have eaten some watercress, in which the newt was concealed in its larval stage and it had subsequently grown in her stomach. Sarah was given the amphibian in a specimen jar and would ever after tell people, 'I swallowed an h'alligator and am still alive, and here is the little gentleman!'

Surely this story has to be an urban myth. You will have to make your own mind up.

CHAPTER 9

MYSTERIES OF THE SKIES

INTRODUCTION

Wherever one lives in Northamptonshire, and in whatever era, there is – and always will be – a fascination with aerial phenomena. Of course, much of those phenomena are wonderful, natural displays that fall into the realm of atmospheric and astronomical oddities; some, however, fall into the category of UFOs and the paranormal. Of the former, there have been numerous noteworthy instances recorded by astronomers.

On 20 September 1676 a meteor was observed in Northamptonshire that appeared to be exceptionally low in the skies; it was the dusk of evening but the meteor was so bright that it lit the county as though it were daytime. One observer commented, 'The smallest pin or straw might be seen lying on the ground.' It was visible for about half a minute and had a very long tail that threw out sparks.

The rash of earthquakes that shook England in the year 1750 were mysteriously accompanied by various aerial activity which terrified the populace. A spectacular aurora borealis accompanied a tremor in the Lincolnshire Fens on 23 August, while another 'quake at 2.15am in Northampton on 30 September was preceded by multiple phenomena. A Dr Doddridge wrote that he had seen a fireball a few days previously, a red sky the following night and the night following that 'the finest aurora he ever saw'. (Indeed, the earthquake of 27 February 2008, which was centred on the Lincolnshire Wolds but which also rattled Northamptonshire, was apparently preceded by mysterious lightning flashes in the sky and ball lightning.)

The *Gentleman's Magazine* reported how on 9 September 1799 'all England' had seen at 8.30pm a beautiful ball of blazing white light which moved very fast in a south-easterly direction, noiselessly and 'with a gentle, tremulous motion'. It was visible from Northamptonshire and was observed to emit red sparks as it made its soundless way through the heavens.

As noted earlier, such sights – like the comet observed prior to the Geddington rising of 1607 – were sometimes viewed with fear as portents of doom and disaster. One can imagine that the as-yet unexplained event chronicled as taking place in 1387 was seen as heralding the end of the world. The contemporary *Knighton's Continuator* recorded that in November and December of that year a 'certain appearance in the likeness of a fire' was observed in the sky from many parts of England. The appearance of the phenomenon varied from where it was observed, or on what night. Apparently, this spectacle was observed with particular clarity in Leicestershire and Northamptonshire where some saw a 'burning revolving wheel'. On another occasion it displayed itself as a round barrel of flame which emitted fire from above; on other occasions it took the form of a long fiery beam. Quite what this worrying astronomical oddity was remains open to speculation. Whatever it was, it was apparently visible in the lower atmosphere for some weeks.

Many aerial spectacles from folklore – rains of blood, dragons, 'sky battles' and so forth – have since been attributed to spectacular auroras, meteors and weather extremes. It is easy to see how our ancestors viewed the clear night sky with awe and reverence, implying as it did (and still does) a mysterious whole other realm, full of endless cosmic possibilities. In the last two or three centuries such astronomic spectacles were viewed by the learned with much less superstition but no less an amount of amazed curiosity. By May 1909 when a 'brilliant green light, similar to a rocket' was reported by the *Northampton Evening Telegraph* as having been seen shooting through the heavens by an observer in Thrapston, it was recognised for what it was: a rare atmospheric oddity and nothing more portentous.

Advances in rational thinking and science aside, the mystery of what was up there in the blanket of space had by then become stuff of lore. Antiquarian Thomas Sternberg noted how the wonder

The moon, just visible at midday, seen from Everdon.

of space, with its suggestions of unfathomable secrets and higher forms, reflected itself in the folklore of the Victorian Northamptonshire peasantry. It was considered very unlucky to point at the moon or the stars, and if one were to first see the new moon through glass then this was fatal. The new moon had, in fact, to be gazed at over the left shoulder upon first viewing and the beholder should make a wish. One can imagine, then, on the advent of a new moon, thousands of people around the country all craning their necks on the same evening in an effort to procure better fortunes than their neighbours. Perhaps the strangest belief was the one that held that a Sabbath-breaker sat alone on the moon awaiting death, having been whisked up there for some offence on a Sunday, and that he gazed back at the Earth even as those in Northamptonshire gazed up at him. Even the poet John Clare referred in his piece *The Woodman* to a curious haziness sometimes observed around the moon as though cosmic fog had blanketed it. In Northamptonshire this was referred to as the moon being 'burred', and *The Woodman* has a line:

> And burred moons foretell great storms at night;
> In such-like things the woodman took great delight.

Theories as to what was up there seem to depend upon the era one lived in and the atmospheric phenomenon concerned. From dragons and fiery portents, to sky battles and fairy tale men in the moon, we now find ourselves scientifically aware of a lot of what is out there and what is natural; but still the mystery is there, and in the modern age it has become the Unidentified Flying Object, or UFO, that is now witnessed.

A correspondent to the *Astronomical Register* noted how he had observed a strange thing through his telescope at his home in Northampton on the night of 2 May 1869. He had been observing Venus and to his bewilderment had seen a fleet of what looked like shiny objects. They looked to be different sizes, and as he watched them for an hour and a half he saw that the larger of the objects had a blueish hue to them on one side. Charles Fort, the collector of all things out-of-place, noted of this that 'the planet Venus and her veil [are] dotted with blue-fringed cupids!' This is one of the few incidences that would indicate – to the believer – that alien civilisations were scoping out other planets in our solar system before making their way to Earth. Today modern unidentified aerial objects spotted above the region are usually supposed to be either of extraterrestrial or top secret human origin.

The *Northampton Chronicle & Echo* reported in August 2007 that since 1998 there had been 27 reports of unidentified airborne objects in the county judged as credible by the Ministry of Defence. However, the MoD was at pains to point out that these are not necessarily spacecraft from another world, merely that they are 'unidentified'. In order to try and get away from the fanciful supposition that all these observations concern alien spaceships, the term UAP (Unidentified Aerial Phenomena) is now gradually replacing that of UFO; this term, however, still clearly recognises the actuality of objects/lights in the sky that cannot be identified. While the earliest unidentified aerial phenomena do suggest a misinterpretation of some spectacular natural sky activity or something of earthbound construction, the glowing metallic objects, extraterrestrial harassment and weird 'sky jellyfish' of today's Northamptonshire perhaps suggest something truly out of this world…

SKY BATTLES

Mythical phantom battles in the skies above the British Isles have occurred since Roman and Anglo-Saxon times. Around AD 230 'armies of footmen and horses were seen in the air over London and diverse other places, fighting', or else parts of England would see 'rains of blood' during some monumental shift in government. Sometimes it was fiery crosses or flaming spears which shot through the heavens that were visible. In those times such natural phenomena were taken to be portents of famine or war, but in the Stuart and Hanoverian eras 'sky battles' were seen as frightening supernatural curiosities, and it is hardly surprising that such an event is said to have occurred in the skies above Naseby following the decisive battle there on 14 June 1645.

Perhaps because of the fame – and violence – of the event it is still said that for a century or so afterwards generations of locals from the surrounding villages gathered at Naseby Field on the anniversary of the battle and watched it re-enacted in ghostly form in the sky. The booming of the guns, the cries of the charging cavalry and the screams of the wounded were all to be heard emanating from the skies. With time, so I understand, the phenomenon faded.

The historian John Morton heard of such 'sky battles', although his *Natural History Of Northamptonshire* (1712) makes it clear that he gives them little credence: he considered that extreme bad weather such as thunderstorms, coupled with the superstitious mind of the country folk, explained the entire mystery.

By 1883, when Alfred T. Story wrote his definitive *Historical Legends Of Northamptonshire*, the legend of the phantom battle in the sky above Naseby Field was commonplace. He wrote, 'It would be curious to trace the antiquity and genesis of these superstitions.' Perhaps the ferocious weather explanation when combined with the turning over of bullets, bone fragments and decayed pieces of armour at the site for generations afterwards *did* fuel this story. As late as 1830 historian Henry Lockinge had noted that the depressions of the graves of 'cannon fodder' who had fallen during the battle and been buried at the site could still be observed.

It is possible that the legend of the Naseby 'phantom battle' is a misremembering of a more thoroughly documented incident of a similar nature in the neighbouring county of Warwickshire.

Naseby: could phantom echoes of clashes still resonate in the skies?

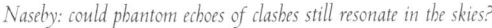

Here, the Battle of Edgehill was the first major clash of the English Civil War, and occurred on 23 October 1642. The following January a pamphlet told its readership the particulars of the '*Prodigious Noises Of War And Battle*' which had been widely reported as occurring the Christmastide immediately *following* the actual battle itself. 'Strange and portentous apparitions of two jarring and contrary armies' had fought a spectral battle in the sky in view of some shepherds shortly after midnight, with others further afield being alarmed by drums booming, muskets going off, horses neighing and wounded men screaming in pain. The rumours caused a sensation in this part of the Midlands and the hellish spectacle – obligingly – re-enacted itself with even more warlike intensity on subsequent nights for the benefit of prominent and trustworthy witnesses, including emissaries of King Charles I. The pamphlet noted that the phantom battle occurred at 'Edge Hill, in the very confines of Warwickshire, near unto Keynton, in Northamptonshire.' Subsequently this became repeated as '*Keinton, in Northamptonshire*': in fact this is Kineton in Warwickshire, so the whole episode appears to have occurred in the neighbouring county. It is therefore easy to see how Northamptonshire became associated with phantom battles after this. The Kineton 'sky battle' is usually cited as one of the most impressive accounts of such supernatural phenomena; so if such an incident could occur there then why should it not also occur at such a place as Naseby itself, where the decisive battle in the conflict occurred?

STRANGE RAIN

Occasionally, strange falls from the sky have been recorded in Northamptonshire. Among these have been the still-debated falls of 'star jelly', a clear, apparently organic, gelatinous substance that would be found deposited in fields or clinging to hedgerows. It gave off a foul odour, and county folk would refer to this matter as star jelly, star shot or star falling – the supposition among the local peasantry being that it had fallen from the stars. The antiquarian Revd John Morton wrote of star jelly, 'As to the origin of this body, it has, in many particulars, a near analogy with animal substances: it appears to me to be only the disgorge or casting of birds of three or four sorts; of those sort of fowl in particular that at certain seasons do feed very plentifully upon earthworms, and the like.' He even went so far as to dissect some of the substance and observed what he thought were blood vessels, pieces of skin and blood clots.

These observations were made in the early 18th century, but the cause of star jelly is still open to question. It was still a well-known phenomenon in the mid-19th century when folklorist Anne Elizabeth Baker noted that it was sometimes called fairy butter and was, 'A yellow gelatinous substance found on rotten wood or fallen timber and supposed by country people to fall from the clouds.' Modern cases are still sometimes reported throughout the world, and there are many who still believe that star jelly is extraterrestrial in origin. Some go even further and claim that such substances, which often dissolve shortly after having fallen, are the remains of 'atmospheric beasts' – unidentified, living organisms that inhabited the Earth's upper atmosphere and weigh less than the air, and which have since died and drifted to earth.

These notions aside, there have been other wonders that have fallen from the skies in the past. Morton also noted in his *Natural History Of Northamptonshire* of an instance when it had supposedly rained frogs. He had little time for such fancies, but was nonetheless told by a former county resident of an event that had occurred on the estate of Sir William Langham at Walgrave. The witness asserted that he had been walking the grounds when a summer storm gathered. To his surprise he saw '...in the court, kitchen-garden and coppice-close' hundreds of tiny frogs, a little larger than tadpoles. They appeared to have fallen with the rain, but displayed no sign of any injury; in fact, they seemed exceptionally lively. The air above was no darker than would be expected, and the gentlemen who witnessed the curiosity affirmed that frogs had never before been seen at the site, or in such numbers anywhere else.' He certainly believed that they had fallen with the rain, but the Revd Morton dismissed the whole allegation as preposterous. He detailed other similar accounts from Northamptonshire and suggested that perhaps the storm had enlivened hordes of frogs and

Bulwick, where 'black rain' fell.

encouraged them to 'come marching on from place to place.' Of all the people he talked to, he commented, none would admit to actually seeing the frogs *fall* from the sky, merely that it was supposed they had done.

Although not an explanation, the power of the wind can play strange tricks. In October 1690 a Mr Templar observed a single struggling jackdaw buffeted so violently by the winds of a hurricane at Braybrooke that it 'forced the guts out of the body and made it bleed plentifully at the mouth'. However, one wonders what Morton would have made of the following account that appeared in *Timb's Year Book Of Science And Art* (1851), which reported an ominous rumbling 'as of wagons' that was heard above the skies of northern Northamptonshire for almost an hour on 16 July 1850. Three days later *black rain* fell above the rectory in the village of Bulwick.

THE PHANTOM SCARESHIPS

In the early 1900s Northamptonshire, along with other parts of the British Isles, was menaced by phantom airships, or dirigibles, of unknown origin. It is a mystery that even today raises more questions than it answers.

The phantom 'scareship' enigma first gained public attention across the Atlantic in 1896. The first shaky test flights by airships in Europe were some way off, but in the autumn of that year people in San Francisco, California, were reporting that huge cigar-shaped objects with bright lights were being spotted floating through the sky. In 1897, with genuine airship activity still some months away, another wave of mysterious 'phantom airship' sightings were reported across the western and mid-western states. Rival newspapers speculated wildly as to what was going on and unknown, unnamed 'eccentric inventors' claimed the airships were their handiwork. However, the sightings died away.

The unexplainable sightings proved to be a bizarre forerunner of what was to come in other parts of the world. For in 1909 mysterious phantom Zeppelin invasions were reported in New Zealand, Australia and the UK.

In the early days this bizarre airborne horror that so fascinated the imaginations of the Edwardian public seemed to favour the region where the borders of Northamptonshire, Lincolnshire and Cambridgeshire all converge. The first major sighting of a 'scareship' in Britain occurred in the early hours of 23 March 1909 when PC Kettle's ears were alerted to the steady buzz of a high-powered engine while he patrolled Cromwell Road, Peterborough. Looking skyward, he was utterly dumbfounded – and not a little unnerved – to see a gigantic '...object, somewhat oblong and narrow in shape, carrying a powerful light', which sailed speedily through the starlit sky. PC Kettle told the *Peterborough Advertiser* this, and, although the sighting was at first dismissed as nonsense by his red-faced superiors, it was followed by reports of giant airships from all over the British Isles in the proceeding months.

On 5 May the mysterious sky-borne object was sighted again in the region. A Mr C.W. Allen was driving through the village of Kelmarsh, accompanied by some friends. All heard a loud 'bang' in the night-time sky and looked up. They heard a 'tock-tock-tock' noise as of a motor engine and saw above them a 100-foot-long, torpedo-shaped object with bright lights at either end sailing swiftly through the heavens. Although the sky was dark, they could make out a platform suspended beneath the object where figures appeared to be visible. Once again the strange object sailed in the direction of Peterborough. The bemused Mr Allen and his companions, who had slowed down their car to look at the object, thought it must be the product of an 'English inventor.' Their account appeared in the *Daily Express* a week later.

On 9 May the phantom airship was seen over Burghley House at about 11 o'clock at night – when it appeared to be shining a bright searchlight into the woodland on the edge of Burghley Park. The object had apparently found something that interested it in this extreme south-western part of Lincolnshire. The searchlight rose and fell into the woodland some eight times before the object turned and sailed south east, in the direction of Peterborough.

Also on 9 May reports came in not only from Burghley House, but Wisbech and Northampton, where another PC reported that he had seen mysterious lights sailing through the sky at around 9.30pm. Apart from the constable, hundreds, apparently, stood in the town and watched this bizarre airborne object silhouetted against the blanket of stars. It was even seen in Southend that night (20 minutes before being seen in Stamford, Lincolnshire), over the county of Essex, making it possible to give the 'scareship' an approximate speed of 210mph.

By this time PC Kettle's original account had been dismissed: the luckless constable, the public was assured, had been the victim of a practical jape, as had the people of Northampton. Pranksters had sent up a kite with a lantern tied to it and the wind had given it the appearance of movement; the motor noise that drew the constable's attention was the 'motor which goes all night in the Cobden Street bakery.' This was according to the Chief Constable of Northampton, Frederick H. Mardlin. Charles Fort, the compiler of all that did not appear to make sense, commented of this supposed hoaxer that he '…could not have been a very *practical* joker. He must have been fond of travel. There were other reports from various places in England and Wales. There were reports from places far apart.' In July an eccentric English inventor claimed that the airships had been his secret project, but this was also dismissed as nonsense.

However, by this time sightings of the objects had been reported almost daily across the south east of England, and a man walking along a lonely road over Caerphilly Mountain, Wales, claimed that he had stumbled across one of these objects at about 11pm on 18 May – and it had touched down. Two men in thick fur coats and caps were stood by the roadside, studying something in depth. The Welshman's arrival spooked them and, jabbering furiously in an unknown tongue, they clambered aboard a carriage swinging beneath a 'long tube-shaped affair', at which point the whole contraption rose clumsily in a zigzagging fashion. Newspapermen who visited the site found flattened grass, newspaper clippings and assorted random debris. Witnesses in Cardiff independently confirmed the sighting of the airship that night.

The occupants of these carriages, or 'swinging boats', beneath the airship were variously described as Germans or Orientals. Or else they were clean-shaven Americans or rude Frenchmen. They were foreign agents spying on strategic locations and were paving the way for an invasion. Or they were all hoaxes. Some even thought the clumsy contraptions contained men from the Moon, or Mars. However, as Fort recorded in *LO!* (1931), 'the stoppage [of sightings] was abrupt. Or the stoppage of publication of reports was abrupt.'

Three years later there was another wave of phantom airship sightings that began with a report of one over Sheerness, Kent, in October 1912. In 1913 they were reported in Dover, Merthyr, Swansea, Liverpool, Manchester, Scarborough…but again the whole scare came to naught.

So who sent the scareships? Given the build-up to World War One, the first and most obvious answer is that they were, indeed, German Zeppelins on reconnaissance missions. However, by 1909 there were only three working dirigibles in Germany, owing to financial difficulties and a series of crashes. Only two were in the hands of the German army, neither of which was thought technologically capable of travelling as far as the British Isles nor of undertaking the complicated manoeuvres the British scareships had done. Perhaps, then, the scareships were prototype British army airships? Again, this is unlikely, as the army's two airships – the *Nulli Secundus I* and the *Nulli Secundus II* – had been dismantled by 1909.

By 1913 the British public at large were increasingly familiar with concepts such as flight and Zeppelins, and in the tension of pre-war Europe the question of the mysterious airships ended up being debated in the House of Commons. When questioned about an unidentified dirigible spotted in Glamorganshire, MP Mr Joynson-Hicks replied, 'I don't doubt the report at all, for though our own aircraft can only do 30 or 40 miles, the Zeppelin vessels can cross the Channel. I believe, in fact, that foreign dirigibles are crossing the English Channel at will. It is a very serious matter.'

However, if the technology and capability had simply not been there in 1909, and no nation was prepared to admit responsibility in 1912, then what were the scareships that frightened the inhabitants of Northamptonshire during this time, and seemed – always – to head away eastwards towards Peterborough?

MISSING TIME IN LITTLE HOUGHTON

By 1978 the British public was greatly familiar with the concept of the Unidentified Flying Object as being 'from outer space'. A bizarre story, repeated recently in the *Northampton Chronicle & Echo*, indicates that Northamptonshire's 'first' UFO encounter took place *c.*1954 when an eight-year-old boy digging in his back garden in Rushden looked skyward and saw an oval-shaped 'cloud' from which came voices giving him instructions. The lad later claimed that he had seen several UFOs since and he may therefore be a so-called contactee. On 22 August 1960 the *Chronicle & Echo* reported that earlier that month a resident of Little Houghton had seen from his garden a yellow, circular, solid object shooting through the sky from the direction of Northampton.

Little Houghton is just east of Northampton and off the A428 Bedford Road. The little village is one of only a few in the county that has retained its oaken punishment stocks, a two-man affair, and also its whipping post dating to 1835. To the south is a dismantled railway, to the north the ancient remains of an 11th or 12th-century castle motte near the River Nene. Its antiquities aside, this place is now famous county-wide (if not nationwide) as a prime UFO 'hotspot'.

The reason for this attention is that a very strange incident occurred here in 1973, as noted in Jenny Randles' books *Abduction* (1989) and *Time Storms* (2001). It is unclear whether the phenomenon concerned was caused by a UFO or a natural wonder like ball lightning, or even some kind of time travel episode, but the story follows these lines.

Ms Randles was told the story by a man named P. In September 1973 P had been driving through Little Houghton; it was the early hours of the morning and P was returning home from a dance. He had not been drinking. As he passed the 13th-century St Mary's Church in the centre of the village, he glanced at its clock and noted that it was about 2.00am.

The next thing P knew was that he found himself stumbling about in a field in daylight, and soaking wet – although it was not raining. He recognised that he was at Bromham, a village just west of Bedford, but there was no sign of his car anywhere. It was now about 7.00am. P managed to make his way to a friend's house, where he explained that he assumed he had been in some kind of car accident and lost both his car and his memory, although he appeared to have sustained no injuries. The friend offered to drive P back along the A428 in the direction of Northampton to see if they could locate the car. Sure enough, they found the car in a field near the village of Turvey, where the borders of Northamptonshire, Bedfordshire and Buckinghamshire all meet by the Great Ouse River.

The car was in the middle of the field, undamaged and locked, although P found the car keys in his pocket. The gate on the field was closed and the car was in deep, wet mud – so deep, in fact, that P could not drive it and had to employ a farmer to tow the car out. The mud had been softened, he learned, by a torrential rainfall, which he assumed accounted for his being soaked to the skin. The strangest thing was that, despite the mud, there were *no tyre* tracks leading into the field – it was as though the car had materialised there.

In 1975, two years later, P suffered a flashback to that strange night in which he suddenly remembered that as he passed the church in Little Houghton, a 'fuzzy white glow' in front of the windshield filled his vision. There was never really any explanation for this mystery, although it bears all the trappings of a classic 'alien abduction' scenario. Jenny Randles noted in *Time Storms* an astonishing sequel to this incident: in February 1983 a motorcyclist who had just passed through Little Houghton and rounded the bend, heading towards Great Houghton, found that his bike unaccountably cut out, lights and all. It was around 7.00am, and as he wondered what to do with his malfunctioning bike he became aware of a strange 'white, egg-like glow clinging to the ground in the field next to him'. The whole area was plunged into an unnatural silence and stillness, and in this trance-like state the witness saw the mysterious misty white glow begin to wobble and gyrate 'like a spinning top'. Suddenly he realised that he was in a different position, and that he was holding the bike's keys – although previously they had been in the ignition. The bike engine worked when he turned the ignition, and, somewhat shaken, he motored back to Little Houghton – where he realised from St Mary's clock that it was now 8.30am. An hour and a half had been lost to him.

The *Northampton Chronicle & Echo* commented in 2001 of these tales that, 'while sceptics will dismiss the stories as nothing more than urban myths, for the internationally-acclaimed author (Jenny Randles) they are evidence that time-travel is a real possibility.'

Quite what was going on is unclear, although the author was inclined to class these experiences as some kind of time phenomenon. It is interesting to note that the local media picked up on stories concerning weird lights in the sky in April 1973, at Hanging Houghton to the north of Northampton, predating the Little Houghton 'time-loss' incident by five months. Here a couple spotted two glowing orange lights in the night-time sky hovering some 500 yards from their own house. They were visible for around half an hour and appeared to revolve slowly before floating away.

The *Chronicle & Echo* of 3 August 2007 covered claims of *another* such incident during that strange year, only this had taken place to the south of Northampton, at Roade. It had been mid-1973, and a couple claimed that upon leaving a friend's house in the small hours they had spotted strange red lights hovering in the sky and above the road. The area was illuminated by a huge tube of brilliant white light which prompted the couple to stop and climb onto the roof of their car to see where it could be coming from. The newspaper was told, 'That's when we saw the disc object on the ground of a field. It was as big as a football field. It was majestic, we were absolutely stunned. It was incredible.' Some 40 minutes later the couple found themselves suddenly driving down the road, unable to account for the time loss.

The coincidences are too striking to ignore. Could they all be the same thing? What were the mysterious, misty white lights that at one time haunted the area of Little Houghton, and possibly other areas on the fringes of Northampton, causing such bewilderment?

CLOSE ENCOUNTERS OF THE CHURCH STOWE KIND

In February 2008 the *Northampton Chronicle & Echo* celebrated the 30th anniversary of one of the 'classic' UFO encounters, a bizarre and frightening event which had occurred right here in Northamptonshire. It remains one of the most mystifying incidents in UFO folklore.

In the early evening of 22 November 1978 Elsie Oakensen was driving to her home in Church Stowe and had turned off the A45 onto the A5, heading in the direction of Towcester. Although there was other traffic on the road, she suddenly became aware of two unnatural lights up ahead of her – one green and one red – which appeared to be above the road. At the same time her surroundings became surreal and dreamlike (a sensation often reported during paranormal encounters) and the other traffic appeared to slow down as her surroundings grew darker and quieter. The lights, however, had taken on a 'form': it resembled a greyish dumb-bell shape, very smooth, as though made of plastic, and which had no apparent windows or doors. The green and red lights were on either side, and the object seemed to be about 100 feet above the road.

Elsie drove right underneath this weird shape and then turned off the A5, pulling the car over to a spot where it was quieter so she could observe the strange airborne object more closely. She did not stay parked for very long, however; a green light began to flash on the object and at this she decided to resume her journey. As she approached the village of Church Stowe her car engine unaccountably cut out. Frantic attempts to key the ignition soon got the car going again, but only as far as another 100 yards before the engine cut out a second time.

As the car rolled to a halt the lane in which Elsie now found herself stranded became devoid of any natural light, as though a switch had been flicked. The area was plunged into an unnatural blackness. Then, as she told the *Chronicle & Echo* on 4 February 2008, '. . .a brilliant white circle of light about a yard in diameter shone on the road.'

The next thing Elsie recalled was that she found herself driving the car normally along the same road and the natural light of early evening had returned. Strangely, some 15 minutes had passed for which she could not account. She later underwent hypnotic treatment the following year to help her remember what may have occurred; this, if anything, further mystified the whole episode. She recalled having been sat in her car with a blazing white light shining at her through the windscreen, when out of the whitish haze two strange shapes, barely defined, appeared. One was thin and long, while the other was a curious rectangular shape. They faded from view, but when they reappeared they seemed both to be silvery-grey in colour and smooth, as though polished, with rounded edges. The temperature within the car grew hotter and she began shaking but could remember little more.

Elsie's own account of her bizarre experiences were later reproduced in two books in which she clearly considers herself an abductee: *One Step Beyond: Personal Abduction Experience* (1996) and *Into The Unknown-Or Is It?* (1999). Although some have explained the whole episode to me as a combination of a monotonous drive, an unusual kite or firework being let off, flashing car headlights, hot flushes and perhaps a blackout, the *Chronicle & Echo* notes that this is 'one of the most famous UFO experiences in Northamptonshire'. The aforementioned Jenny Randles – a recognised world authority on such phenomena – took the incident seriously enough to mention it in her alien-harassment piece *Abduction*.

THE UFO PHENOMENON IN NORTHAMPTONSHIRE

The 1970s were the heyday for such weird scenarios, although perhaps the ultimate encounter occurred near Corby in September 1982, as recalled by *The People* newspaper of 20 February 1994. A couple had been driving to visit a friend when all of a sudden a white light engulfed their car, apparently caused by something hovering above. A flying object then became visible parallel to them as they travelled, and then the car engine died. The female passenger recalled that she had then blacked out and the next thing she could remember was that they had arrived some three hours later at their friend's house. The woman who gave the account claimed that she later remembered being in unfamiliar surroundings and being confronted by two strange creatures which were three and a half feet tall and had large, black, almond-shaped eyes. These beings also had slits for mouths, their skin was a greyish colour and they had no ears, but they did have two little holes for nostrils. They were hairless, and the woman recalled that she had found herself laid on a table while a taller entity – seven feet tall – prodded her and took skin samples, before inserting a needle into her stomach. She believed her ovaries had been extracted during this encounter. The story is almost unbelievably by the book; if one were asked to imagine the stereotypical alien abduction scenario, this is what they would recount. What is immediately apparent is that the media ran this story in February 1994, just as *The X-Files* became a worldwide TV hit, which says a great deal. Either the popular depiction of 'alien abductions' is an accurate one, or else the encounter was an invention, a delusion or a case of sincere misinterpretation. The same, it should be remembered, could also be said of every single 'close encounter' anywhere.

It is also clear that in many respects these encounters mirror the fairy abductions of bygone eras. Sadly, however, from the point of view of the researcher, these types of time-loss/possible abduction scenarios seem to have disappeared from Northamptonshire in the post-*X-Files* era, although the local media still report strange incidences of possible UFO activity. Some close encounters must have caused quite a stir at the time for people can (and do) remember hearing of such events. I understand from merely discussing the subject with people in Northampton that *c.*1985 there was a great furore caused in the town because something resembling a gigantic 'Chinese lantern' with different coloured lights on its edges had been witnessed swooping very low in the sky as though it were losing altitude. Furthermore, it emitted sparks and flashes as though some kind of power failure had doomed it to crash. Above Raunds a blue disc-shaped object shot through the evening sky at a height of 45,000ft on 18 August 1997.

Like the many reports of mysterious 'black panthers', it may appear to some that these UFO stories crop up on 'slow news days' across the United Kingdom generally, but this is not always the case. On 3 August 2007 the *Northampton Chronicle & Echo* published compelling evidence that some remarkable UFO encounters in Northamptonshire never made the newspapers, but were taken seriously enough to be logged by the Ministry of Defence. Under the Freedom of Information Act of 2005 it transpired that there had been 27 credible accounts of unidentifiable airborne objects in the county since 1998.

On 26 January 1998 a 'large light bulb' some 100 feet across was seen above Corby in the early hours of the morning. On 5 June 2000 there appeared three bizarre objects above the towns of Towcester and Brackley further to the south. They were bigger than a plane, glowed a brilliant orange and were shaped rectangular, squared, and the third appeared to be the shape of a hook. That same year a bemused police constable spotted a large, round pinkish object above the eastern edge of Northampton; it was the night of 23 November 2000 and this unidentified aerial curiosity appeared to have a number of smaller, circular objects attached to it. In February 2002, around mid-morning, a silver disc was spotted above Corby that appeared to be being pursued by two terrestrial aeroplanes...

Categorising unidentified aerial phenomena (UAP) is a near-impossible task due to the diversity of the sightings. Some of the sightings are undoubtedly natural, but some appear to be solid objects, and the astonishing range of weird things spotted in Northamptonshire's skies can be gleaned from a simple look at the recently released MoD archives. In one eight-month period, between February and September 2003, there was spotted an immense ball of light shooting over the county, while a brilliant orange ball made two appearances over Wellingborough. Over Northampton two large white objects moving at jet speed were spotted and appeared to be refuelling; over Wellingborough a white cylindrical object was spotted shooting very fast up into the sky; and in February a very bright white light that 'looked like a barrage balloon from World War Two' was spotted on multiple occasions. It had five smaller lights flying about it. On 17 September 2003 a witness observed two 'star-size objects' which seemed to be a rusty, orange metallic colour and which were joined by two more of the same; all four appeared to be doing manoeuvres in the night-time sky.

So it goes on. In the early afternoon of 9 January 2004 one of the notorious 'black triangles', making a rumbling noise as it shot through the sky, was witnessed *yet again* above Market Harborough. These have been spotted very frequently in the Midlands and there is speculation that they are of human origin; an above-top-secret, technologically advanced triangular aircraft of American origin referred to as TR-3B, or a so-called Unmanned Aerial vehicle (UAV) piloted by remote control.

The UAV aside, if alien visitors *are* taking an interest in earth then all one can assume is that they are from an unbelievable number of planets and piloted by a range of species, given the diversity of sightings experienced. A bizarre observation was made in the skies above the town of Daventry in 2003 which appears to fall into the realm of the completely unidentifiable – in that if they were airborne craft which were spotted then the general impression given in the media is that they swam and pulsated as though 'alive'.

Around 10pm on the evening of 22 July a man standing in his backyard with his young son spotted what he initially thought were two birds in the distant sky. Before long these objects were almost above his house in Daventry and appeared to be two brown jellyfish-like objects about the size of a coin held at arm's length. They 'swam' through the sky, pulsating at they went. They appeared to have an organic-type propulsion system which made a 'swishing' noise as they sailed slowly overhead. The witness described the objects thus: 'They were like two brown jellyfish in the sky, they looked like they were swimming'; perhaps this is the best description available to describe something completely strange which was in fact more of a 'craft' than a 'life form'. For the benefit of the sceptical it was also reported that an hour earlier a BBC cameraman in Worcestershire had apparently filmed footage of similar objects in the sky. These sensational claims were reported in the *Daventry Express* and have since been widely circulated on the web, becoming an 'internet classic'. The world's media also covered the story. Given this, even if the story turns out to be a mistake or could be explained fully, the strangeness of this claim will doubtless become part of Northamptonshire's shared folklore in generations to come. Although they may have been airborne 'craft', I am reminded of the strange, invertebrate fish-like organisms called 'Rods' that (allegedly) float around the upper atmosphere of the earth. Evidence of Rods, or 'Roswell Rods' as they are sometimes known, was first discovered by a Mexican named Jose Escamilla in the 1990s. They are thin, unidentified organic life forms that generally move through the air quicker than the human eye can perceive – but which can be captured on camcorders and the like. They appear as string-like organisms playing among the clouds and it would seem they can be anything up to 100-feet long. These objects spotted over Daventry, then, could fancifully be imagined to be their enormous 'queens'. There is even a possible link here to the organic 'star jelly' noted earlier. Interestingly, an unidentified shape in the sky in East Kilbride, Scotland, around the same time was described as a 'flying jellyfish'.

Despite the modern trappings of such observations, it is clear that UFOs are a form of new folklore. It is a kind of realm where the Anglo-Saxon world of the fiery flying dragon and mediaeval abductions by earthbound fairies collide with a more technologically advanced age. It is also clear that the 'early' UFOs took a form dependent on the technology of the times: 1909 was the year of the scareship invasion – these mysterious airships were thought to be of foreign origin. They were not seriously thought of as 'spaceships' at the time, but some 40 years later such mysterious sky borne objects became 'alien craft'.

As with ghosts, it is notable that the way strange aerial phenomena are perceived has changed over the decades and centuries. 'Close encounters' are rarely reported these days: could this be that in this

RAF Grafton Underwood, north east of Kettering – a salute to a different type of aerial activity.

internet age they would no longer stand up to scrutiny? You will have to make up your own minds. However, in instances such as the strange 'sky jellyfish' over Daventry it is difficult not to believe the sincerity of the witnesses who can be assumed to have at least seen *something* strange, even if it was not a *bona fide* alien spacecraft. People on the whole are not fools and have enough intelligence to recognise very rare *natural* phenomena in the sky for just that. What this brief study of unexplained aerial activity in Northamptonshire shows is that for all the tall tales or misidentifications, there are still instances where people with nothing to gain make credible observations: people, it is assumed, capable of correctly relating what they think they have seen – or actually *did* see – in the skies above Northamptonshire.

CHAPTER 10

INEXPLICABLE INCIDENTS, BIZARRE BEHAVIOUR AND PECULIAR PLACES

INTRODUCTION

The scholarly Gervase of Tilbury wrote in his giant *Otia Imperialia* (1214) that there could be found 'in the diocese of Lincoln in a place called by the inhabitants Rodestrim' a large stream, which could be awkwardly crossed by way of a small ford. There the local peasants claimed if two horses of unequal size were driven into the waters, at no matter what point, when the animals alighted up the bank on the other side they were always found to be wet to exactly the same levels on their bodies. Nearby, Gervase noted, was 'a tomb open to the air which will fit any grown man.' Historians have tentatively placed these curiosities at Roade or Radstone in Northamptonshire, both of which have nearby streams.

It is assumed that Gervase meant that should a corpse be put in the tomb then it would 'mould' itself to fit the exact proportions of the body, and this oddity is intriguing as it foreshadows a pattern of marvels and natural wonders linked to the beautiful Northamptonshire landscape. Collected by a somewhat sceptical Revd John Morton, there appeared in his grandly titled *The Natural History Of Northamptonshire, With Some Account Of The Antiquities To Which Is Annexed A Transcript Of The Domesday Book So Far As It Relates To That County* (1712) a curious – not to say terrifying – anecdote attached to the mediaeval motte-and-bailey earth mound at the crossroads between Farthingstone and Weedon Bec. Morton was told by workmen who had been digging for stone among the remains of castle dykes that their excavations had revealed a great square room within the earthmound. As they looked at the moss and lime-covered stone walls in curiosity, they laid a ladder against the wall so they could move the stones up and out of the strange place and to the surface. As they set about this, the ladder almost immediately began to sink into the ground, carrying one fellow into the ground up to his waist with it as though it were quicksand; for under the room was another, and the disturbing of the earth released a horrendous stench of death and decaying corpses, sending the workmen scrambling out of the depression and onto the surface. Revd Morton noted that the sinister site was afterwards filled in and he appears to have had little patience for the un-scientific manner in which the discovery was handled; he would have had even less time for the superstitious claims that the woodland was, or is, haunted, or that the workmen had discovered the very entrance to Hell.

Daniel Defoe's 18th-century *A Tour Thro' The Whole Island Of Great Britain* (1724–27) took him to Boughton House, built in the manner of the Palace of Versailles. The grounds of the house exceptionally impressed Defoe, but he was less than impressed by the 'petrifying spring' within the grounds. He commented that he was told 'so many stories of its turning everything that was laid in it into stone, that we began to discredit the tale as fabulous; but I have been assur'd, that the water of this spring does really petrify, and that in such a manner as deserves the observation of the curious.' It was even said that at Sidney College, Cambridge, there resided a skull taken from this spring which had been literally turned to stone by its qualities. On one occasion this curiosity had been brought to King Charles I so he could see it for himself. There were held to be several such springs in Northamptonshire, which were referred to as 'stone-water' springs and to which local farmers led ill livestock: two or three drinks of the water and any animal suffering from 'the fluxes' would recover.

Revd Morton also noted in the early 18th century that the slopes along the River Welland, as it flowed along Northamptonshire's north-western border, were commonly known as 'moot-hills'. In times past folk had taken themselves to these hills along the valley of the river whenever any danger threatened their district; there the hills were 'consulted' and one can imagine delegations of villagers attempting to ritualistically appease Mother Nature herself when, say, flooding was imminent. The veneration of the natural landscape of Northamptonshire is something that has survived long beyond the lingering superstitions of the age of Morton and Defoe, and there are modern examples to be found in this final chapter.

Indeed, it is noticeable that such veneration of the wonders of the natural landscape forms one of the staples of Northamptonshire folklore – alongside the county's curious associations with beliefs and legends linked to the animal kingdom, and of course its ghost stories. However, as the previous chapter on the mystifying aerial visitors seen over the skies of the county indicates, such love of the bizarre and out of the ordinary is more universal these days.

There are many examples and anecdotes of things that do not appear to make sense in any kind of rational way. Sometimes this can take the form of human curiosities; such as extreme old age or unusual physical characteristics. There are also several well-attested examples of human behaviour that cross over into the paranormal: astral projection, and an equally well-attested example of what appears to be some kind of time-slip, something apart from a routine ghostly encounter.

However, some anecdotes are just utterly random: the *Daily Express* of 12 June 1919 reported that a woman was shocked to witness a basket of clothes simply fly into the air accompanied by a loud 'bang'. The incident happened at Islip, west of Thrapston, and the unaccountable 'force' shot the clothes upwards and flung them all about the premises. Charles Fort, the Albany-born compiler and

A memorial near Brixworth to Viscount Chesham, killed in 1907 during the Pytchley Hunt.

chronicler of all things irrational, thought it may have been due to some kind of cosmic – but ineffectual – teleportation incident. In July 2003 it was reported that several inches of water was somehow flooding the cellars of homes in Argyll Street, Northampton – although where the water was coming from was a total mystery. The weather conditions were very dry, and yet after being pumped out the cellars would always be found flooded again within hours. Exhaustive tests revealed that it was not sewage or tap water from a burst pipe, nor water from local rivers, leaving the Environment Agency scratching its head as to just where it was coming from.

Fort was also fascinated by coincidences, particularly coincidences where patterns emerged. In 1873, he noted, even the *New York Times* had found a string of deaths, serious injuries and accidents across England linked to foxhunting noteworthy. All had happened within the space of a couple of days, in places as diverse as Gloucestershire, northern England and Lincolnshire. In Northamptonshire, added to this list of disasters was the fate of one General Mayow, who had collapsed and slid off his horse, dead, during a hunt in Pytchley. Fort remarked that there appeared to be either an invisible hunt-saboteur travelling around England or else an 'incident force related to the common character' was at work. Certainly a wounded partridge had 'revenge' of a sort in 1797 after being shot by members of a hunting party at Old. A servant attempted to finish the bird off by clubbing it with his gun; unfortunately the weapon went off, and one of the shooting party, the vicar of Pytchley, was shot dead.

After phantom battles, walking dolls, witchcraft, unidentified flying objects and black panthers, this chapter is concerned with all the rest: everything that does not quite fit the perceived order of things in Northamptonshire.

HUMAN ODDITIES

Apart from the gravely interpreted births of monstrously deformed infants mentioned elsewhere, there are other allegations of truly bizarre and wonderful human characteristics of the sort that P.T. Barnum would have given his right arm for. For example C.H.M.D. Scott, the Edwardian poet who drew upon Northamptonshire's folklore for inspiration, heard that a bearded lady had lived in Bulwick. Apparently, at one time this woman had been a celebrated beauty in London's society during the reign of King Charles II (1660–85). Scott even heard that she had fought – and won – a duel to gain her husband. However, by the time she inherited Bulwick Hall from a cousin, the husband had died and she had become a bedraggled, hunchbacked crone with a great beard. During her reign at the hall, servants were terrified of her, as were the villagers. Quite who this 'old crusted harridan' with her 'horrid beard' was is not known, but if she was a real person then presumably she was related to one of the Tryon line who historically owned Bulwick Hall.

Stories of those who lived to great age have also fascinated the county. John Mastin's *The History And Antiquities Of Naseby* (1792) recorded that a farmer by the name of Corby, who resided in the village, had died aged 94. This quarrelsome old man had astounded his family by cutting an entirely new set of teeth at the ripe old age of 70, which served him with no problems until the day that he died. However, surely the champion of all age-related mysteries is the following amazing story.

In Northampton a button-maker named John Bayles died on 4 April 1706 – allegedly at the unbelievably old age of 130. His sinewy, wizened and ancient-looking figure had been familiar at market for as long as anyone could remember; even those in the town who were in their 80s and 90s said that they remembered Bayles from their childhood and he had seemed like an old man even then. It appeared that the parish registers did not go back far enough to record his birth some time in the middle of the Elizabethan era. Bayles himself had always affirmed that as a young man he had been at Tilbury, Essex, on 9 August 1588 when Queen Elizabeth herself had famously inspired the troops during the war against the Spanish Armada. There was general agreement that Bayles was *at least* 120 years old when he died, and possibly much older. A surgeon, Dr James Keill, who was privy to his death and dissection, commented that there was nothing noticeably different about Bayles's diet; he had eaten what he could get his hands on. In the end he conceded that in all probability Bayles had lived, '…in three centuries and seven reigns.'

We can add to these curiosities the phenomenon of extreme stature. *The History, Gazetteer & Directory Of Northamptonshire* noted that in the village of Alderton a surprising find was made during renovations to St Margaret's Church in 1847. Workmen removing the ancient altar tomb of William Gorges, Esq (said to have built a large manor house in the area during the reign of King Henry II) found a stone coffin in which was contained the giant skeleton of a mysterious man of 'large dimensions'. In the late 1700s the celebrated 'Irish Giant', Patrick Cotter O'Brien, who died in 1806, stayed for a time in Northampton. Anthropologist Edward Fawcett's *Journal* (1909) recalled that Cotter stayed in Northampton around 1785, and some 20 years after Cotter's death aged 45 there were still those who remembered how the giant had gotten into an argument in a barber's shop and how he had picked his antagonist up off the ground and held him by the scruff of the neck, shaking him like a rag doll. Folklore recalls Cotter's height as being anything up to 10 feet: in 1972 his skeleton was examined and it was established that his height was a no-less-impressive eight feet one inch – making him the tallest reliably recorded human ever at that time.

Perhaps a less reliably recorded human feat is another staple of Fortean strangeness: prodigious vomiting. Joseph Glanvill's *Saducismus Triumphatus* (1689) recorded a truly remarkable instance of this. In 1658 a 10-year-old girl was reckoned to have vomited three full gallons of water in under three days at her home in Welton. Shortly afterwards, the girl's elder sister told adults that the victim was now vomiting stones and pieces of coal. Before long she had produced some five hundred stones and coals in this unconventional manner, some of which weighed a quarter of a pound. Some were so big that those assembled had to force open her mouth in order to get them out of her system. There is a suggestion that the whole episode coincided with outbreaks of poltergeist-like activity and was laid at the door of witchcraft or possession – but what was *actually* happening is now unclear. Glanvill apparently found the tale at least half-believable; there were certainly eyewitnesses who testified to the truth of events. Gilbert Clerk of Loddington first wrote of this mystery 'at the house of the widow Stiff' in a letter to Sir Justinian Isham: Clerk apparently thought that the father of the girls may have been encouraging them somewhat in their claims.

Following the Battle of Naseby on 14 June 1645, there was a remarkable story of recovery. A Mr Trussell was seriously wounded in the chest and his corpse was thrown on the pile of dead. In the chaotic aftermath his blood-caked body was carted back to his home in Thorpe Malsor. As he was prepared for burial, the daughter of the apothecary – out of sympathy – held the hand of the slain man and commented, 'This certainly was a gentleman' since his hand was so soft. However, the body was not yet cold; a weak pulse was discovered and frantic efforts managed to revive the 'dead' man. Mr Trussell ultimately fully recovered, and handsomely rewarded the young lady who had been his saviour.

Perhaps the most outrageous – but likely true – story about such phenomenal human ability comes from Edge Hill, and the battle that occurred there on the morning of 23 October 1642. During that bitter, indecisive clash in the hinterland of the region, where Warwickshire, Oxfordshire and south-western Northamptonshire all meet, a truly remarkable incidence of survival occurred that almost defies belief, and which was noted at the time by the Royalist chronicler of events Sir Richard Bulstrode. During the battle Sir Gervase Scroope (who fought for the king) fell as he attempted to leave the scene of the conflict at about three in the afternoon; he was wounded and losing much blood. By the time he collapsed, he was close to death and did not have long. When the fighting receded into small-scale chases and skirmishes, local people appeared from the surrounding villages and, like scavengers, began to strip the bodies of the slain. Sir Gervase was stripped completely naked and thrown where he was found. It was the following Tuesday before his son, Sir Adrian, managed to get to the site, where he found his father lying in the dirt surrounded by the corpses of 60-or-so from his Lincolnshire-raised regiment. Sir Adrian had only recently made peace with his father following a family quarrel and so now – sure his father was dead – the body of Sir Gervase was sadly taken to a nearby tavern somewhere in the region of Kineton.

The nobleman had suffered no less than 16 serious wounds, but unbelievably he began to stir when he was laid out before the fire. Frantic massaging managed to restore movement, and gradually Sir Gervase – only half an hour before thought dead – was managing to mumble and beginning to move again.

The two nights that Sir Gervase had been laid in the wilderness had been freezing cold, and it appeared that these frosty conditions had slowed down his metabolism to put him into a state of suspended animation just long enough for his rescuers to find him. Fearing there may be others in the same state, a party scoured the region of the battle – and unbelievably found another man named Bellingham who had suffered the same indignity. Bellingham too was brought back from the dead, but lived for only 10 days as his 20 wounds were too severe. However, Sir Gervase lived for another 10 years, dying in May 1655.

THE FOLKLORE OF BLOOD

Daniel Defoe's *Tour Of A Gentleman Vol II* notes the following: 'From Daventry we went a little out of the road to see a great camp, called Burrow Hill…They say this was a Danish camp, and everything hereabouts is attributed to the Danes, because of the neighbouring Daventry, which they suppose to be built by them. The road hereabouts, too, being overgrown with Dane-weed, they fancy it sprang from the blood of the Danes slain in battle; and that if, upon a certain day of the year, you cut it, *it bleeds.*'

Dane-weed, or Danewort, is actually the European Dwarf Elder plant. The site mentioned is Borough Hill, on the eastern edge of Daventry, and the discovery of coins bearing the features of Roman emperors here indicates that it is, in fact, vastly older than the Anglo-Saxon era.

For centuries the Danes formed a part of Northamptonshire's folklore in their own right. The natural historian Morton recorded that numerous hill forts were supposed to be Danish settlements, and that bone deposits were always assumed to be the remains of some slaughter they had carried out. In AD 870 the Abbot of Peterborough and 84 monks were butchered by an army of marauding Danes, who largely conquered the area for some 45 years before being forced out by King Edward of Wessex c.AD 918. Northampton itself was pillaged and burnt in AD 1010 by armies under King Svein Forkbeard of Denmark, who was enraged by the murder of his sister during unprecedented anti-Danish rioting eight years before in south and central England. The riots and the Danish backlash claimed tens of thousands of lives, and the folklorist Sternberg noted that these events, even a millennia later, had left the Danes despised in Northamptonshire as a kind of collective bogeyman figure. This was even despite such incidents as the massacre of AD 1065 when the county was laid waste by the marauding armies of Earl Morcar – the earl of Northumbria and not a Danish invader. Houses were burned, the men murdered and the crops were either stolen or destroyed and the county was for 'many winters the worse' as near-famine and depopulation threatened the region. Yet, Sternberg wrote, 'innumerable legends are still current of battles, burnings etc in which the Danes play the most conspicuous part. There would appear still to remain a traditional remembrance of their oppression.' No later battles or outbreaks of vicious rioting in the region appear to have eclipsed this sentiment.

Vegetation that grows spontaneously from the blood-soaked ground of battle sites is a common theme in British legend, as is the supposition that such plants will bleed when cut. A story with a similar theme was told to Sternberg in the 1850s as having happened 'a few years ago'. A man had been passing by a tree at Syresham when a little boy asked him if he would cut a branch off the tree for him to play with. The man obliged, but upon cutting the branch a stream of blood jetted from its severed limb. Some time later, an old woman from the village was seen with her arm bound up and it was assumed that she was a witch who could transform herself into a tree. Quite why she would do this is unclear, but at any rate the villagers ducked her in the pond to teach her a lesson.

Nearer the present day it is the phenomenon of indelible, or phantom, bloodstains that are perhaps most familiar. The ominously named Haunt Hill House on Kettering Road, Weldon, was built c.1640 and has been a listed building since 1951. This Jacobean building, also known as Weldon Cottage, is claimed locally to be very haunted, although whether this is on account of its name (or whether its name is on account of the haunting) I cannot seem to verify. A gentleman is supposed to have hanged himself above the staircase, and it is this very staircase which I have heard is supposed to leak a red liquid, which proves very difficult to remove and will always reappear. Despite its gloomy reputation, this eerie-looking building (with its stone lions flanking the lobby entrance and its gothic chimney stack protruding from the middle of the roof) was sold in July 2007, as reported in the *Northants Evening Telegraph*.

Haunt Hill House.

HEALING SPRINGS AND WELLS

We have already seen that there were instances of miraculous 'healing springs' being utilised by the more affluent in days gone by, but the phenomenon was a wide-reaching one. The petrifying spring at Boughton House, Saint Rumbald's Well at Astrop House, St Thomas's Well at Northampton, the well of Boughton church, even the 'presaging' Marvel-Sike well of Church Brampton...the list goes on, and there are many other sites with their own stories. There must be, as they say, something in the water.

The antiquarian John Cole wrote in 1837 that it was supposed that Wellingborough had developed its name from its associations with healing springs and wells; historically, the town had been called Wendlingburgh. One spring, called the Red Well, was particularly famed. Cole wrote, 'This chalybeate spring rises in a field about a half-a-mile northwest from the town.' It even received the patronage of King Charles I who visited with his wife and the royal physician in 1628. A grand marquee was set up at the site and a band played; in fact, the whole town turned out to cheer as the king partook of the healing qualities of the waters 'at source'. For 200 years the Red Well was a place of pilgrimage, but by the early 18th century its fame had dwindled and it was by then difficult to find. In fact, many of the sites of these healing wells and springs had fallen out of favour with the fashionable set by the time their fantastic properties were written of, their grandness only recalled by folkloric tales. Near the Red Well was another called the Stan Well, which legend said held the same petrifying properties as the waters at Boughton House. Cole thought this worked by the water 'encrusting different substances with *calcarious* earth.' Out in a field on the Thrapston road was the Lady's Well, which, it seemed, had been the subject of veneration since Roman times; this was indicated by the discovery of a Roman-era silver coin at the site. Another on the outskirts of Wellingborough was called the Rising Sun Spring, which faced to the east and was reputed to contain waters that could heal any eye ailment. In days past, the Well of St Loy at Weedon Lois was thought to cure even the blind and the leprous without fail. At the Spring of St Denis, Naseby, it was customary to bring sick and injured children and dip them in the waters for nine successive mornings to affect a cure. The waters were said to be exceptionally cold, even in the middle of summer. This spring was to be found a mile west of the village but by 1791 had become neglected and overgrown. A nearby spring, called the Scrough Hill Spring, was observed to be yet another 'petrifying well', as was judged from the 'yellow *ochreous* colour of the earth and stones'. At some time a piece of prehistoric wood had been found in its waters, petrified almost into the texture of stone. In Barnwell there were seven wells, it being the custom among the peasantry to dip sickly children into the waters. From their alleged healing properties it became the supposition that angelic beings had 'purified' the water, and villagers are said to have performed 'mystical and puerile' rites at Barnwell in honour of this.

Thomas Sternberg noted in 1851, however, that many of the ancient healing or holy wells were still called by these names: 'Many of these [mineral springs] still retain their title, and their waters are still considered efficacious for external application. Such names as Rood-well, Cross-well, Monk's-well, are of frequent occurrence.' It was certainly remarkable and curious, noted the *Provincial Medical And Surgical Journal* in 1844, that Northamptonshire appeared comparatively free from the epidemics that took such a huge toll of life in other parts of Britain.

The alleged mystical healing properties of such springs still greatly fascinates; the local media speculated in February 2007 that with 'traditional forms' of healing becoming popular there might be a resurgence of interest in Northamptonshire's numerous sources of pure water. However, the locations of some are lost in time, while still others have fallen into dilapidation; some are now inaccessible, being on private land, while others are waiting to be found. On 30 September 2005 a 30ft well, covered by earth and rusted corrugated iron, was discovered by chance on the football field of the Community Primary School at Bugbrooke – when a child partially fell into it. As reported at the time, 'Mystery surrounds the history of the well, as no one in the village seems to remember it being there.'

WONDERS OF THE NATURAL WORLD

Notes And Queries reported in 1890 that in Mears Ashby there was an old elm tree, probably about 300 years old, which had become known as the 'Tinker's Tree' on account of the belief that a passing tinker had thrust his staff into the ground there – and it had subsequently blossomed into the mighty tree. A nearby house bore the sign 'The Tinker and Tree' in recognition of this event. There are other phenomena rooted in the natural world of Northamptonshire that inspire wonderment, including the following amazing event which took place on 30 November 1872 and was first reported in the *Banbury Guardian*. At about 1.00pm the sky above Banbury, Oxfordshire, became very dark and heavy rain began to fall. There was an enormous thunderclap accompanied by vivid lightning, With this, a strange force of nature materialised and tore its way through the region between Banbury and Brackley, in the south of Northamptonshire. It was described in the newspaper thus: '...something in the shape of a haycock, accompanied with fire and dense smoke, revolving through the air, making a noise similar to a railway train in motion, but a great deal louder, and travelling much faster.' Sometimes it was high in the air, and sometimes near the ground. Between King's Sutton and Aynho this frightening spectacle ripped up trees while making its way north west with a screaming, whizzing noise like an oncoming train; it apparently changed direction and ripped up a tree that a man had previously been sheltering under. By the time it reached Newbottle it resembled a ball of flame and was tearing up trees, smashing down walls and whipping thatches off roofs as it made its destructive way. The destructive element was apparently an exceptionally aggressive localised tornado, but the description – 'a huge revolving ball of fire travelling from six to 10 feet off the ground' – is confusing, and not to mention a little unnerving. It destroyed everything in its way, even sweeping up water from a pond, and made a horrific noise. However, at Newbottle the whole thing simply disappeared in a second before terrified spectators without even a bang: it just simply vanished. It had travelled a distance of roughly two miles and had left the smell of sulphur in its path. Some fled, apparently thinking it was the Devil; rational voices, although recognising that this was not the case, were nonetheless bemused by the event.

Many scientists studied this incident, and it was fully examined in *The Meteorological Magazine*, which drew attention to thunderstorms in Newbottle earlier that June and horrific gales that pounded Oxfordshire not long after this strange event. The 'ball of fire' was later explained by friction from the whirlwind causing the vegetation it swept up to combust, but the behaviour of the phenomenon appears to suggest some extreme example of ball lightning accompanying a tornado.

Ball lightning itself is a phenomenon still largely unexplained, and there is a suggestion that such 'earth lights' can haunt a particular spot for years and even display behavioural patterns: people have even reported what sounds like 'interaction' with earthlights, such as being chased by them or observing them 'switch off' when approached. Atmospheric conditions appear to have to be correct and scientists (while acknowledging their existence) still find the nature of these incidents puzzling. This is a realm where some of the curiosities noted within these pages all converge; for ball lightning/earthlights have been put forward as a possible explanation for such assorted things as ghosts, UFOs and the 'trickster sprites' such as the Shag Foal. It has also been suggested that ball lightning is responsible for creating the crop circles that today's generation are so familiar with – although why it should have started doing this only fairly recently is another unanswerable question.

The first time crop circles materialised in the county was in 1978 when a 'double-ring' was discovered in a field at Twywell, between Kettering and Thrapston, but they have been found all over the county since then. Some of them (including the majestic Woodford Rings of 1991 and the complex, 160-metre-wide five-pointed star shape found at Cranford St Andrew the following year) have been claimed by hoaxers. In June 2001 a giant circular crop circle was discovered in a barley field at Wakerley, which resembled an intricate Aztec tribal design.

There is a persistent urban legend that during the making of the Cranford St Andrew circle the hoaxers saw what appeared to be a glowing orange ball of light over the field about a quarter of a mile away, which faded away before the stunned group. However, some folk do appear to be able to 'connect' with nature. *The Builder* (2 April 1891) notes that a committee from the Northamptonshire County Asylum had recently 'employed the services of John Mullins, of Grantham, Lincolnshire, a self-dubbed "water-diviner" who pretends to find water through the action of a fork-shaped twig.' Staff and patients were treated to the bizarre sight of this individual walking round the grounds to see where his twig would point out the presence of water. Perhaps a good modern example of the veneration with which Northamptonshire's beautiful rolling countryside is still held is the following anecdote, submitted to *Fortean Times* magazine in 2004. Three years earlier, the correspondent wrote, he had been walking through Wakerley Great Wood on a sunny summer's day with his girlfriend when the attention of both was drawn to a strange rhythmic noise that was almost akin to a sensation – 'a dull throb, best described as a kind of chthonic heartbeat.' This 'heartbeat' was apparently all about them, as though it somehow inhabited the woodland itself, and the pair found it quite unpleasant, as if they were a mere part of the inner workings of something much greater. There were no roads anywhere nearby and the mystified correspondent could only note, '...whatever was producing the vibration was massive, as it seemed to pervade the Earth and air.' True believers might be tempted to speculate that it was the very life force of the Earth itself that the couple tuned in to.

CURIOUS CURES

Springs and wells aside, the belief that the natural world harboured many 'miracle' cures for a variation of ailments is long gone in the county. The science of the application of such cures has also died out, leaving us to wonder whether these remedies actually worked and who the desperate, brave and stupid people were who actually tested some of the cures concerned. Well into the 1800s, such cures were practised by Northamptonshire's 'white witches', or 'cunning men', as a trade plied alongside the counteraction of witches' spells. This is an area where veneration of nature, phenomenal human healing ability and even harmless witchcraft collide, and it says much about the county in days gone by. Thomas Sternberg noted in *The Dialect And Folk-Lore Of Northamptonshire* (1851) that in the whole county, but especially in the south, there were few villages that did not employ '...a professor of the healing art, in the person of an old woman, who pretends to the power of curing diseases by charming.'

The general routine was something like the following. The invalided or sick person would arrive at the premises of the white witch to seek a cure. The sufferer had to turn up absolutely convinced that the cure they were about to receive would work, and during the whole consultation they must not say 'please' or 'thank you'. The healer would cross the afflicted part of the body and whisper 'certain mysterious words'. Sternberg was unable to discover what these words were, or even *might* have been, due to the belief that once disclosed the healer would lose their powers, and all cures affected by them would fail. An old woman in her nineties, who lived near Brackley, had gained a great reputation for healing agues; the most information she would provide Sternberg with was that she had received the secret incantations from the lips of her mother as she lay on her deathbed, who had received them in a similar fashion from her own mother before that. Sometimes little pendants or pieces of leather had to be worn round the neck of the sufferer, never to be removed – for once they were the healing powers of the charm would be broken. In Brackley there was great sadness because it looked as though the old woman might die without passing these secrets on to anyone.

Some cures were more widely known about, however, and needed no secret rites. Someone suffering from a painful sty on his or her eyelid needed to procure a black cat on the first night of a new moon. A single hair was pulled from the tail (an act which usually resulted in 'sundry severe scratches' from the annoyed cat) and rubbed gently nine times over the sty. If one were suffering a nosebleed a toad needed to be captured. It was then stuck through with a pin or a nail and hung in a little bag around the sufferer's neck. For those afflicted with warts, a snail had to be obtained; then for nine successive nights the snail had to be rubbed on the wart and then impaled on a thorn. As the snail withered away and died so too would the wart, it was believed.

Some cures were not so disgusting, however, just surreally bizarre. The wearing of a nut in the pocket as a prevention against toothache was apparently commonplace at one time in Northamptonshire. In the 19th century *Notes & Queries* frequently featured such oddities from the county as observed by its readership: a female suffering from epilepsy could be cured if nine pieces of silver money and nine three-halfpences were collected from nine bachelors. The silver money was fashioned into a ring to be worn by the afflicted person while the rest of the coins were presented to the blacksmith for his trouble. If it was a male suffering fits, then the charge was levied upon nine females. Quite why or how this was supposed to work is not clear. In Marston St Lawrence it was the custom to collect any rainwater that fell on Holy Thursday as this was supposed to cure diseases of the eye. Ascension Day of 1854 thus saw the entire village out with their buckets during a heavy rainstorm.

One 'cure' that says much about how times have changed was the ghoulish belief that the dead hand of an executed criminal had to be rubbed over a wart three times in order to get rid of it. Edwin Radford, writing in 1949, noted that this belief prevailed 'especially in the county of Northamptonshire' where a queue of people would form at the foot of the gallows and pay the executioner outrageous fees to be allowed to touch the hand of the swinging corpse. The act was called the 'dead stroke'.

There is a general impression that there was thought to be something 'miraculous' in the properties of nature which, when applied correctly, might even save lives. One assumes that by the time they were noted for posterity by writers such remedies were well established across the county. Presumably, then, some of them must have worked to one degree or another in order to have persisted for so long. However, those days are long-gone now, and I would defy anyone in this day and age to touch a corpse or hang a toad round their neck in a bag to cure some ailment…although I cannot help but wonder what the results would be.

STATUES THAT COME TO LIFE

One of the great staples of supernatural legend is the supposed instances of images coming to life. In most cases the story is related to faith: images of the Virgin Mary or Jesus Christ weeping tears or else displaying wet blood, or even stepping from stained-glass windows bathed in an ethereal light. There are mythical instances, however, of *statues* that are believed to come to life. Perhaps the best known is the story of Pygmalion, a Cypriot sculptor of the pre-Christian era who supposedly carved a beautiful woman out of ivory; the goddess Aphrodite eventually granted this carved woman the gift of life, and Pygmalion married her.

The romanticism of this notwithstanding, there are a couple of instances of statues that are supposed to possess 'life' in Northamptonshire. The palatial Boughton House, a stately home in the parish of Weekley with foundations that date to the 15th century, is the seat of the Duke of Buccleuch. From the impressive northern front it gives the impression of a French chateau and its grandness has led to its being labelled the 'English Versailles'. A Dutch landscaper named Van der Meulen was employed to furnish the estate with lakes, ponds, fountains and ornate gardens, and by 1706 it was noted that Van der Meulen had completed the immense, rectangular ornamental pond, which was the pride of Boughton House and was called the *Grand Etang.* Today this remains only as a depression in front of the stately home.

The water features within the grounds were fed by a complicated system of sluices, springs, natural contours and streams linked to the diverted River Ise. One of the springs that fed the system was located on the fringes of Weekley itself, and here there stands (hidden among all the bracken at the end of what was once called Wash Well Lane) a badly weather-damaged statue of a bearded, biblical-looking man who for at least two centuries has been known as 'Stone Moses'. The duke is said to have moved Stone Moses from Boughton Park to this out-of-the-way spot around 1700, perhaps because he tired of the image; although he did apparently place Moses in an ornamental pond of his own. The job must have been an expensive one as he stands upon an exceptionally large and heavy-looking stone platform. It is perhaps this move that has given rise to stories locally that say he can move atop his stone platform. Despite his poor condition, Stone Moses is reckoned to be physically capable of stepping down from his gigantic plinth at midnight 'on certain times of the year' in order to sup from the nearby River Ise.

Stone Moses hides in virtually impenetrable woodland at Weekley.

In trying to find this curiosity I had to ask someone in the thatched cottage village of Weekley. I was told, intriguingly, that if one were to shine a torch on Stone Moses at midnight and then return an hour later, a slight shift in his position could be noted. I suspect, if anything, this has more to do with the fact that his hands and face are badly damaged; the emphasis of the position of the moon may further explain the phenomenon. Interestingly, there are other instances of this type of myth in Northamptonshire, which involve carved or stone images climbing down church faces to go to a nearby brook to get water before returning to their cubby holes or plinths.

In August 2008 I made a valiant attempt to try and locate Stone Moses and was pointed towards a great patch of woodland and thicket near the southern edge of Boughton Park. Unfortunately much of it is securely fenced off and the parts that are not are so inaccessible it would make any search impossible. Once or twice I thought I could espy him, deep in the woodland, and although this may have been a trick of the light I am sure he is in there. In the end I had to abandon the search, soaked and scratched from the effort. The fact that he is now so inaccessible adds an even more curious aspect to this tale. There is something a little unnerving about Stone Moses – and the thought of this battered, hidden, centuries-old statue with no face managing to move of its own volition through the woodland, as if some tortured soul were trapped within, is an intriguing one.

ASTRAL PROJECTIONS AND PAST LIVES

Northamptonshire has produced some remarkable examples of phenomenal human behaviour that transcends natural boundaries into the realm of the paranormal.

Some people appear to have mastered the psychic ability of 'astral projection'; *Miracles And Modern Spiritualism* (1896) cites a Victorian example of this. The spiritualist Stainton Moses was expected to attend a friend's funeral in south-western Lincolnshire but could not go. About the hour of the funeral, however, he fell into a trance, and from his manner of talking appeared to be visualising himself there. Upon becoming conscious once more, Mr Moses wrote down everything he could remember visualising while under, including details of the service and the fact that a replacement vicar had had to be obtained at very short notice. He also described the subsequent burial at a churchyard over the border in Northamptonshire and the exact location of the grave by a particular tree within its grounds. He put the details down in a letter to a friend who had attended the funeral; subsequently, this friend wrote back, astonished, as everything Mr Moses had said had been true. Mr Moses, it would appear, attended his friend's funeral in astral form, without his physical body actually ever leaving his house.

Spiritualism and experimentation with psychic abilities were very fashionable in Victorian Britain. Frederick W. H. Myers' authoritative *Human Personality & Its Survival Of Bodily Death* notes two believable instances of astral projection. In the autumn of 1877 a Mr Carroll had been about to retire to bed at his home, Sholebrook Lodge in Towcester, when, in the act of moving the lamp to the bedside, he suddenly saw a ghostly likeness of his brother appear within the room. 'It seemed to affect me like a mild shock of electricity,' he commented. His brother was at the time still alive and well, and Mr Carroll could only gape in astonishment as the apparition faded away before him. Amazingly, about a minute later, his brother appeared in the flesh: he was outside tapping at the window pane and asking to be let in, having made a surprise journey all the way from London.

However, the most incredible instance of such a feat occurred in the house of one Sarah Hall at Wansford. The Hall family house, Sibberton Lodge, was a converted church, and in the winter months of 1863 Mrs Hall and her husband were paid a visit by a cousin and her husband. One evening all four were sat round the dining table having supper, when there suddenly appeared a solid-looking figure by the sideboard. The group could only stare in amazement – for the apparition was of Mrs Hall herself, even as she sat there looking at it. She wrote that her doppelgänger wore 'a spotted light Muslin summer dress' of a type that she herself did not even possess. As her husband stammered, 'It is Sarah!' and pointed, the apparition simply vanished. There is no suggestion that the group were experimenting with – or even talking about – spiritualism; Mrs Hall wrote, 'The apparition seemed utterly apart from myself and my feelings, as a picture or a statue.' The most bizarre feature of this already weird anecdote is the detail that the phantom Mrs Hall wore a dress that the *real* Mrs Hall did not own.

There are also incidences that point to past lives and reincarnation. In 1993 *Fortean Times* carried an interview with a 39-year-old Northamptonshire woman, Jenny Cockell, who all her life had dreamt details about the life of someone called Mary Sutton – a woman who had died in a Dublin hospital in 1932, leaving her eight children to fend for themselves. So sure was Mrs Cockell that there was something more to this than mere nightmares that she actually set about patiently trying to locate the details of who the long-deceased Ms Sutton might have been, and ultimately managed to track down her surviving children.

Mrs Cockell's book, *Yesterday's Children*, explains her long search for the answer to her strange dreams, a search which took her to Mary Sutton's homeland of Malahide in Ireland, and where Mrs Cockell realised that many of the locations she had 'dreamt' about were familiar to her already. She also uncovered numerous events from the Irishwoman's life that fitted the patterns of her dreams and accounted for the torment that she knew Ms Sutton had suffered in her lifetime. When Mrs Cockell ultimately managed to bring together the surviving children in an astonishing reunion, the by-now elderly Suttons were amazed by the intimacy and sympathy that Mrs Cockell shared with their late mother, and equally amazed by the details of her life that she appeared to know. For example, she 'knew' that one of Mary's brothers had relocated to Kettering. There is a strong suggestion that Mary Sutton was reincarnated as Jenny Cockell 20 years later, and the affair received much printed and televised publicity: *Yesterday's Children* was even made into a TV movie.

Perhaps this phenomenon is a two-way experience. Jenny Randles wrote of Mrs Cockell in *The Unexplained*: 'In October 1993 Jenny Cockell told me that she was now researching further dreams and memories emerging under hypnosis. These told of a future life in the 21st century where she knows 'tomorrow's children' – yet to be born.' Well, we are here now and it would interesting to know if Mrs Cockell has yet met any of 'tomorrow's children' that she dreamt of all those years ago.

TIME SLIP

By its very nature much of the content of this book is difficult to categorise. While some will view the following as a 'ghost story', it bears all the hallmarks of a 'time slip' – that is to say the witness found *themselves* in another era, rather than seeing a ghostly re-enactment in their own time. The story was passed on to the late folklorist Katherine Briggs and concerned a school inspector called Mr H.G. Lee who had been working in Northamptonshire in the late 1940s. Frustratingly, the exact location is no more specific than this.

One lunch hour, during his school visits, Mr Lee decided to go to a church which had been recommended to him for its architecture, although there was general agreement that the 'modernising' of this particular church's interior was not an improvement. Mr Lee sought out the church and as he viewed the exterior of the building an immense thunderstorm broke out above him so he dashed inside. Once within he found the church had not been subject to restoration as he had been led to believe. The most modern piece of furniture he could see was the Jacobean-era stone pulpit; there was not even an organ visible, and the place looked remarkably unspoilt and bereft of any modern trappings. As he sat by the font Mr Lee was startled by a voice behind him that echoed round the chapel: 'So you are interested in our fine old church!'

Mr Lee turned to see a middle-aged cassocked clergyman, whom he assumed to be the parish vicar, and agreed with him that the church was in a wonderfully preserved state. The vicar nodded and replied, 'We have seen troubled times, and some churches have suffered great damage. But I trust in the Lord Protector to see that my beautiful church is safe from harm. You see, the Lord Protector is an old friend of mine. We were at college together.' At this the vicar offered to take Mr Lee (who assumed the man was somewhat eccentric) on a tour of the church.

Eventually the weather cleared, and Mr Lee walked down the aisle and then – still accompanied by the vicar – out of the church and into the now sunlit churchyard. An aeroplane passed noisily overhead and Mr Lee glanced upwards; when he looked around he found that he now stood alone and the vicar had vanished. Walking back into the church he was shocked to discover that it was like entering a different building. An unsightly modern organ now masked a beautiful chapel arch he had admired earlier, and it now began to register that the vicar's footfalls had made no sound on the stone slabs of the floor. A notice board – which had not been visible before – displayed a list of all of the incumbent vicars at the church, and on impulse Mr Lee jotted down the name of the one who had served at the church in the 1640s and 1650s. His later research turned up the fact that this particular parson had been educated at Sidney Sussex College, Cambridge, in 1616 and he could, therefore, have known Oliver Cromwell – the Lord Protector – himself.

Postal Black Holes

Among the more whimsical mysteries of Northamptonshire is the enigma of the so-called 'postal black holes'. Mail can get lost for decades, somewhere in the system, and yet 50 years later *somehow* reach its intended destination. Local and national media picked up on just such a bizarre story in January 2008. A wedding invitation arrived at an address in Wakefield Road, East Ham, in December 2007 inviting a George and Ivy Atkins to the wedding of Valerie Wynn and Henry Parrott at All Saints' Church, New Eltham (Greater London) – on 1 September 1956! The envelope was dated 4 June 1956 and bore a tuppence ha'penny stamp. The address at which it arrived was by 2008 a shop that sold motor vehicle parts.

What was even more curious was that the faded envelope contained, apart from the invite, some black and white photographs and a newspaper cutting of the actual wedding for the benefit of the recipients. The yellowed clipping noted, 'The happy pair left for Jersey. On their return they will reside at Northampton.' So had the mystery envelope been sent before or *after* the wedding? Its post date evidenced it had been sent before, while its contents indicated it had been sent just afterwards. Where had it been for 51 years?

A Short Conclusion

It is clear that there are 'themes' that Northamptonshire mysteries follow. It is evident that some of its ghost stories contain money as a central theme, or else that they appear to be fatal to witness. The county's association with royalty and events of historical significance have left their mark upon popular belief, and this is particularly evident in the case of legends attached to the alleged burial sites of famous figures, such as Cromwell and Boudica. This kind of story has a modern incarnation: on the Round Oval island in the ornamental lake within the grounds of Althorp, there are already – not

Northampton today.

surprisingly – modern urban legends circulating. European media reported in March 1998 how an unnamed billionaire was offering a fortune to anyone who could procure for him the nameplate from the Princess of Wales's coffin. This had led to a gang invading the Round Oval island and digging indiscriminately. Guards on the estate spotted their lanterns and immediately rowed out to the island, where they found only abandoned shovels and muddy footprints. There is no evidence that this event *actually* occurred, and it is clearly a piece of outrageous tabloid fiction. However, it does well to illustrate how urban myths reinvent themselves for successive generations.

Northamptonshire is a beautiful county, and indeed still is 'the county of squires, spires and springs', although many of its antiquities and curiosities are well hidden. The true origins of its folklore are often lost to history, and many of its ghost stories are confused; sadly many of its cures, customs and beliefs appear to have faded from our shared memory, but it is somehow reassuring to know that a whole generation is growing up with modern equivalents. Phantom stagecoaches have been replaced by phantom vehicles, fairies and goblins have been replaced by bright lights and 'aliens', and Victorian urban legends of moving statues have been superseded by such things as telephone booths giving out eerie messages. Where there were once Will o' the Wisps, there are now crop circles. Indeed, some anecdotes are representative of the modern generation: stalled cars and time slips could not have been comprehended 100 years ago. Gigantic felines that prowl the Northamptonshire countryside have supplanted Black Shuck…

It is also reassuring to know that people are *still* familiar with the ancient legends that haunt their particular village. One wonders what form these urban legends, supernatural encounters and paranormal events will take in the future, but either way hopefully total scepticism of such events will not overtake us too soon.

INDEX OF PLACE NAMES

BV - #0093 - 280426 - C0 - 234/156/12 - PB - 9781780913056 - Matt Lamination